BIG RED

BIG RED

Memoirs of a Texas Entrepreneur and Philanthropist

By Red McCombs
As told to Don Carleton

Dolph Briscoe Center for American History
The University of Texas at Austin
Austin, Texas

Printed in the United States of America.
First edition, 2011
Requests for permission to reproduce material from this work should be sent to Office of the Director, Dolph Briscoe Center for American History, 1 University Station D1100, Austin, TX 78712-0335.
∞The paper used in this book meets the minimum requirements of ANSI/NISO z39.48-1992 (r1997)(Permanence of Paper).
Library of Congress control number: 2010934923

Frontispiece: Red McCombs, owner of the Minnesota Vikings, 1998.
Photo by Rick A. Kolodziej.

CONTENTS

Red McCombs with University of Texas head football coach Mack Brown.
Courtesy of UT Athletics.

FOREWORD

THE ONLY THING BIGGER THAN RED MCCOMBS IS HIS HEART. HE is a Texas icon and an American hero. And he is a hero to all of us who are lucky enough to call him a friend—and that's a bunch.

Before Sally and I ever met with people from Texas concerning the head coaching job for the Longhorns, Red McCombs was at work on my behalf. He made phone calls and offered recommendations, all before I ever met him. So it was natural that when we got to Austin, one of the first calls I made was to Red. We struck up a close friendship, and that wasn't hard. He's an easy guy to like, especially when he's on your side.

Red and Charline have been on the side of the Longhorns for more than fifty years, but I have also been amazed at his commitment to sports that has led him to become an owner of both a pro basketball and a pro football franchise. He and Charline have given millions of dollars to great causes, including, of course, the University of Texas.

When we came to Texas, another friend told me that the University of Texas was a place full of diverse ideas and opinions. He suggested that to succeed, we should pick five or six close confidants to whom we can turn in both the good times and the bad. Coach Royal made that easy when it came to Red. He was a guy who helped him when he was a young coach at Texas over fifty years ago, and he's a guy who helps me every day.

Once, when some of our staff were concerned about the long hours it took to sign autographs during our fan appreciation day, Red told me, "Look, there are a lot of teams in the country that would like to have that many fans turn out for anything. You don't have a problem, you have an opportunity."

You not only appreciate Red for what he does to help you, you admire him for who he is. Roots are very important to him. He remembers where he came from, and he has a keen sense of where he is going and of the new roads that are still out there to travel. I remember a couple of years ago he was talking about future land development, which takes a lot of energy for a guy who was darned near in his eighties.

He reflects the passion and pride for what he has built and for his state. I remember a few years back when an official at another university made what he thought was a disparaging remark about the University of Texas. He said, "All Texans are rich and arrogant."

Red called me and said, "You tell that guy that he's right. I am rich and I worked hard to earn it. And I am arrogant and proud of it."

He's really not arrogant. He is a proud humble man who has never forgotten his small-town beginnings. But you get the point.

Red's a wonderful friend and a better man. He obviously has a keen business mind, is extremely bright on any subject, and he cares deeply about people and his country.

Some would say he's larger than life. In an old western movie, he'd be John Wayne. In truth, he's simply Red McCombs.

MACK BROWN
Head Football Coach
University of Texas Longhorns

Red McCombs giving his own personal Stetson to former Texas governor Dolph Briscoe at the luncheon announcing the Dolph Briscoe Western Museum on West Market Street in San Antonio, November 28, 2006. Courtesy of the McCombs family.

INTRODUCTION

IN HIS NOVEL *WAR AND PEACE*, LEO TOLSTOY FAMOUSLY OFFERED THE concept of the "unknown X factor" when predicting the success or failure of an army in battle. That unknown factor, according to Tolstoy, "is the spirit of the army." During my work with Red McCombs, I frequently thought of Tolstoy's "X factor," not in the military sense, but as an indefinable spirit that is an essential component of Red's character.

The fact is that, throughout his life, Red McCombs has had an uncanny ability to perceive business opportunities that most others were unable to see. Red calls them his "McCombs moments." Some simply call them "hunches," which are as much intuitive as rational decisions. Anyone can have a lucky hunch or two. What gets one's attention when examining Red's business record, however, is that he has had far too many successful "hunches" to have just been lucky. As you will see in this memoir, there is no doubt that Red has enjoyed good luck in his career, but his success as an entrepreneur goes well beyond random good fortune. Whatever one chooses to call this unknown variable—hunch factor, basic instinct, or "X factor"—Red has had it his entire life.

Red has other, less mysterious, character traits that have played a critical role in his business success, including his high tolerance for risk, his intensely restless energy level, his vivid imagination and curiosity, his deeply felt self-confidence, his ability to cut rapidly through irrelevant issues to perceive the true essence of a deal, and his absolute refusal to be satisfied with the status quo.

Red enjoys a gift for decisiveness. His ability to make decisions quickly may seem to some like a propensity to "shoot from the hip," but that is an illusion. Red has a mania for information and data, and he always does his homework before he makes a business decision. That decisiveness can also mean unpredictability, making Red's business ventures a fascinating study—you just never know what's next. As we sent this book to the printer, for example, Red announced his major investment in bringing Formula One racing to Austin. Time will tell if this new venture will prove to be as wildly successful as his others, but it is quintessential Red—a combination of sports, risk, and showmanship, based on a solid foundation of research and business.

As this memoir makes clear, Red is also imbued with the traits of the winning athlete and sportsman, both of which he has been most of his life. Those traits, which have carried over into his business life, include a fiercely competitive nature, a keen awareness that discipline and hard work are critical ingredients for success, and an almost unquenchable thirst for victory. In many respects, entrepreneurship has been, and continues to be, a sport to Red. That's not to imply that the money doesn't matter to him, but in the several decades since Red became financially secure, profit has in some ways been a means for him to keep score.

But Red's moneymaking is more than scorekeeping. It also makes it possible for him to carry out his wide range of philanthropic activities. One of Red's most intense passions is education, a passion shared by Charline McCombs, Red's lifelong partner, best friend, and most trusted confidante. Red and Charline believe that an educated citizenry is essential to the good health of a democracy and the viability of the free-market economy. Accordingly, they are among the leading philanthropists in Texas. As detailed in this memoir, they have been extremely generous donors to a number of educational institutions, especially Southwestern University in Georgetown, Texas, and the University of Texas at Austin. In addition, Red and Charline's generosity has included a number of other institutions and organizations dedicated to furthering the public good, including the M. D. Anderson Cancer Center in Houston.

Working with Red McCombs on this memoir has been an exciting and informative experience for me. Red is a formidable person when one encounters his physical presence, his stunning achievements as a no-nonsense entrepreneur, and his forceful personality. He is not a person who puts up with anything that he feels is a waste of his time. And it doesn't take him long to figure that out. That's why I was so pleased that he not only agreed to work with me on this memoir, but also willingly gave up much of his valuable time to see it to completion. I have come away from this project with deep respect and affection for Red McCombs. I also have learned a great deal about how an authentic wheeler-dealer actually goes about his business, which is not something historians typically learn.

Having that opportunity made this project even more satisfying and fun.

A portion of *Big Red* is based on *The Red Zone: Cars, Cows, and Coaches: The Life and Good Times of a Texas Dealmaker,* a memoir that Eakin Press published in 2002. Famed sports journalist Mickey Herskowitz, who for many years was a celebrated columnist for the *Houston Post* and later the *Houston Chronicle*, was Red's coauthor. That book had a troubled editing, production, and marketing history, none of which was the fault of Red McCombs or Mickey Herskowitz. I want to acknowledge the superior job that Herskowitz did in pulling together and articulating the Red McCombs story. His efforts were invaluable to our work. In Red's acknowledgments in *The Red Zone*, he thanked the following individuals for their help: Lowry Mays, Henry Cisneros, and Dr. Charles "Mickey" LeMaistre. Because some of the information that Red and I used in *Big Red* came from those same sources, I want to thank them again.

I also want to acknowledge and thank some other people who were strongly supportive and helpful to me during this project. Red's business associates Gary Woods and Rad Weaver, as well as Red's daughter Marsha Shields, provided important information and answered a number of my questions. Red's dedicated and talented longtime assistant, Suzy Thomas, played a critical role in scheduling interviews, helping with photographs, and serving as my chief contact for anything related to Red. Sheree Scarborough conducted oral history interviews with Red's wife Charline and his daughters, Marsha, Connie, and Lynda. Sheree's work was invaluable, and I very much appreciate the time that Charline and her daughters gave for these interviews. Diana Claitor gave me able assistance with research. Barbara Woodman, Dolph Briscoe's able assistant, also was helpful. Briscoe Center staff members Duvall Osteen and Hal Richardson did an excellent job with additional photo research and photo scanning, respectively. Erin Purdy, the Briscoe Center's associate director for communication, and Dr. Holly Taylor, the Briscoe Center's head of publications, did an outstanding job in carrying out the complex tasks necessary to get this book into print.

Red and I both want to convey our sincere thanks to Mack Brown, the head coach of the University of Texas Longhorn football team, for his thoughtful foreword.

The individual most responsible for making this book possible was my dear friend and patron, the late Dolph Briscoe Jr., former governor of Texas. Governor Briscoe greatly admired and deeply respected Red

McCombs as a businessman and philanthropist. In June 2008, Governor Briscoe, who was not satisfied with Red's first published memoir, called me and said that if I would work with Red to revise, expand, and update that earlier book, he would provide the necessary financial support. Governor Briscoe felt fervently that Red's story deserved a better telling, a more attractive physical book, and a wider distribution. I readily accepted his offer. I have long been interested in Red McCombs's career, and I welcomed the opportunity to collaborate with him. Besides, anyone who ever had the privilege of knowing Dolph Briscoe will understand how difficult it was to say no to such a decent, soft-spoken gentleman. I'm pleased that he was able to read the final draft of this book, but, sadly, Dolph Briscoe died on June 27, 2010, at the age of eighty-seven, five months prior to publication. Making this book possible was Dolph Briscoe's tribute to his dear friend, whom he so admired as a businessman and philanthropist.

Don Carleton, Ph.D.
Executive Director
Dolph Briscoe Center for American History
University of Texas at Austin

BIG RED

Red McCombs with his mother, Gladys, c. 1927 in Spur, Texas. Courtesy of the McCombs family.

Chapter One

SPUR

PEOPLE HAVE OFTEN ACCUSED ME OF BEING A TYPICAL wheeler-dealer Texan. Born and bred in the little West Texas town of Spur, I certainly plead guilty to being a Texan. And at six feet, three inches in height, I guess in the physical sense at least, I do fit the popular image of the typical Texan. Besides that, I do speak with a West Texas drawl, I wear boots, and I have been seen with a Stetson covering my red hair. And, like every other Texan that I know, I do love Texas as a place and as a state of mind. I simply can't imagine living anywhere else.

As for the wheeler-dealer part, I guess I have to plead guilty to that as well. The fact is that in my business life I have dabbled in automobiles, cattle, oil and gas, broadcasting, insurance, racehorses, motion pictures, real estate, politics, minor league baseball, and pro football. I've even been deeply involved in pro basketball, having owned a majority interest in the San Antonio Spurs twice and the Denver Nuggets once.

To be perfectly honest, however, I'm not sure that I qualify as a typical anything. I don't mean to brag or even to imply that I'm better (or worse) than any other Texan, but I have been much blessed with the good fortune of having been able to do a lot of things that most of my fellow Texans have not been able to do—whatever the reasons.

Now that I've claimed I'm a proud, if not typical, wheeler-dealer Texan, who has had some success in life, the burden is on me to provide some proof. Which is one of the reasons for this book. Another, more important, reason for this book is that my family and friends have flattered me by arguing that knowing my life story might be useful to others, especially to youngsters who are looking at the possibilities in life and the challenges that they will inevitably face in making a place for themselves in the world. And finally, my historian friends have flattered me with the argument that I owe it to the cause of history to preserve my memories of a special time in Texas and the nation.

I never refuse my family, I don't like to argue with my friends, and history is one of my favorite subjects, so this book is the result. I'm not sure that my life is a good example for anyone else. It hasn't been easy, and it hasn't always been fun, but I can't imagine living my life any differently from the way I have lived it. Of course, the tales told in memoirs are not always to be trusted. Some people supply themselves with too many victories, while others cling to hard times, real or imagined, to excuse what they have become. Aware of those pitfalls, I will do my best to tell my story as I felt it and as I can best remember it.

My Parents

This story begins with my birth in 1927 in Spur, a small farming and ranching town in southern Dickens County in West Texas. My hometown was named for one of the legendary ranches in Texas history, the Spur Ranch. My dad, Willie Nathan McCombs, known to his friends as "Slim" or "Mac," never Willie, was born in Groveton, a town in East Texas in the rural area known as the Piney Woods. Dad was born on June 5, 1903, the eldest of nine children. His family had migrated from Mississippi. He attended a one-room country school, which he left in the third grade to help work on the forty acres his family sharecropped and to earn extra cash by cutting timber.

When he was still a young man the word spread to Groveton that out in West Texas families could sharecrop as many as three hundred acres. His family decided to seek whatever opportunity they could find in this new promised land. Unfortunately, this promised land was what Texans call hardscrabble and subject to frequent drought. I once asked my father why he left the lush greenery of East Texas to settle in a place where it never rained. His answer was simple: "Well son, we didn't know that until we got here." He rode in a railroad boxcar and got off at Spur, the end of the Burlington rail line. Dad worked that dry, rocky farmland with his father, brothers, and sisters until he was nineteen, when he talked the local Ford dealer into letting him become an apprentice mechanic. He worked at the dealership for two years for room and board and tobacco before he drew his first paycheck.

Dad was born with a gift for understanding anything mechanical. He was self-taught and brilliant at analyzing what was inside a motor or an engine. He was attracted to airplanes with the same passion he felt for cars. There was a small airstrip in Spur, and he went down there whenever the stunt pilots of that era put their planes down. He would bombard them with questions about flying.

My mother, Gladys McCombs, came from a family of farmers in Central Texas, who had known far better economic circumstances than Dad's clan. Mom was a high school graduate and a bit of a snob about it. Her father later settled in a fairly fertile area near Jayton, about twenty miles from Spur.

My earliest memories are of the house we rented and then bought in Spur. The white frame house had three bedrooms and one bath. I was seven when Dad signed the purchase papers in 1934. It was a pretty little house by the standards of those years. Dad bought the place from Clifford B. Jones, who later became president of Texas Tech University, for the grand total of $900. This was during the Depression, and just about everyone in our part of the country was having a difficult time making ends meet. I remember my parents gravely discussing whether they could make the twenty-five-dollars-a-month payments.

When I was a kid, Spur was an interesting little speck on the map, a quiet, well-behaved town of maybe two thousand citizens, most of them churchgoers. Eighty percent of my schoolmates lived on farms and ranches, and a good many of them rode horses to school and tied them to a hitching post. In that area of West Texas, Spur was a hub for supplying the big ranches, and a train ran through it. Well, not all the way through it. The train actually made a U-turn and headed east, hauling its cargo of cattle from the ranches.

My childhood was just about right. It was during the Depression, and times were lean, as times often are, but we had a loving family, and the McCombs kids suffered no hardships.

Mom's mother, my grandmother Dempsey, belonged to the Church of Christ, and to the most orthodox segment, which believed that if you belonged to any other church you were going straight to hell. I can recall visiting Grandma Dempsey and hearing her say, "Gladys, are you still going to that Baptist church?" My mom's response was, "Yes, I am, and I love it more every day." And without raising her voice, my grandmother would say, "You're going to hell, Gladys. I'm sorry, but you're going to hell." As a kid, I thought, how can this be? My mother was always the one who was right. And in the end, I have to say that really was the case.

There was a slight contradiction in my father's family. While Dad was a dedicated churchgoer, he and his kin were Scotch-Irish and not opposed to drinking. They were not drunkards by any stretch of the imagination. But, like a lot of backwoods people and dirt farmers, when they had access to liquor they would drink until nothing was left. Then they would pass out and sleep it off. I never saw any of them do anything violent or even disorderly.

But my mother hated liquor. If anyone in Dad's family, including Dad, came to the door with alcohol on his breath, she would not let them in the house. My father had to visit with his drinking friends out in the yard, never in the house. One time we were going to a picnic at a place called Roaring Springs, which is about thirty miles north of Spur. One of the old cars had a blowout, and when the men got into the well to retrieve the spare tire, my mother spotted two bottles of whiskey that had been placed there by Dad's brothers, or perhaps his father. Mom busted the two bottles on the hub in one fell swoop, and all they could do was stand there. Dad never said a word. Mother absolutely detested liquor. She said many times over, "I would rather see any one of you children in a coffin than with a glass of whiskey in your hand." So, even as I grew up and got into my social drinking days and beyond, I never drank in front of my mother nor served any liquor around her.

Educational Influences

My mother believed in education, not only as a way to stay out of trouble and to learn life skills, but also as a child's best chance to escape the lower rungs of society. She had graduated from high school when that was not a priority for girls in the poor, rural Southwest. She was an avid reader, and to the pleasure of both of us coaxed me into reading to her. To her, education didn't end when school let out. You started over every day. You learned as much as your brain could hold, up to the point of actually feeling pain.

Although Mother played the most important role in my educational development, I also have to give a lot of credit to two wonderful grade-school teachers in Spur. My third-grade teacher, Mrs. Wadzek, was a tremendous influence on me. In the third grade, I thought school was for fun and a place to get your hand slapped with a ruler. Mrs. Wadzek saw through all of that and encouraged me to raise my sights, to see how much fun it was to do positive things. She showed me that I didn't have to be involved in mischief to enjoy school. The fact that she was the wife of the high school football coach had a lot to do with it, because that put her close to hero status. It was important to me that I please her. She made me realize how much fun it was to fix something instead of breaking it down and how to travel the world through books.

Mrs. Wadzek liked to bring me up to the front of the class and tell me how special I was and that she wanted me up there to help her. This was in contrast to other teachers who made me stand in the corner. She took me home after school to help her work in the garden.

My seventh-grade teacher, Miss Francis, introduced me to classical literature and inspired me to reach beyond my limited understanding of the world and read outside my experience. Doing so, she said, would stir my thought processes. She could tell if my interest was wandering, and she would ask the questions that made me think: What is the author saying? What point is being made? I had some interesting and influential teachers in college, but no one had as much impact on my educational development as those two grade-school teachers in that little school in Spur.

Kid Entrepreneur

I don't know where it came from—neither of my parents were dreamers—but I had an entrepreneurial instinct very early in my life. In fact, I was an entrepreneur before I knew what the word meant, and certainly before I could spell it. When I was ten years old I went into business for myself. (I don't know why it took me so long.) Somehow I had figured out one of the first rules of private enterprise. If you identify a need, and know where the buyers are, all that is missing is the product. I decided to sell roasted peanuts for a nickel a bag during the four weeks in winter that the migrant cotton pickers passed through Spur. If you have ever been to a ballpark or on an airplane, you know that peanuts comprise one of the major food groups.

The migrant workers normally came into our area in late November and early December. This was an annual pilgrimage. They stayed no more than a month, leaving the fields on Saturday and Sunday afternoons to visit Main Street, four blocks long. At the end of the street, certain ambitious townspeople would set up stands and sell homemade foodstuffs.

The idea of selling peanuts was inspired by the appearance of the Harley Sadler Medicine Show, which toured small towns peddling tonics and elixirs that would cure everything from baldness to lumbago. Sadler was a real character. His career included being an oilman, showman, and member of the Texas Legislature. Sadler's crew put up a tent, staged a play (usually a melodrama), and peddled Cracker Jack and peanuts during the entertainment.

I didn't know where or how you bought quantities of Cracker Jack. But I found out that the Kimball wholesale grocery in Lubbock sold peanuts, and we had a delivery station in town. I went right over and asked the manager if they carried peanuts. He said that they sold them in one-hundred-pound sacks.

The next step was to ask my dad to be my banker. I explained that I was going to put the peanuts in brown paper bags and sell them to the cotton pickers. I knew, as children always do, that if I pestered him enough I would win. He knew it, too. But I don't believe Dad was displeased by my ambition. He had to quit school as a ten-year-old to work beside his father in a logging camp in the Piney Woods to provide support for his younger brothers and sisters. Eventually there would be eight of them.

I eagerly waited for the day when my load of peanuts would arrive on the truck from Lubbock. I worked early and stayed late, filling the brown bags, flipping them over by the corners to make ears on them. By the end of the week, I had sold my one hundred pounds of goobers and had a mountain of nickels.

Proudly, I showed off my haul and took for granted that my dad would finance my next order. Dad was a big man, at six-foot-three, with a sweet disposition. With his usual patience, he counted the nickels and said, slowly, "We have a little problem, honey boy. The peanuts cost more than you took in." I was dumbfounded. But I learned a priceless lesson. I had a ready source of capital, my father. I had a labor source, meaning me. I had a market because I went right to the customers. What my business plan didn't include was figuring out how many bags I had to sell to make a profit.

Dad wasn't critical. He just said, "When you get the next hundred-pound sack, cut the number of peanuts per bag in half. That way you'll double your money." That week, when I balanced my account, I had two mountains of nickels—one to pay off the peanuts and one to keep.

I did not see myself as a kid who was industrious in any special way. I mowed lawns, carried out groceries, and picked up a dime here and a nickel there in tips. I got my first ongoing job when I was about ten years old. It was a paper route to deliver the *Lubbock Avalanche-Journal.* The boy who had been throwing the papers was moving to another town, and he offered to introduce me to the distributor.

From selling peanuts four weeks out of the year, I now took on a job that was as daily as it gets. There were two lessons learned, quickly and not painlessly. Number one, not everyone pays his or her bills. It was disheartening to throw the paper all week and not be able to collect. Number two, people expected their paper whether it was snowing, sleeting, freezing, or storming.

My mother didn't want me delivering the papers—period. But, bless her, many of those freezing mornings when I rolled out of bed at five a.m. to ride my bicycle, she got up to drive me instead. She would be angry about the hour, the weather, and the inconvenience, but she insisted on taking me in the car. I never once asked her to do so. In fact, I dreaded it because she complained so incessantly. One morning she commanded me, "Sit down. I have to talk to you. I want to know why you are doing this? You don't need to do it. I do not enjoy getting up before dawn, in the bitter cold, but I am not going to let you go out on that ice on a bicycle and kill yourself. So tell me, why do you do this?"

She really could not understand my persistence. Her questions hinted that I was making my parents look bad. I didn't need the money. My dad had a job. He always had a job. My mother would shake her head and say, many times, "I gave birth to him and raised him, but I never have known what made that boy tick." To me, it was so obvious. This was a resource, a chance to have a job, to make my own money. I didn't analyze how I felt. It was just as natural to me as breathing.

After nearly two years of delivering the newspaper, I had an opportunity to land a better job—riding the fender of a milk truck and jumping off to leave the customer's dairy order at the door. The job paid a little more than tossing papers, and was seven days a week, morning and night. I took home all the milk the family could use.

I looked around to see if I could find a buyer for my paper route. It's odd to look back over the years and see how, and when, we learn to value ourselves. I had paid nothing to the boy before me, but I had built up the route so that it turned a profit of three or four dollars a week. I just assumed that it was worth money. The town had one general insurance agency and the owner had a son a year older than me. He wanted his son to have the job, and I offered to sell it to him for fifty dollars cash. The father said that was fine. The day the newspaper distributor came down from Lubbock, the father asked him if the price was fair.

The distributor responded that the routes weren't for sale. The newspaper decided who got them. I sensed that the distributor regretted having to say it. The father turned to me and said, "Well, Red, it looks like we can't pay you for the route." I said okay, but in that case I would keep the route. At that point, the distributor said, "Let's step outside for a minute." Once we were alone, he said, "I'm sorry I said that, but it's the truth. We can't allow you to sell your paper route, but I think I can fix this."

We went back inside. "Red can keep the route," he told the insurance agent. "He does a good job for us. But if you want it, give Red fifty dollars, not for the route, but to show your boy how to do it." The son threw the papers for six months, and then quit. The distributor wanted me to take it back, but I had moved on. I was riding the fender of that Model A Ford and bringing home all the milk my family could drink, plus cash.

I soon took another job washing dishes at a local cafe after school and on weekends. An elderly woman named Mrs. Smith owned and lived over the cafe, which seated about ten at the counter in addition to tables that seated four each. She usually retired to take a nap when I got there after school. The cook and waitress was a woman in her thirties named Evelyn, who had been divorced. In our town, in that era, a divorced woman carried a stigma. She was not considered a "good" person. Evelyn lived on a farm nearby and had little or no social life.

I liked her. She was helpful and considerate and taught me short-order cooking and how to make stews and chili con carne. She represented my first encounter with the abrupt and random turns of life and personal relationships. One night during my second year at the cafe, less than an hour before closing time, a man unknown to me and to the town walked in. I watched through the service window as Evelyn went to the counter to wait on him. She drew him a cup of coffee, and I saw him reach inside his suit coat, pull out a pint of whiskey, and pour some into the cup. I just knew that God was going to send a lightning bolt through that cafe and strike us dead.

I was a green kid, and my eyes opened wide. Evelyn had gotten herself a cup of coffee and was leaning over the counter. The stranger poured some whiskey into her cup. I couldn't hear their conversation, but after a few sentences she walked back into the kitchen. I was literally petrified from what I had seen. She untied her apron and wiggled into her coat. She said, "Red, when Mrs. Smith comes down to check the register, tell her I quit and not to worry about the three days' wages she owes me. I don't care. I'm giving it to you." I asked her where she was going. "I don't know," said Evelyn, "but it will be better than where I am now." And a minute or two later, she walked out the door with a man she had never seen before. With that Baptist church bell ringing in my ear, I watched Mrs. Smith, in her high-necked collar, make her way down the stairs. When she asked where Evelyn was, I answered that "she just took off her apron and said to give the three days' wages she had coming to me. She was quitting and she wasn't coming back."

I thought a lot about what had happened. The man was traveling through town, probably heading west, and he saw a reasonably attractive woman. In the movies, this would have been Veronica Lake leaning over a Formica counter, having a cup of java with a stranger. This was 1939; the Depression was still a reality, jobs were short, and money was scarce. I hope they grew to care about each other and stayed together a long time, but I doubt that it turned out that way.

The story stirred a few days of town gossip. The offshoot was that Mrs. Smith took Evelyn's place and showed me how to do the sandwich orders, so she could go upstairs and take her nap. The business wasn't much in the afternoon hours, and we usually closed around eight or eight-thirty p.m. I was the cook, waiter, and cashier, with no increase in pay. At the outset, I'm sure she intended to hire a replacement for Evelyn. But as time went on, she saw that I could handle it. We never had more than five or six people at a time. I had a repertoire that consisted of sandwiches, hamburgers, chili, and beef stew.

I don't mean to imply that because we were a little better off than many, I wasn't keenly aware of the Depression. I had seen with my own eyes hungry, jobless, defeated men, called hoboes, straggling through even our little town, which was not on a main route going west. I saw people who slept in our yard at night, wanting to work, knocking timidly at the door, asking, "Is there anything I can do to earn a meal?"

I saw my mother feed hundreds of them. Many times I saw entire families—men, women, children, aunts, and uncles—on the move through town. Mom fed them whatever she could spare. Mom always had food and a place for them to stay, even if it was just a quilt on the yard in front of the house. I heard Dad say, "I wish I could do more," as he handed a man a dollar. Gasoline was a nickel a gallon, and that dollar was to get them farther down the road. We didn't have social services. It wasn't part of our world at the time. The Depression left its stamp on my brain, and it will always be there.

I witnessed the end of the Depression in 1940 when I became a part of one of the most profound changes that ever swept across America. That was when large numbers of people left the rural areas and went to cities to work in the factories that had expanded to produce the equipment and materials that were needed for the military, which was preparing for the possibility that we would be drawn into the war that was raging in Europe. We called these factories "war plants," and they had plenty of new, well-paying jobs. Many of these war plants were in California, but some were closer to home. For example, the North American Aviation Company built airplanes on an assembly line in Fort Worth.

News started drifting back to Spur that these plants not only were hiring nearly any man who needed a job, but they also were hiring women. On top of that, the women were making as much money as the men! This struck me as unbelievable. When I was growing up, the only jobs women had were teaching school, nursing, and waiting tables. Even the banks had male secretaries. There weren't many jobs for women.

In 1940 and 1941 stories about German victories in Europe and the imminent threat to our country filled the newspapers every day. I was struck by the enormity of the changes taking place, of people going off to what I perceived to be the outside world. When Japan bombed Pearl Harbor on December 7, 1941, we were pulled into the war that had begun two years earlier in Europe. The war changed America forever. I was very much aware of the times and fascinated by them. I was little different, I suppose, from most teenage boys on the threshold of becoming men, excited by this good war being waged against the forces of tyranny.

When I was fifteen, and the war had scooped up most of the young men, I had the opportunity to leave my job at the cafe and step up to the best job in town: working in the drugstore. I owed this break to the wife of a doctor named Blackwell, who owned the pharmacy and let the druggist manage it. The Blackwells were considered "moneyed" folks. The doctor's wife was a gentle and pleasant person who befriended me in small ways and large. She got me the job. I worked with an older boy, probably seventeen or eighteen, who had finished high school. I was a typical soda jerk, mopping the floors, stocking the shelves, keeping the syrup dispensers full at the fountain. I worked after school, and by summer I had hit the big time, earning a dollar a day—seven dollars cash a week. As a reference point, my father was making only twenty-five dollars a week and raising a family.

Life was on a downhill pull. I was buying Arrow shirts—not many people could afford Arrow shirts back then. I played the French horn in the school band. On one memorable day we played marching songs as the first of Spur's young soldiers and sailors boarded the train to serve their country. My hormones kicked in, and I was doing pretty well in the girlfriend department. I gave girls extra dips of ice cream and refilled their cherry Cokes on the sly without charge.

By accident, I learned that Leon, the guy I was working with, was making a buck and a half—more than ten dollars a week! This was my first lesson in negotiating, and it was a difficult one. After getting paid one Sunday night, I told the druggist that since I was doing the same work as Leon and doing it well, I wanted to be paid the same money. The druggist looked at me and said, "You do work as well as Leon. You have been a good employee," with the emphasis on HAVE. "Fact is," he went on, "I've been stretching things to keep you on and I enjoyed having you here. Good luck to you."

I didn't think I had given him an ultimatum. In my mind, I had asked him for a raise, but I didn't tell him I was going to quit. I turned this over in my mind and concluded that I had made a major error. It was painfully clear that Mrs. Blackwell had leaned on him to give me the job and maybe he didn't really need me at all. I was truly upset. I had blown the best job for a teenager in Spur, Texas.

I couldn't wait for the sun to come up. As soon as it did, I jumped on my bicycle and hustled over to Mrs. Blackwell's house. I told her I was embarrassed and explained that the disaster of my life had taken place. She very gently said, "Let me explain what probably happened here. You do the same job, and you do it as well, but Leon is a full-time employee. You are part-time, even though you work full-time in the summer. So you were not necessarily wrong in what you did." She let me down beautifully. She promised to go back to the druggist and ask him to reconsider. He did, and I got the job back.

Another huge lesson was learned. It was one of those moments that helps shape your character.

Red McCombs, high school graduation, Corpus Christi, Texas, 1945. Courtesy of the McCombs family.

Chapter Two

PERSUASION WITH A TENNIS RACQUET

IN 1943 I WAS STILL WORKING AT THE DRUGSTORE WHEN MY folks announced we were moving to Corpus Christi. There were virtually no parts left to fix cars with, and even though his employer, the Godfrey and Smart Ford Company, kept him on the payroll, Dad was eager to do something for the war effort. He found out that he could get a job as a mechanic at the Corpus Christi Naval Station, so he decided to go there. It was incidental to him that the job paid four times what he made in the Ford service department. They wouldn't need him again until the war was won.

My family moved to Corpus, but I stayed in Spur that summer, moving into a house with a boy named Leon, whose family also went to work in a defense plant. Leon had a car and I didn't. To stay in Spur, I used the excuse that I wanted to graduate with my high school class in two years. That was partly true. But I still had no intention of ever leaving Spur. After all, I had a choice job at the City Drug, had discovered girls and vice versa, and was living about as well as I thought possible.

While I was enjoying this arrangement, my mom called once a week to press me about moving to Corpus Christi. I stalled as long as I could. I assured her that the drugstore really needed me, at least until school reopened in the fall. I thought it had been easy enough to convince Mom to let me stay in Spur. That was my first experiment at making a quality-of-life decision. Like all parents, however, Mom was perceptive. She knew I wasn't going to come voluntarily, so she just elected to come fetch me.

One afternoon in late August, I looked up from the soda fountain and saw my mother walk in, unannounced. We embraced, and she invited me to dinner at a friend's house where she was spending the night. I promised to be there right after we closed.

I had no guarded thoughts at all. I went sailing into the house and didn't even get all the way through the screen door when my mom confronted me. She had gone to the place where I was boarding and collected all of my clothes and personal items. "It's all in the car," she said. "I packed us something to eat. We're going to drive to Corpus Christi tonight because it's cooler." My response was to make a nice little speech to the effect that I would not be leaving, now or ever. My life was in Spur, Texas, and I would stay in touch.

Mom said, "I thought that was what you would say, Billy Joe." That was a name no one else called me. With that, she reached behind a chair and brought out my Wilson tennis racquet. I loved to play tennis, which in those days in my part of the country was seen as a game for rich kids. That tennis racquet was one of my first prized possessions. The racquet cost $2.50, and it took me eighteen months to earn the money to buy it. I still have it. At any rate, without further warning, Mom swatted me up the side of the head with the racquet, prized possession or not. I was addled, very addled, the way you are when you are knocked senseless. I actually fell to my knees. She said she didn't want to hit me again, but I'd better get in that car. I believe she may have popped me one more time, but the first smash busted most of the strings on my tennis racquet.

I should explain that when my brother and sisters and I were growing up, Mother was free with the switch and the belt and rightfully so. My dad never swatted me or even raised a hand to me or to my little sisters, Mildred and LaWanda, who adored him. And he certainly never spanked my brother Gene, who became a preacher and who led the purest life of anyone I have known. The simple fact is that Mom was the decision-maker in the family. Dad worshipped Mom, and he was quite happy to let her make the calls.

I got into the car, of course, and we set off for the long drive to the lower Gulf Coast. I was mad and upset and didn't say three words on the trip to Corpus Christi. Because my dad worked at the Naval Air Base, he had rented a little place nearby on North Beach. The next morning, I walked on the beach near the water's edge, feeling very sorry for myself. Then I met a group of kids hanging out and, in fifteen minutes, I decided my whole world belonged in Corpus. I just hadn't realized there was anything else but Spur, Texas.

I didn't return to Spur until the late 1980s, when my brother Gene, a distinguished Baptist minister living in Memphis, Tennessee, was conducting a revival in town. I flew with Mom out there for the day.

Sundeen and Southwestern

I was fifteen years old when I moved to Corpus Christi. I enrolled in a brand new high school called Sundeen, which the state created by consolidating a couple of rural school districts. The school no longer exists. The federal government constructed a new building for the school because it served naval families and civilian employees of the Naval Air Station. It was a wonderful scene because there were people from all over the United States being brought together as a group. I had never been exposed to kids from such diverse backgrounds and experiences. We lived in a new government housing project made up of duplexes. This was a new residence for everyone living there, so everyone was a stranger.

I skipped a year in high school. What happened is that when I went to enroll in the new high school for the first time, I recognized the administrative turmoil and chaos in the office. Everyone was a new student, so the admissions office was overwhelmed with paperwork. As I watched all of this confusion, I decided that I would rather be a senior than a junior. So, when it was my time to step forward, I very proudly announced my name, that I was transferring from high school in Spur, Texas, and I would be a senior. The registrar asked for my documentation, and I said it was in the mail. He said fine, thank you very much. That was the end of that.

No one ever checked, so I entered school as a senior. I didn't play sports in high school at Spur because I moved to Corpus Christi after my sophomore year. This, of course, reduced my ability considerably to compete as an athlete. But we played these little bitty schools in the area and I was good at that level. I was a big kid, so I played end and tackle. At that time, I was about six feet two inches and 180 pounds. I was in a very small high school with only sixteen students in my graduating class. I had limited talents, but a lot of desire. I played football, basketball, and baseball.

Growing up in Spur, I had made a crucial discovery. The three people in town who seemed to be involved in all the decision making were the banker, the lawyer, and the doctor. Wherever I lived, I was fascinated by those who were in charge of things. I thought about it for hours on end: how do you get to be one of those elite few? I wanted to be in that role.

In high school, I didn't do well in science, so I figured that ruled out my becoming a doctor. I didn't have a clue about what kind of education you needed to be a banker, or what path you took, so I scratched that one. It seemed clear to me that if I was going to achieve my goal, I had to make it as a lawyer. And, of course, to be a lawyer I needed to go to college. To do that, however, I needed to get some financial help. I planned to solve that problem by winning a football scholarship from whatever college would give me one.

After my graduation from high school in 1945, I hitchhiked across the state trying to persuade a college to give me a football scholarship. I was big, willing, naïve, and raw as a crate of turnips. I made a tour of six or seven campuses, but the coaches rejected me on sight. I had a letter from my high school coach, but I didn't have much of a background. I really hadn't done anything. Nobody really knew me. I refused to give up, so I decided to go to Waco and try out at Baylor University. Baylor had suspended its football program for three years because of World War II, the only school in the old Southwest Conference to do that. But, with the end of the war on the horizon, Baylor was organizing a new team. I figured I would have a better chance to get on the team under those circumstances.

Baylor's regular football coach was still serving in the military, so Athletic Director Bill Henderson was the acting coach. He gave me the opportunity to try out. Since Baylor hadn't played football for three years, about 150 kids showed up on the field hoping to make the team. After about three weeks of workouts in late August, I really thought I had made that team because a bunch of kids had already washed out, and I was still around. But, after the last day's practice, Coach Henderson called me in with two other ragged candidates to his office. We were the last players to be cut. "You kids can't help us," he said as gently as he could, "but you have all worked hard and I appreciate it. I've arranged for you to go to another school if you want." He had taken the time and effort to call around to see if he could place us.

He said we had a choice of scholarships at Southwestern University, just down the road in Georgetown, or Tyler Junior College, over in East Texas. I asked him if Southwestern was a four-year school and he assured me that it was "a fine little college." So I decided to go to Georgetown. Coach Henderson wrote a letter asking them to give me a scholarship. I will always be grateful for Bill Henderson's help and kindness. That made my college education possible. I was the first member of my family, on either side, to attend college. Years later, after Coach Henderson died, I made a contribution to Baylor in his memory.

I will always be grateful to Southwestern for giving a full scholarship to a mediocre athlete. I'm not being modest when I say that. I was a pass receiver and I played both ways in the line. I didn't get to play much, but I loved going to that school.

The Boxer

Our coaches wanted everyone who was on scholarship to stay physically active during the off-season. I had a friend at Southwestern named Burt Guin, who was from the Rio Grande Valley. Burt was a middleweight who had boxed in the Golden Gloves for two years down in Harlingen. He needed someone to train with for a tournament in San Antonio in the winter of 1946, so Coach let me skip some workout sessions to train with him. Burt was a pretty good little boxer, so I learned a little about boxing from him.

I went with Burt to San Antonio for the tournament. We hitchhiked and stayed with a family friend. When we went downtown to Memorial Auditorium, the site of the tournament, for Burt to sign in, the guy running the tournament asked me if I was going to participate. I replied no, that I was just with my friend. He said that they were very short of heavyweight boxers and urged me to sign up. Burt egged me on, so I agreed to do it. I didn't realize that they had a novice class, which is where I belonged. I had never boxed in my life except for that little bit of training with Burt.

They entered me in the open class, which is where the experienced guys were placed. I got lucky because my first three bouts were with older guys who were fat and big but they had no clue about how to box. To my shock, I beat those guys easily and wound up in the finals. I thought, boy, I must be pretty good. In the finals, however, my opponent was an experienced guy in his mid-thirties who was a very good boxer. He just played around with me in the first round. In the second round, the first thing I heard was the referee counting "eight . . . nine . . ." I stumbled up, but my opponent had knocked me senseless, and they declared him the winner. They gave me a runner-up medal, and the school newspaper printed a story about Red McCombs, the famous heavyweight boxer from Southwestern University.

A Tour of Duty for Uncle Sam

I turned eighteen in October 1945, which made me subject to the military draft. I was in college, but I didn't have a deferment. Two of my buddies were in the same boat, so we checked around and learned that the army had a special enlistment program that allowed one to volunteer for the regular eighteen months of duty, but you got out in sixteen and a half months. That would satisfy your time. So in April 1946, to avoid the draft, my two friends and I left school and went to San Antonio and enlisted at Fort Sam Houston.

The army sent me to Fort Benning, where I was selected for Officer Candidate School. I made the Fort Benning football team, but didn't get to play much. I enjoyed my time at Fort Benning. The instruction I was getting there was as good as any I ever got in college. We had been in class three or four weeks when the major who was our instructor came in one morning and gave us a form to fill out and sign. I read the form and discovered that if I signed, it would extend my enlistment by one year. I told the major that I was sorry, but I was not going to sign the agreement. I had enlisted for eighteen months and I was going to stick to that. He took a hard line and tried to intimidate me. The major made it clear that I would not receive my officer's commission and that he would ship me off to Korea, which he called the armpit of the world. Well, in 1946, none of us had ever heard of Korea, much less knew where it was in the world.

I was only nineteen at the time, so I'm a bit surprised that I didn't give in, but I didn't. My buddies signed, however. When they found out I had refused, they told the major that they wanted to cancel their agreement. All of a sudden, the major had a little rebellion on his hands, so he brought in a colonel, who lowered the boom. Nevertheless, about seven or eight of us held our ground. The result was that we soon received orders to report to a transport ship in Oakland, California. We were bound for Korea.

We arrived in Korea on Thanksgiving Day, 1946. I got lucky, however. The army assigned me to a signals battalion where we had steam-heated rooms in very cold downtown Seoul. Some of the other guys were sent up to the thirty-eighth parallel, which was the demarcation line between the Soviet and U.S. occupation zones in Korea. I also got lucky as a result of my hanging out in the recreation room. The captain in charge called me in to his office and said, "Private McCombs, I see that you are a Texas boy and that you have boxed in the Golden Gloves program." I said that was true. He then asked if I would like to be his duty sergeant. Of course, I answered that I would do whatever he wanted. "Well," he said, "I need for you to be my 'gofer.' But I've also got my wife and two daughters over here, and I need for you to look after them." This was a great assignment: it was easy duty, and I loved his family.

Everything was rocking along until February 1947, when the captain asked me to put together a boxing team for the unit to compete in a tournament at the thirty-eighth parallel. I agreed and pinned notices on the bulletin board asking for volunteers for the boxing team. Several guys came forward. I recruited a trainer, and we prepared for the tournament. When the captain asked me how the team was coming along, I told him that we had a couple of guys who might be pretty good, depending on the competition. He asked if we had a full team. I replied that we did not. "We don't have a bantamweight or a heavyweight," I replied, "but we are okay otherwise."

The captain smiled and said, "Well, we do have a heavyweight and that's you." I replied, "No, I've already tried that. I'm not very good." He responded that he didn't care if I was any good or not, "you find a heavyweight or you're it." So I became the designated heavyweight for the boxing team.

The team and I traveled to this army facility on the thirty-eighth parallel for the tournament, which was held in a freezing cold arena. The room was filled with cigarette smoke and GIs drinking beer. It turned out that the first two boxers I faced were in terrible physical shape. Although I wasn't much of a boxer, I was in excellent condition, so I was able to handle them. Then I got a bye and wound up in the title match. I got lucky again. My opponent was scared to death, and I sensed it immediately. So I just got rid of him in the first round. Suddenly I was heavyweight champion of Korea.

My captain was delighted by this outcome. He decided that we would go to the Pacific finals, which were scheduled for August 1947. When I told him I would be out of the army by then, he said no, "I'll get you a commission and you can stay." I wasn't tempted by that offer. I went to the captain's wife to see if she could help me with her husband. Afterward, the captain called me to his office and said that it was pathetic that a heavyweight champion had to go to a 120-pound woman to cry on her shoulder. "I caught enough trouble from her last night," he complained, "so go on, you're out of here."

Back to School Again

After sixteen and a half months in the army, I happily received my discharge, retired from my boxing career, and headed home to Corpus Christi. One of the first things I did after I got back to Texas was buy a new car. At the end of World War II, my dad had taken a new job as service manager for the Ford dealer in Aransas Pass. As part of his compensation, the dealer gave him a certificate giving him permission to buy a new car. In 1947, new cars were still scarce, and there was a kind of rationing in place. Dad gave me the car certificate when I got out of the army in August.

While I was in the army, I had sent money home to be saved. When I got out, I had a nice stash of money put away, most of which came not from my army pay but from extra money I made hustling. I hustled everything. I just found a number of ways to make a few bucks here and a few bucks there. For example, when I was in Korea, I traded whiskey and cigarettes. And I did a lot of bartering. At any rate, I saved some money, and I was able to pay cash for my new car.

My primary goal after the army was to enroll at the University of Texas, which had been my plan ever since the first day that I had heard of the place. Under the terms of my enlistment in the army, I got credit for the full eighteen months of service. That gave me the right under the GI Bill to have government financial support for three full years of college, which is what I needed to complete my law degree.

I needed to earn a few more credits, however, before I could begin the three years of course work at the University of Texas and take advantage of my veteran's benefits. To earn those credits, I decided to enroll at Texas A&I College in Kingsville, near Corpus Christi, but I had to come up with a way to pay for it. I still had one year of eligibility to play college football, so I decided to try out for the A&I football team. If I made the team, I would have a scholarship.

Before going to Kingsville to meet the A&I coaches, I learned that Del Mar Junior College in Corpus Christi was putting together a football program to play that fall. I drove in my new car over to Del Mar, which had only one building, and found the head coach and his line coach. I told them my background and where I had played. I stressed that I could really help their new team, which was called the Vikings, but I was not going to use my GI bill benefits to go to school at Del Mar. I needed to save those benefits for my full three years of law school. If they wanted me, I would need full support for tuition, room and board, and books. I also wanted one hundred dollars a month in cash. They would only have to pay me for nine months because I would be leaving for the University of Texas after that.

They immediately replied that they didn't give anyone cash to play football. I responded that A&I was going to give me one hundred dollars in cash, which was a lie. We talked a little longer but didn't get anywhere. Finally, the coach told me that he would think it over. He asked me to come back the next morning. When I returned the next day, the coach said that he could pay all of my school expenses. In addition, he noted that I owned a car. He offered to give me ten dollars a week for the full nine months of school if I would agree to drive my car to the games and let other guys on the team drive with me. I accepted the offer.

The deal with Del Mar was one of the best I ever made because it resulted in my meeting the woman who would be the love of my life. When I went to the registrar's office to enroll, there was a line of students waiting ahead of me. In that line was one of the prettiest girls I had ever seen. She was wearing a little peach skirt, brown-and-white saddle oxfords, and had long brown hair. Her name was Charline Hamblin. I was fascinated immediately.

When she got up to the registrar's window, I heard Charline say that she was transferring one year of credits from Southwestern University. When she finished her business and started to walk away, I stepped out of line and told her that I had heard her tell the registrar that she had attended Southwestern. Charline answered that, yes, she had finished her freshman year at Southwestern. "Well," I said, "I want to transfer credits too, but I'm confused and I don't know how that works. I have a few questions. Would you have time to help me?" I asked her for a date, but she wasn't interested. It took me two or three months to get her attention, but I got it. I've always said that from the day I realized I was a salesman, I have signed only one lifetime contract, and that was with Charline.

I played one season of football at Del Mar. I was the co-captain. We didn't have a good team, but we got through the season. When I left Del Mar, my athletic career was over. By the end of spring 1948, I had completed my two semesters at Del Mar. I could now go to Austin and enroll in the University of Texas in the fall. That summer I took a temporary job with Magnolia Oil Company as a roughneck in the oil fields around Falfurrias and Freer in South Texas. It was hot and hard work, but I made good dough and saved most of it.

The University

When I enrolled at the University of Texas in the fall of 1948, my goal was to get as much formal education as I could, just as long as it didn't slow me down. I had to earn some additional credits in the business school before I could go to law school. I enjoyed both, but I was your basic B student with an attitude. In between classes, I played intramural sports and hung out with the athletes who were on scholarship.

My entrepreneurial instincts were alive and well while I was at the university. I was doing a few things around the campus, making three or four hundred bucks a month. I had been an entrepreneur from the time I was ten. I enjoyed college, especially the social life, but I felt the extra hours that were required to be a better student could be better applied elsewhere.

That was my outlook when late in the fall semester of my second year in UT Law School, one of my Alpha Tau Omega fraternity brothers, who had graduated, dropped by and stayed for supper. He had ranked in the top 5 percent of his class and had helped me with some courses as a tutor. I was shocked to find out that he had come back to school to earn some extra hours working on campus and doing some practice teaching. The reason he had returned was that in 1950 the range of pay offered to the top graduates was $350 to $375 a month.

Of course, this was before we had become such a litigious society. But I knew I was not by any definition a top student, so where did that leave me? I went over to the law school and confided my misgivings to one of the deans. He gave me a royal ass-chewing and said that the best lawyers entered the field because it was an honorable profession, not simply to make money. One did not expect to make "big" money until one had labored for years—at least.

I left his office in shock. I wanted to be a lawyer so I could be one of the select few who made the wheels turn. For advice, I talked to an economics professor I admired. I mentioned that I might drop out of school. He understood my concern. He told me that if I wanted to make money, I ought to get in the selling business. "Like what?" I asked. "Oh, high-ticket items," he replied. "Commissions won't have to wait until you learn all the ropes. You get paid on production."

I finally realized that a career in law was going to be too confining for a guy like me. It's hard to explain how significant a change that was. I'd always just assumed that law school was going to be my ticket to get there—wherever there was. But I really hadn't understood what the practice of law was about. When I did figure out just exactly what an attorney does, it was like I fell into a black hole for a day or two. I was really angry with myself. Why hadn't I found out what it was all about before I wasted this time in law school? Here I was twenty-two years old and I had no idea what I was going to do. The law was supposed to have been my ticket to success and the answer to everything.

The Awakening

But I quickly emerged from the gloom. I thought about that economics professor's advice. I realized that I should try out the selling profession, but it had to be selling big-ticket items that paid good commissions that would allow me to work as hard and make as much money as I could on my own initiative. I didn't want to work in some organization where I had to wait most of my life before I could get to the top of the ladder.

Within a couple of weeks, I had lined up a job in Jackson, Mississippi, with a University of Texas grad who was selling heavy equipment to build highways, roads, and dams. He agreed to pay me a commission on sales plus a small salary. The job didn't start until six weeks after the end of the spring semester, so I finished my classes, took my last final exam, and left school for good.

With six weeks to burn before I could report to work in Mississippi, I needed a temporary job to earn some money to tide me over. I accepted an offer from a friend who was with the Magnolia Oil Company to work temporarily as a roughneck on oil drilling rigs, work I had done previously as a summer job. On my way to Falfurrias, where the oil field was located, I stopped by Corpus Christi to visit my parents and to see Charline, whom I was still courting.

One night after Charline and I had gone to a movie, I dropped by a drive-in restaurant where some of my friends liked to hang out. One of them was a salesman at a Ford dealership owned by Austin Hemphill. He asked what I was doing at home. I told him I was on my way to a temporary job roughnecking on a drilling rig and then on to my new job in Mississippi. He asked why I would want to do that. "You're going to work those dusty oil fields, pull iron, and live on the ground with the snakes," he argued. "Charline is here. Why don't you come down to the car lot where I work and get a sales job there? We don't have to work hard. We spend half the day shooting pool. And they give us a new car to drive." When he told me what he was making, it didn't take me long to do the math. I said, "That's as much as I'll make working double shifts," which meant sixteen hours a day. He lifted his glass. "Come on down. I'll introduce you to the sales manager."

The irony of my agreeing to check out the car dealership job was that I had grown up certain that was the last thing I ever wanted to do. My father was an automobile mechanic most of his life and proud to be one. He was the best I ever saw at diagnosing a problem and fixing it. But as a kid, I hadn't seen anything attractive about the car business. I only saw long hours and low pay.

I went to the Ford dealership. Right off the bat, I knew this was something I would enjoy. The economy was booming, and cars were easy to sell. They gave me a job. I've never been shy about meeting and getting to know people, so I set out to make friends with the people who made the dealership work. I looked closely at the business setup to see how it operated. I got acquainted with the business manager, who let me examine the operating statements. He was impressed that a car salesman had an interest in the accounting. I studied the financial statements and thought, wait a minute, this seems to be a pretty good business. I realized that this was an opportunity.

I slipped around and got acquainted with the parts manager and found out what his role was. Whatever entry level you took—parts, sales, service, or accounting, any of the four—you were only about three steps from the bottom to the top. I found it to be an interesting business. Look out, I thought—I could be a dealer in a year!

In 1950 the national sales average was more or less ten units per month. I had no training, but they put me with another salesman and I learned the procedures and how to do the paperwork. After three weeks of training, I set a goal for myself to sell one car a day. I sold thirty-one cars a month for three years, which really grabbed the attention of my boss, Austin Hemphill. I still have all my pay slips to this day because I was proud of them. I had found my business! As it turned out, going to work at Hemphill Ford was one of the most important decisions I've ever made. The beautiful thing is that I am a natural entrepreneur. Buying and selling and trading things and seeing business opportunities that others don't see, that's always been a part of me, even to the present day.

I had found my calling, and I was making money. My gloom about my law career going south was in the distant past. I had a new plan and it was succeeding. Now I was ready to have a family. I knew I had the perfect partner in Charline, so in 1950 I decided to ask her to marry me. Charline went away for about two weeks to visit friends in Comfort, Texas. As soon as she returned to Corpus, I asked for a date. We were sitting in my car in her grandmother's driveway afterward when I pulled out a ring. Charline played coy and told me that she would think about it, but I knew then what her answer would be. This was in August, and we were married in November 1950.

Our wedding was at South Bluff Methodist Church, which had been founded by Charline's great-grandfather. I was so nervous at our wedding that the people sitting on the front pews later told me that my feet were shaking. The night we were married we drove to San Antonio. On the way, I told Charline about some of my goals and dreams. At one point I told her, "I want you to be prepared because we are going for a ride! I don't know what life holds for us, but it's going to be great. Some day I may come home and tell you we're going to South America, and I expect you to be supportive." Charline just looked at me and smiled. Then she said, "I've always wanted to go to South America." That was how we started our marriage. She keeps reminding me, by the way, that we've never gotten to South America.

The first of our three daughters, Lynda Gay McCombs, was born on December 29, 1951. Two more girls soon followed, Marsha and Connie. I had a family and a business career and I lived in the United States of America. Life was good and getting better with the passing of each day.

Red and Charline McCombs, November 9, 1950. Courtesy of the McCombs family.

Chapter Three

HEART LIKE A WHEEL

IN MY FIRST YEAR AT HEMPHILL FORD, I HAD SOME NOVEL CONCEPTS about how we should do business. But, because I was only twenty-two, my ideas were not welcome at the dealership. Like every other dealership in 1950, we were perpetuating the myth of a postwar car shortage. In a given week, as few as fifteen cars would be available for sale, even though seventy-five were being stored out of public sight in a warehouse. I told our sales manager, "Hey, why not pull out those cars we're hiding and hold a major sale?" He just stared at me, and that was the end of that. Later on, after I had my own business, I encouraged young people to speak their minds if they thought they knew a better way. I've often benefited from their suggestions.

At the end of my first year, I was recognized as the top salesman in town, but I was still considered too young to get a position in management. That didn't dampen my ambitions. There were other chances to make money, and I jumped on them. I got my license to sell car insurance. And if a person called to ask if I sold residential insurance, I said, "Sure, I can take care of that." I would turn it over to a real estate agent and take a commission. I met a builder who was doing one or two starter homes at a time for war veterans who had access to GI mortgages. I asked him why he didn't build three or four instead. We went to a bank, set up a line of credit, and became partners in building houses. I made a little money out of that.

I also got involved with the Chamber of Commerce. But I was itching to take the next step. Our dealership had good, solid management and no openings, so I contacted some of the other dealers. The response was the same. I was still too young. Didn't they realize that Alexander the Great was twenty-four when he conquered the world?

Not long after I got my feet on the ground selling new cars, I realized that while everyone is in love with new cars, the real leverage in the business was in used cars. I understood that the car manufacturer doesn't make your new car any different than he does for the next guy down the street who buys the same kind of car. Except for a few minor accessories, the new cars were all the same in those days. If you wanted to buy a new Ford convertible, it was the same at your place as it was at the next dealer's place. They didn't make them any differently. It's the manufacturer who sets the price on new cars, and they don't price them any different for any other dealer.

But every used car is unique. Even if you had five of the same year's model, different people would have owned each car, and those people would have used their cars differently from the others. That gives the used car salesman a story. And people like stories about the things they might be interested in buying. So you can have a story about how every used car had been driven and maintained. And the bottom line is that the percentage of profit on the mark-up is far better on a used car than it is on a new car.

For every new car sold there are two and a half used cars sold. Nevertheless, in those days, selling used cars was a business that most new car dealers largely overlooked or ignored. But they are the largest component of overall car sales in this country, and I figured that out quickly. A lot of new car dealers are new car dealers their whole career and never figure that out. They look at trade-in cars as a problem, and they don't want to get stuck with them. A lot of dealers don't even really stock used cars. They wholesale them or move them all out.

Once I realized that the used car business was more lucrative than the new car business, I also figured out that there was a market for people who had never had bank credit. These are good, working people who pay their bills. I saw a market that wasn't being recognized at the time, and I was determined to make a move. In 1953, I decided to put my ideas to the test and go out on my own with three years of selling experience behind me.

To get started, I needed a loan to buy inventory, as well as a ready source of money to finance used car purchases by people with no credit. The problem was that I had to convince a bank to make credit available to people who had never purchased anything on credit. This was during the old days, when the only people who could get loans from a bank were people who could prove to the bank that they had so many assets that they didn't really need the loan. And that's only a slight exaggeration.

I made an appointment with a local banker, Eugene Dabney of the Corpus Christi Bank and Trust. I spread my business plan across his desk, and I asked him for a loan to open a used car lot. I proposed to finance all my contracts with the bank and let them keep the reserve. I planned to sell my house and put that money into the deal, along with about $7,000 I had saved.

Mr. Dabney looked at the plan and after a long and very uncomfortable silence, said, "That is the silliest thing I ever heard of. You can throw that in the trash." I didn't understand. I asked him what there was not to like. "I don't like any of it," he replied. "You're twenty-five years old. You have a new house, a wife, and a baby. You're working for the best car company in town. What else do you want?" That question was easy to answer. I told him that I wanted my own business. What could be simpler? I straightened up the papers and continued, "Let's go through this again. You have always been supportive of me and I'm grateful for your advice. You are the smartest banker in town." Actually, he had never done anything for me.

Mr. Dabney didn't try to conceal his disbelief. "You don't show that you're taking down any of the finance reserve." I replied that I had no intention of doing that. "I'm going to let the bank apply it to my debt." He pointed out that I had not made provisions for taxes. "Yes, I have," I said. "Take a closer look at the plan." He replied, "Well, you can't operate without keeping the reserve. It can't be done."

I insisted that it could be done, because I was going to handle everything myself—buy, sell, finance, and keep the books. I told him that if I didn't succeed, I would pay him back every dime and admit the plan had failed. "But there is one thing I can always do," I stressed. "I can sell cars."

Dabney was a stereotype of what we used to think bankers should look like—a bald, cigar-smoking, dour man. I wore him down. "This is the silliest thing I've ever done," he said. "I'm going to do it, but I will be keeping a close watch on you." Armed with that loan, I quit my job at the Ford dealership and left with the blessings of Austin Hemphill, the kindly gentleman who was my first boss. Austin had been like a father to me. I had worked for him for three years, the only boss I ever really had. I would never have another.

My new business, McCombs Used Cars, began with two salesmen, including myself. I bought cars out of town and drove them back to Corpus. To Mr. Dabney's surprise and relief, I quickly paid off our loan and opened a second lot. Both lots prospered. Gene Dabney and I became good friends. He followed my career until he died. He was very proud of my success and the role he had played to help make it possible. The result was that by the age of twenty-five I had my own successful used car dealership.

Adventures in the Big State League, 1953–1957

By the end of 1953, I was doing real fine selling used cars in Corpus Christi. It was a rewarding and fun time. Late in 1953, I got a phone call from Bob Hamric, a former classmate of mine at Southwestern whom I had known since high school. Bob had been an all-around athlete. The New York Yankees signed him after college, but he never rose above Class A in the minor leagues. Bob was managing a baseball team in Harlingen when he called me. "I'm doing okay, but I'm not going anywhere. I see where your ball club in Corpus Christi might have to file for bankruptcy. Why don't you buy the team before that happens and I'll run it for you?"

It started out as one of those conversations you throw away the instant you put the phone down. I told Bob that my car business was booming and I couldn't take on anything else. I'll never forget what he said—"Red, as creative as you are, you'll figure that out." That was a challenge I found hard to decline. So Bob came to town and, before I had time to think up any good excuses not to do it, I agreed to get involved.

Bob and I decided to buy the Corpus Christi Aces, a club owned by the Schepps family, whose dairy company supplied milk products to towns all over Texas. We paid the princely sum of $10,000. Bob and I split the cost, fifty-fifty. The $5,000 I invested was just about all the savings that I had. Bob had to hock his wife's engagement ring to come up with his share. We also needed to keep the club out of bankruptcy, which meant that we would have to assume responsibility for the club's debts. For this plan to work, the club's creditors would have to agree to give us time to earn enough money to take care of the debt.

For help with the creditors, I went to Bob Sorrell, a brilliant lawyer in Corpus who also happened to be a regent for the University of Texas. He was a great sports fan. Bob agreed to help. He made a plan to keep our deal from going into bankruptcy. Bob called a meeting of the creditors to sell me to them. Bob had great credibility in Corpus. I had none. The creditors didn't know me. During the meeting with the creditors one guy asked Bob why he thought they would want to go along with me. "He's just a kid," he said. "We've already lost our money on this deal. In bankruptcy we'd at least get a little something out of the remaining assets. Why would we want to go with McCombs? He doesn't know anything about running a baseball team; he's never done anything like this."

Bob Sorrell asked if they "had ever thought about how much value there is in soiled jock straps?" He pointed out that the main asset with any monetary value was a little old baseball stadium, "but there's nobody to play in it, which means it's worth nothing." He argued that I was "a young, aggressive, healthy guy who's going to put everything he's got into getting the stock in this company." And Bob said I had a partner who was going to run the baseball team, and I would manage the sales and marketing end of the business. Bob asked, "What better shot have you got? This thing's been for sale for six months and nobody's touched it. You're not taking much of a chance with him, and he'll give you 70 percent of the cash flow for each of the first two years to liquidate the debt. And if he doesn't liquidate it then you release him. So you have the best end of the deal." The creditors went for it, and the deal went through.

It had taken everything we could do to get the money together to buy that stock and then make the operation work. We had no other choice. The first thing we did was change the name of the team from the Aces to the Clippers. Then it was Bob's job to assemble a roster. Bob was a very bright guy. It was his job to put the baseball team together, and he knew exactly what he was doing. We were an independent club, which meant that we were not owned by a major league team. We had a working agreement with the Milwaukee Braves, who had recently moved from Boston to Milwaukee. They held the contracts of half our players. We signed the rest and had our own scouts, who were paid a small fee to seek out talent that we could afford in Cuba, Mexico, and South America.

We had taken a team that had lost money and gone bust, and we were having the time of our lives. This is every fan's fantasy—making deals and moving the pieces around.

Down there in the dungeons of pro baseball, you gained a real healthy respect for a dollar or you didn't last. About a year after we bought the team from the Schepps family, it developed that they had not paid the government any withholding taxes. The feds sent the bill to us. Although it was only $3,000, we would have had to sell out the ballpark and have a big run on snow cones to make that kind of money. Bob and I informed the Schepps family that we didn't owe this tax bill, since it was not a baseball debt and not part of our original deal.

After going back and forth about who owed the taxes, we wound up in a hearing at the Shamrock Hotel in Houston with George Trautman, the commissioner of minor league baseball. George Schepps, a delightful man who spent the better part of his life owning teams in the Texas League, represented his family. I remember thinking that Bob and I had been in baseball for a year, and here we were in a beef with a man who probably knew Abner Doubleday!

Hamric, my twenty-six-year-old partner, and I put on our case. If we owed the local merchants, the bus companies, or the cafes where we fed the players, those debts were what we had agreed to pay since they were baseball related. But my interpretation did not include the federal government. Mr. Schepps, however, claimed it was a debt like any other. After Trautman listened to our arguments for an hour, he told Schepps, "George, you ought to know better. Taxes are a personal debt. I find in favor of the present owners."

George Schepps spent the last decade of his life running and promoting the Texas Baseball Hall of Fame, whose membership includes Dizzy Dean, Rogers Hornsby, Carl Hubbell, Joe Morgan, Brooks Robinson, Nolan Ryan, and Tris Speaker. Schepps was a feisty man right up to his last breath in 1997 at the age of ninety-four. I feel privileged to have engaged George in a negotiation, much less to have won.

Minor league baseball was once a way of life in America. Local fans could see some of next year's major league rookies playing for teams in cities such as Nashville, Minneapolis, Denver, and Louisville, which had teams at the top rung of the minor league system. At the lowest levels of the minor leagues, the caliber of play was not much higher than that of company teams, who played to see who bought the beer. There was always a railroad track near the ballpark, maybe a bakery, and an organist whose music pumped up the crowd. The players were there to chase a dream, or just for the love of the game.

The owners counted their pennies. Whether you made or lost money might depend on the cost of your phone bill. In those days we actually had a kind of salary cap in the Big State League, even though you couldn't enforce it. The way ours worked, you could pay 80 percent to one player and the balance to all the rest. The club had mostly older players going nowhere and young kids on the way up. We had a pretty decent shortstop making $325 a month, and I sent him a contract that gave him a raise to $340. In that league, an increase of nearly 10 percent was significant and, as the new owner, I included a nice letter saying that he deserved it.

When I didn't hear from him, I wrote again. This time he sent my letter back folded and with cutouts, like paper dolls. It read: "Dear Mr. McCombs, I don't know you, but you must enjoy a good joke. Enjoy this one." I called and asked him if we had a problem. He said, "You didn't mention anything about my cash. In addition to the three and a quarter the club has on the books, I get five hundred dollars each month in cash." Welcome to the real world, Red McCombs. The shortstop, by the way, was no amateur when it came to money. In the off-season he worked as a plumber.

After our first season, we attended the winter baseball meetings, where Robert Creamer, a correspondent with *Sports Illustrated,* introduced himself. I didn't know it then, but Bob was a wonderful writer who later would author an acclaimed biography of Babe Ruth. He said he had heard that "you guys" have a pretty good operation down in Corpus Christi. I realized this was our chance to attract some priceless recognition. I laid it on and, sure enough, Creamer wrote a feature story for *Sports Illustrated,* praising the Clippers as "the best lower minor league operation in baseball."

Thanks to Bob Hamric and our manager, Connie Ryan, the Clippers won the playoffs and the Big State League championship in our second season. I put people in the stands, paid off our debt, and retired the bank note for the ten grand we had used to buy the team. We just turned the town upside down. There I found again the magic of sports. I became a big deal overnight because I had the only sports team in town, and it was winning. Who wouldn't want to identify with that? It was a big deal.

In our first three years we continued to thrive on the field, and we led the Big State League in attendance, averaging 100,000 a year. We won the Big State League championship in 1955 and sent two players to the majors: Don Leppert, a catcher who went on to become a coach with several teams, and Ed Charles, a third baseman and part-time poet. He played on the Miracle Mets of 1969, and gave himself a nickname, "The Glider." His teammate, Nolan Ryan, told me that Charles hit a home run in the playoffs, and when he returned to the dugout he announced, "You never throw a slider to The Glider."

We had a Cuban pitcher, a left-hander named Rene Vega, who claimed to be twenty-six, but was probably ten years older, at least. He won thirty-plus games for us, and we were able to sell his contract to a club upstream, but that was as far as he went. We made our money that year by selling off our players to teams in Double-A and Triple-A.

We won our third straight pennant, but attendance began to fall despite our winning ways. The problem was that people had fallen in love with the television set. By 1956, those hard wooden bleachers in a ramshackle minor league park, the mosquitoes, and the muggy weather were no match for Jackie Gleason or *I Love Lucy.* I saw the end coming when my best friends, who owed me their loyalty, started to miss a few games.

As objective as I like to think I usually am, I blamed our decline on the local newspaper, the *Corpus Christi Caller-Times.* The beat writer was Roy Terrell, a young, crew-cut, good-natured guy. I'd watch the lights of the cars coming into the parking lot, the numbers growing smaller, and I would tell Roy, "If your paper had put a border around that box, we'd have some fans out here."

After Roy had heard all he wanted to hear, he said, "You know, Red, it might be worth your time to look around. You might find that people have discovered some things more interesting than this raggedy-assed baseball team of yours." He was right, and I apologized. Later, *Sports Illustrated* hired Roy, and his rise was something to see. He eventually became the magazine's editor and then publisher.

Whatever I didn't learn in kindergarten, I learned in the Big State League. Against all the odds, I made more than $100,000 and had a good time. But after the 1957 season, I called Hamric and said we should get out. Bob thought we ought to buy a club in the Texas League. I said, "Not me. The difference is, this is slow death. That would be sudden death." Pulling some papers out on my desk, I said, "I'm selling you my stock for ten bucks." I sealed an envelope and dropped it in the mail. I don't know if Bob loved baseball more, or money less, but he stuck it out for three or four more years. It was a financial disaster for him. Later, he had a chance to become a car dealer in Baytown, less than an hour out of Houston, and he called and asked for my help. He bought the dealership and rebuilt his wealth. Over time we made other deals, including cattle.

This was my "romance with pro baseball" story, and I wouldn't take anything for it. That was a huge boost to my ego, because I'd done something that other people couldn't do. Mr. Schepps, who had owned the club, was a very wealthy man from Dallas, and he couldn't do it. But I'd done it. That was a big boost to me. I also learned a lot of practical stuff from the experience. The elements of running a sports franchise are pretty much the same at any level in every sport. For example, everybody lies to you, and they all want to win. And later, I discovered that the big difference between running a team in the minors and one in the majors is the number of zeros on the checks you write.

Partners Red McCombs and Austin Hemphill at one of their San Antonio dealerships, 1964. Courtesy of the McCombs family.

Chapter Four

LIFE WITH EDSEL

EARLY IN 1957, MY OLD BOSS AND GOOD FRIEND AUSTIN HEMPHILL helped me secure my first new car dealership, which was with the Ford Motor Company. After two years of prepping, Ford was coming out with the Edsel in 1957, its first totally new car since World War II. It was going to be the most expensive new product launch in history. I was the youngest dealer in the country, and I could not have been more proud or excited.

To launch my new Edsel dealership, I hired three of the best car salesmen in Corpus Christi and brought in Charlie Thomas to work as my general manager. I first met Charlie Thomas a year earlier, when I had stopped by a Dodge franchise in Corpus that he was managing. I was looking for used car trade-ins. It didn't take a minute to size him up: he was bright, honest, and committed to the long hours the business required. I tried to hire him on the spot, but he decided to stick it out with the Dodge dealership. A few months later, he quit, called my office, and said, "I'm ready to take that offer. If you can pick me up right now, I'll be standing on the corner with my briefcase."

That began a friendship that has lasted more than half a century. No two people could have been better friends or less alike than Charlie Thomas and me. Charlie is compact, trim, tidy, quiet, reserved, soft-spoken, and modest—a man with very little packaging. I'm big, and I live big. I enjoy people, and I don't mind crowds. When I'm in a good mood, the normal force of my voice can frighten the birds off of tall trees. I have tousled red hair, and people say I look like Grizzly Adams, without the beard. If the weather forecast is partly cloudy, Charlie will carry a raincoat, a hat, and an umbrella. I'll have sunglasses in my shirt pocket.

Within a month, Charlie and I knew the Edsel wouldn't sell. It had taken the company five years to bring this vision to the marketplace, and it had endured a good bit of infighting in Detroit. Ford president Robert

McNamara, who became the first person outside the family to run the company, kept his distance from it. He followed the same philosophy at Ford as he later did as secretary of defense when he ran the war in Vietnam for Lyndon Johnson: "There is no strategy. There is only crisis management."

The Edsel had no advantage over the other cars in its class in price or new options. Its design drew puzzled reviews. What it had was a grill that people compared to a horse collar, or worse. The car went on sale the first week of September 1957. Given the early hype and the public's curiosity, the initial reaction was promising. My Edsel franchise immediately recorded the highest volume in the state. At the start, we averaged fifty to sixty-five sales a month. We actually made some money.

Even so, within a month I told the Ford company that the car wouldn't sell. As the weeks went by, it became too exhausting an effort to close the sale. There was too much resistance. It's true that the public was fascinated with the car initially, and it had as much publicity as any model in history. But it reminded me of the advertising agency that created a dynamite campaign for a new dog food. The cans flew off the shelves, and every supermarket clamored for reorders. This time they gathered dust, and the groceries were stuck with cases piled to the ceiling. "What happened?" the devastated ad agency cried out—"The public loved our campaign." The grocers responded: "Yeah, but the dogs wouldn't eat the dog food."

At the factory, they thought I was way out in left field. Why was I being so negative, they asked, when I was supposed to be working hard to push this car? And that was why. I didn't want to hand wrestle every customer to get them behind the wheel. I was an Edsel dealer for exactly five months. My friend Austin Hemphill, who had moved to San Antonio, warned me that I was being too hasty by bailing out. My banker urged me not to be too quick on the trigger. "Stay the course," he said. "You're young. Be patient."

Much more personal, and more difficult, was the knowledge that my father disapproved of my decision to jump ship. Over the years, he questioned some of my decisions in depth, but never in anger. When he did chide me, it was always gently, the only way he did anything.

I was frequently critical of the product, the style and design of Ford's cars, and this made my dad defensive. To him, Ford Motors could do no wrong, and he didn't like it when I criticized the company. He reminded me that they had "a lot of smart people at Ford" who surely knew what they were doing, and I only needed to give the model more time. But I thought three months of trying to sell the Edsel was darned near a life sentence.

Dad argued that I should stay with the Edsel for as long as the company did, because the Ford Motor Company would make it work. He set high standards for loyalty. This was that basic loyalty that had been a part of his life since he walked off the farm at nineteen. It was part of the character of a man who never sought glory, recognition, or monetary gain for himself. I saw him cry only twice in his life: when Henry Ford died and when FDR died.

I received very little support for my decision, but I never hesitated. The Edsel was simply not going to be a success, and I would not let it undo what I had just begun to build. I was fortunate in that I hadn't taken on any debt the way that almost all new businesses do. I had bought used equipment and parts bins, and I had a very small staff. I lost no money at all. I still had my two used car lots. I also had a leasing business for used equipment. Charlie Thomas and I went back to my two used car lots, and I learned a life lesson. You have to know the difference between a slump and a situation that is hopeless. Custer did not have a slump at Little Big Horn.

Four years to the month after it was launched, Ford announced that it would discontinue the Edsel. It had cost $350 million to develop. The company stock dropped twenty points. I got no pleasure out of this announcement. It was a sad day. The car had been named as a tribute to Henry Ford's only son, who had died of cancer at the age of forty-nine. As Bill Ford, one of Edsel's three sons, put it, you can't be pleased when your father's name becomes a synonym for failure.

Saving Hemphill Ford

In December 1957, when Austin Hemphill realized I was out of the Edsel business, he invited me to his new home in San Antonio. When I got to his house, Austin asked me to be his partner in his Ford dealership. We drank a lot of Scotch while I analyzed his operating statement. It showed that he was nearly broke.

Austin had built a new dealership a year or so earlier, and now he was on the verge of being wiped out. The country had slipped into a recession. The Ford lineup in 1958 was a dud and sales were off everywhere. The bottom line was that Austin was overdrawn at the bank and had covered it, as many car dealers do, by what is called an out-of-trust maneuver. That's essentially using the proceeds from selling one car to pay off the loan on another car. The original trust agreement obligates the dealer to pay off the lender as soon as the dealer sells a car, but the dealer can float that agreement for as long as sixty days, while he hopes to sell another car to pay that debt. It isn't unlike the common household practice of writing checks to pay your bills and hoping your deposit beats them to the bank.

In Austin's case, he was overdrawn by $100,000. The lender was auditing his inventory even as we spoke. He was a lawyer and understood the consequences. "If I don't get this deal turned around," he said, "I'm busted. Do you have any thoughts?"

I was stunned. I told him that the first thing we had to do was cure the out-of-trust problem. "I can't," he said. "I don't have the money." I told him that I had the money and that I would loan it to his dealership. I didn't know how else I could help, but I told him that I would come back to San Antonio in January to try.

The truth is that I had no strategy, but I was learning fast about crisis management. I figured I would spend no more than four weeks devoting all my effort to the dealership and see if I could salvage it. I still wasn't sure that I could pull it off. After we emptied that bottle of Scotch and talked for hours, I drove back to Corpus Christi.

If I could avoid it, I tried not to spend a full night away from home. It was late when I pulled into the driveway, still reeking of alcohol. As I eased into bed to kiss my beautiful wife, I said, "Honey, this is going to be hard for you to believe, and I'll explain it in the morning, but we're going to have to spend some time in San Antonio." Half-awake, Charline patted me over her shoulder and said, "Honey, go to sleep. You'll feel better in the morning." It was a quarter of three in the morning. My dad taught me that the greatest gift a father can give his children is to love their mother.

On January 2, I met with Austin Hemphill and his management team and sales force. Austin said, in effect, "All of you know about our problems. This is Red McCombs. I have a lot of confidence in him. Whatever he says, it is just the same as my saying it." In short, he gave me full authority over the dealership. After the meeting broke up, he put his arms around me, gave me a hug, and said, "If you need me, call the house." Then he got into his car and drove home.

This was my introduction to a big-time operation. In Corpus, I had five employees on two lots, and I did all the title applications, kept the books myself, and more. Hemphill had sixteen salesmen, and I met with each one individually. I told them that we would operate just as I had with my used car lots. By three p.m. the sales force had reduced itself to five. The others just walked out.

The five who stayed were invaluable to me. They were rewarded later when I was able to help them get their own dealerships. They all became successful dealers. I was disappointed that the others had left. Realizing that I was plowing new ground, I sat down at Austin's desk and wondered what I was doing there. I felt sick to my stomach. I actually threw up in a wastebasket in the office. I excused myself from the dealership and drove aimlessly for an hour, trying to clear my head.

By the time I pulled back into the parking lot, I realized that I had a real opportunity to help a friend. Here was a man who had turned his only asset over to me to do with as I thought best. No compliment of that magnitude had ever come my way. So I went from feeling sick to being exhilarated. It was all a matter of attitude. I met with the remaining five salesmen and told them we were going to do things that were beyond their imagination. All we had to do was stay together. Our comeback would start with me talking to every single person who walked into that dealership or who called us on the telephone.

In the auto industry, the reality is that we operate under the dumbest law any business ever imposed upon itself. In their unbelievably brainless judgment, the auto dealers lobbied Congress for years to get what we know today as the Sticker Law, which requires the manufacturer to post the retail price on the sticker of the car window. And for good measure the manufacturer has always set the wholesale price for the dealer. This is the only business I know where the factory picks the prices, both wholesale and retail.

You can see quickly what happened to the margins in the largest retail business in America. Meanwhile, the dealer has no say as to how the product will be designed or priced. What bugged me most of all was that dealers were so proud of the system. Years of lobbying and multimillions of dollars had gone into this effort.

In car dealerships, you have two invisible partners who are absolutely essential to your success. One is the manufacturer who supplies the product; in this case, Ford. The other is your bank or finance company.

Auto dealerships soaked up capital, not only for the inventory but to purchase the contracts of their customers. In 1958, Ford Motor did not yet have a credit corporation (this came into being in the early 1960s). So the dealers had to arrange their financing through other sources. Just as I had done with my used car lots, I offered a Buy Here/Pay Here program, with coupon booklets and payment notices, and secured a guaranteed line of credit at the bank.

The next problem I encountered was the simple fact that the 1958 model Ford was what the industry politely called a dog. It had no appeal to the customer whatsoever. This happens to the best of them from time to time, but since my role was to help Austin Hemphill, we had to find a way to persuade the public that the line was attractive. The '58 Ford was the only baby I had. This leap would require imaginative marketing and a lot of advertising, and I had not been much involved with either. But I got lucky. I have been blessed all through my career in many ways. This was one of those times.

Looking at the financial resources available to me, I decided to put nearly all of my money into an intensive two-week advertising campaign at KTSA-AM, the most popular local rock-and-roll radio station in San Antonio. I knew that the hottest morning radio program on KTSA, and in San Antonio, was the Ricci Ware show. I decided to buy out all of his advertising time and saturate the airwaves with promotions for Hemphill Ford. In addition, I wanted to take advantage of Ricci Ware's celebrity by personally associating him with our dealership. That would require my working directly with him as well as with KTSA's sales department.

The only problem was that I had never met Ricci Ware. So I had to figure out a way to contact him. People who know me today might find this statement somewhat curious, but at the time I had no identity in San Antonio—period. For me to call the station, to talk to the hottest jock on the air, whose ego was even bigger than his reputation, required some thought on my part. I decided not to be cute. I called the station, identified myself as a new Ford dealer in town, and asked to speak to Ricci Ware. I was informed that I really wanted to talk to a sales executive. I replied, "No, this is a personal matter. I have some information Mr. Ware needs. So have him call me."

A puzzled and haughty Ricci Ware returned my call, and virtually his first words were, "I never heard of you." In that one phone call, I told him I had a grand plan and needed him to help me. I had chosen him and only him for what I had in mind. Within an hour he was sitting in my office. I told him I was in San Antonio to help a friend through a difficult time. I told Ricci that I would give him my entire advertising budget for two weeks to see if he could put people in our car showroom. In addition to the regular spots, I would be using, in effect, his popularity and acceptance. I would actually own his show. He would be talking about the new gang at Hemphill Ford and would put his own personality into delivering much more than just a commercial.

I could not offer him anything under the table to do this, but he didn't even ask. I soon learned that Ricci had as much integrity as any man I ever knew. So I appealed to his ego and the humble nature that he hid under the surface, to help someone in trouble. Ricci bought into it. He delivered people to our dealership in big numbers, and we kick-started our sales campaign with that one strategy. Ricci and his wife, Mimi, and their children soon became some of the closest friends that my wife and I have ever had.

We sold all of our cars basically by applying logic and common sense to our problem. I didn't need fifty thousand people coming to the dealership. I just needed fifteen or twenty visitors a day. So why not concentrate my money in one place? I not only did this with Ricci and KTSA, but my success allowed me to go to the other station and cut a similar deal.

After launching the radio campaign, my next stop was at the office of my new financial partner, Dwight Weir, the manager for the UCIT Corporation, who financed our cars and bought the notes from the customers. I explained to Mr. Weir that the company was overdrawn by $100,000. He wrinkled up his nose in a way that pushed his glasses above his eyebrows. His bald head even had wrinkles. He said, "I've never seen you before. Who are you and what are you after?"

I was totally honest with Weir. I told him I needed his help. I had been told he enjoyed a drink occasionally, so I offered to buy him one. He responded to my offer by saying, "It may take more than one drink if you're over here telling me that my biggest account is broke and you're running the company for him." I told him that was about the size of it.

I knew I had to have Mr. Weir's support. Although we did not buy the contracts, I actually initialed every one. While there was no official guarantee, with a handshake I agreed to buy back any car that did not sell. I would sell it in Corpus instead. Honesty demands that I admit this was a gutsy call on my part and a questionable management decision on his part. But it made both of us very successful. We turned Hemphill Ford around in one week. Mr. Weir and his company were doing very well, and I no longer had to initial the contracts.

The Move to San Antonio

I had not intended to spend more than four weeks in San Antonio, but I got lucky and got some things going, so I decided to stay. In April 1958, I sold my two used car lots and made arrangements for Charline and our three little daughters to move to San Antonio. We did not realize that it would be the move of a lifetime. I brought Charlie Thomas with me to serve as our general manager. By the end of the summer of 1958, Austin Hemphill's floundering Ford dealership had garnered 50 percent of the San Antonio market. Two other dealers were splitting the other half. I was now a certified ninety-day wonder. We restructured the company with Hemphill and McCombs as partners, fifty-fifty. Austin offered me all of it, which he had no obligation to do, and I had too much conscience to accept.

The managers at Ford Motor Company noticed. They decided that I was their golden boy. "We can't sell these 1958 models anywhere in the United States," their general sales manager told me. "What are you doing?" They wanted me to fly to Detroit to discuss putting on sales meetings for them on the West Coast. I told him I couldn't do it. I felt that I was in a fairly good bargaining position, and since I still had twenty-seven new Edsels I offered a swap: if Ford would buy back my Edsels, I would go to California and do their sales meetings. He told me that he had nothing to do with the Edsel, that was another division of the company. I told him, "if Ford buys those cars back, I'll do your deal for you. Otherwise, I'm not going." He bought them.

That was a big deal because I still had those Edsels left. I would have sold those cars, but that was a much faster way to get rid of them. My spirits were soaring in 1958 because we had pulled one out of a ditch. Now Ford wanted me to tell my story. It was a good one to tell.

So I went out to Los Angeles for Ford Motor Company. I had been in the new car business for less than nine months and I was out there telling these dealers how to sell cars in Los Angeles. I really loved it. The heart of my talk was the point that attitude is absolutely the most critical element in selling anything to anyone in America. You can't fake attitude. You either have it or you don't. I'm an open book. I don't usually have to explain myself because people know instantly what my feelings are. If I'm not positive, they can tell. If I'm angry, even my dog can tell. And dogs are not unlike people in this respect: they know the difference between being kicked or stepped on accidentally. If your attitude is poor, change it. Go bust a tree stump or puke or whatever it takes. And what I was telling them was right; it would work. In doing that I kind of got a national reputation.

Trail Blazing in Houston

Late in the summer of 1958, Ford's management contacted Austin Hemphill and me about salvaging a dealership that was dropping like a marble down a drain pipe in Houston. It had lost money for twenty-two straight months. The location was wrong, the showroom was dilapidated, and the roof leaked. If it rained, they needed buckets on the floor. The guys in the service department had to roll up their pants because the garage flooded. The good news was that they didn't need to worry about having to keep a lot of cars dry. They only had three in the showroom.

Austin and I drove over to Houston to visit with the dealer-in-distress. When we met at the old Shamrock Hotel, I looked at their balance sheet and discovered they had $2 million in losses. It was going to take $150,000 just to bring the dealership out of trust. In a torrent of optimism, I figured we could carry that loss forward if we ever made big money. I told Austin that we should buy the company, warts and all. We acquired their 300 shares of stock at a cost of one dollar a share. They were like mice that no longer wanted the cheese—they just wanted out of the trap.

To make this Houston dealership successful, I decided to take an approach that was working in San Antonio. Austin and I had leased four lots around San Antonio, where we put both new and used cars, which at that time was a unique strategy in the car industry. I had persuaded Ford management to sign off on it as a test market. If it worked, to make it fair, other dealers could do the same. The other dealers thought we were crazy, but it did work.

My plan for Houston was to operate from five locations, four of them strictly outdoor lots. Those outdoor lots would have almost no overhead. All I heard was how the idea didn't have a chance. People kept reminding me of how little I knew about the city of Houston. But I could look past the Shamrock, toward Main Street and Fannin, and see that they were building the Texas Medical Center, one of the great facilities in the world. I saw some vacant land nearby, went to the owner, and convinced him to let me use it. I would get out in 120 days if he wanted, but in the meantime I promised to bring so much attention to that location he would have no trouble selling it. He agreed to the deal. If he sold the property in that period of time, I would recover half the money I planned to spend on pavement and lights. But if I stayed there for three years, he would owe me nothing.

This was where I intended to capture the Houston market. I strung up hundreds of lights and put three trailers together as offices. I had one problem: Houston wasn't yet in a building boom, and I couldn't get power to my lights. I called Stewart and Stevenson, the oil field supply company, and asked to borrow a gas generator. I remembered this power source from my summer jobs as an oil rigger.

Car dealers can't operate in this fashion today, and, in truth, they were not allowed to do it back then. Lee Iacocca, whom I met when he was climbing up the management ladder at Ford in the late 1950s, said many times that I had a longer tenure with test programs than anyone in the history of Ford Motors.

I made another trail-blazing decision in Houston. I decided to give my entire advertising budget to only one of the city's three stations. I had their sales managers assemble in my suite at the Shamrock, asked for their proposals, and told them I would commit my money to one station. After they left, I threw away their advertising rate cards. Thirty minutes later, they began calling back. One went for my offer. I would pay the 2 a.m. rate for commercials, but under the table I would be guaranteed half my spots in prime time. I took a six-month option and then signed up for six more.

Now, for me to go on television with all these spots, I had to have a hook. My Christmas lights, strung across a full block out by the Shamrock, were attention grabbing, but what was my sales hook? Every dealer claims to have lower prices or that they can beat any deal. My hook, however, was: "Two to one, the Ford in front of you came from Hemphill." The advertising people told me that I couldn't say that I was outselling my rivals by two-to-one for the simple reason that I wasn't. But that was not my claim. All I did was quote what the odds were. The slogan caught on. Newspaper columnists even wrote about looking at the Ford in front of them and not seeing a Hemphill sticker. You couldn't buy publicity like that.

We broke the Houston market wide open in the second month. That little bankrupt dealership became the most profitable in the city. Everyone who managed one of our outdoor lots ultimately became a dealer and wealthy in his own right. And until 2002 the dealership was operated by my friend and longtime partner, Charlie Thomas, the former owner of the Houston Rockets.

Making two million dollars, and writing off the taxes, gave our little company the capital we needed. The return from that dealership was the basis of everything we have done since. I never calculated the total returns, but it was worth tens of millions.

Ford—Factory Direct to You!

With my success in Houston, I became a big name within the auto business nationwide. In July 1959, Ford asked me to go to Dallas and take over another failing dealership. Ford thought it would be a good idea to have a breakfast meeting between me and the other five Ford dealers to talk about how we were going to work together for the good of us all. That was a laugh. At breakfast they told me, in no uncertain terms, that I had taken San Antonio and Houston by surprise, but it would not happen in Dallas. They would lose money if necessary to keep me from succeeding. This was not exactly the loving embrace you would hope to get from your new neighbors, but I thought we could overcome their hostility.

Not one to run from a challenge, I developed a special marketing strategy for Dallas, one of the best of my career. I found an old three-story building on Cedar Springs Road that used an elevator to bring up the cars. The building had no signage identifying it as a dealership. The string-of-bright-lights strategy that I had used on the open lots in Houston wouldn't work with this building. Then I got an idea. Ford had an assembly plant in Dallas, and it had agreed to build me up to fifteen hundred cars in sequence. I realized that I could use the factory deal in my promotion. I came up with the sales slogan: "Ford—factory direct to you!"

I had a convoy of trucks with these new cars unloaded at the warehouse on Cedar Springs while photographers snapped pictures. There was still no dealership name on the building. Today that would be illegal. You have to identify yourself. But it wasn't illegal in 1959—just a little outrageous. I knew that the other dealers in Dallas would rise up in arms and that Ford's management would come unglued. I kept my plan under wraps until the day we ran with it. I bought big billboards that shouted, "FORD—FACTORY DIRECT TO YOU!"

We needed cops to take care of the traffic jams. I had to fly in salesmen from Houston and San Antonio. I knew the heat was going to be unbelievable, so I hid out in a little motel not far from the site. The flak from the other dealers and Ford was intense. It got to a point where I had to ask Austin Hemphill to tell anyone who called for me that I was "unavailable." I simply disappeared. Ford fired off a threatening message to Austin: "If we can't find Red to stop this, we will have to get a court order to shut him down."

In five days we sold six hundred cars. I never sold that many in that short a time, before or since—and I am not certain anyone else has. When I finally emerged from the motel, like a mole from a tunnel, I apologized to everyone concerned. It was the least I could do. I explained that I didn't realize we were going to create that big a problem. I had my signs removed. I promised to play nice.

In less than fifteen months I went from having two used car lots to having anchor stores in Dallas, Houston, and San Antonio. From then on they couldn't stop me. Suddenly I'm in my early thirties and I've got money. It wasn't easy. I was working seven days a week, but I was loving every minute of it. I really didn't stumble anywhere along the way. It had to work, and it did work. I made it work. And the rest just kept coming.

When I recall that episode of fifty years ago, I realize that there is a certain amount of recklessness and courage that comes with youth. And, I do have to admit, a huge dose of sheer fun and mischief. I believe one of my assets is that I have no fear of losing. And I have no fear of people. By and large, I like most people, but I am not in awe of anyone I ever met. I do try to feel total respect for everyone, with the possible exception of the guy who designed the Edsel.

Buying the Alamo

While I'm on the subject, I should point out that my fondness for outrageous, attention-getting car promotions didn't end with my escapade in Dallas. One particular promotion that stands out in my memory was the one I did in conjunction with the opening of the John Wayne movie *The Alamo*, which had its world premiere in 1960 at the Woodlawn Theater in San Antonio. The movie was filmed over in Brackettville, about 120 miles west of San Antonio. I visited the set a few times while they were filming, and I got to know a lot of the people who were working on the movie. And, of course, I sold a bunch of cars to the crew.

After the premiere, which was a private gala fundraising event, I bought all of the tickets for the first day of the public showing of the movie. I made the deal with the owner of the theater. To get a ticket to the screenings on that first day, people would have to come to my car lot to test drive a car and write an opinion about the car. To promote this ticket deal, I bought a bunch of radio and television commercials. We used an echo effect for the radio ads to make them hard to ignore. The ads would declare very loudly that "RED MCCOMBS HAS BOUGHT THE ALAMO! RED MCCOMBS HAS BOUGHT THE ALAMO?" Then I would come in and calmly state that "Yes, I have bought the Alamo. I bought the Alamo all day for the first day of the public screening. You can get a ticket at our Ford dealership." I did all of my own commercials on television for about twenty-five years. At any rate, this commercial created a big furor in San Antonio, but that's exactly what I wanted it to do. People flocked to my dealership, and we sold a large number of cars.

It was an overwhelming success, but I had anticipated that it was going to offend some people. And, of course, that happened. The Daughters of the Republic of Texas, who are caretakers of the Alamo, were especially unhappy about my promotion. They sent a little delegation to my office at the car lot to express their displeasure. I issued an apology and said that I had meant no disrespect. I promised to take the commercials off the very next day, which pleased them. Of course, the promotion had ended by then, but I did keep my promise. I should add that I have supported the DRT's work over the years with financial contributions, and I admire and respect all that they do to preserve the Alamo. But the Daughters haven't always been happy with me.

"Red Mustang"

When Ford introduced its Mustang model in 1964, it was an immediate hit. The car was styled well and priced right. The list price on the car was $2,350. When you get a hot model like that, it's a hot model for all dealers, so everyone wants to have priority on inventory supply, including me. By 1964, because of having served as the president of the Ford dealers national organization, I had developed a good relationship with Ford's dynamic president, Lee Iacocca. I'll have more to say about Iacocca later in this book, but the point here is that I soon took advantage of my connection with Iacocca to get the Mustangs that I needed.

I called Lee and told him, "Lee, congratulations! The Mustang is as hot as a pistol, which means that I've got to have more of them to sell." Lee replied, "Yeah, well you and everybody else. Now, Red, don't be giving me any trouble about this. There's nothing I can do about it anyway. You are our biggest dealer in Texas, by far, but you are getting inventory proportionate to your size, not any more than that."

I told Lee that there was a little more to it than that. Lee replied, "Why am I not surprised?" I said that it didn't matter what anyone else had done, including him, but no one else had embraced the Mustang the way I had. Lee answered "Oh, is that so?" I replied, "Well, yes. I've changed my name from Red McCombs to "Red Mustang." He told me that I was full of crap and that he didn't believe it. So I held the telephone up to the speaker of a tape recorder and played an ad that I had recorded. It was in the form of a news interview and the "reporter" asks, "Mr. McCombs, I understand we have quite a story here. Let's get to the bottom of it. Is it true that you have changed your name to Red Mustang?" I respond, "Yes I have. I'm so excited about this new car that I want to be personally identified with it, so I've changed my name to Red Mustang. Instead of Red McCombs Ford, our dealership is now named Red Mustang Ford." Then the "reporter" asks, "if you've changed your name to Red Mustang, how does that affect Mrs. McCombs?" My answer was "Oh, she's still my wife."

By the way, Charline heard that commercial on her car radio. She pulled over to a pay phone on the road and called me. "I just heard that spot about me still being your wife. You can do all these silly things that you want to, but use your name, not mine. Get me out of that commercial right now and don't ever do anything like that again." Naturally, I apologized profusely and sincerely, but I didn't change the ad.

After Iacocca heard this commercial, I told him that I had changed my name at the courthouse and filed that I was doing business as "Red

Mustang Ford," so it was legal and official. That did it for Lee. I don't know if he was appalled or excited by my machinations, but for whatever reason, he finally did agree to give me an extra supply of Mustangs.

I put up big billboard ads around town declaring that I had changed my name to "Red Mustang," so why would you buy a Mustang from anyone else? We played that game for a couple of months and then we let it fade out, but not until we sold a bunch of those cars. It could not have been a greater success.

Automobile manufacturers all try to find some little niche in the market in styling or in power plant or in something that will set their cars a little apart from the competition because, at the end of the day, all cars are essentially the same. When a manufacturer can come up with an attractive styling package, particularly in a lower-priced vehicle such as the Mustang, it's like discovering a large oil field. It doesn't happen very often. During that 1964–1965 run the Mustang set sales records that I doubt will ever be broken. Keep in mind that in those days it took about five years from conception of an idea until they got a car actually built. That's a long time lag. If you wind up making a lemon, then you've lost five years of product development. But all of the manufacturers are looking for the next Mustang or whatever will become the hottest car around. It doesn't happen too often, but it does happen. And when it does, I'm ready to change my name again!

Red McCombs with his parents, W. N. and Gladys McCombs, and sister Mildred, 1929. Courtesy of the McCombs family.

Chapter Five

ALL IN THE FAMILY

I BELIEVE MY DAD FORGAVE ME FOR BAILING OUT ON THE EDSEL. He was still working at his job with a Ford dealership in Aransas Pass when I gave up on the Edsel. He eventually realized that Ford had made a mistake, especially after the company finally took the car off the market.

After Charline and I moved to San Antonio, Mom and Dad visited us one weekend a month. In 1959, after we had lived in San Antonio for a year or so, and the folks had just left from a visit with us, Charline suggested that I invite Mom and Dad to San Antonio so that Dad could work in my service department. Her suggestion caught me off guard. That idea had never occurred to me. I was just sure that Mom and Dad preferred to live in a smaller town. I mumbled something like, "Why, Dad would never do that. He likes the small town life. He's happy in the Ford garage where he works. He would never move." Charline replied that she wasn't so certain of that. She urged me to ask him. I don't want to come off as sexist, but there is a feminine instinct that men lack, one that involves the unseen longings in each of us.

The next morning I called my father and told him how much we enjoyed spending the weekend with them. I said we had a large operation in San Antonio, and it was a big city, but if he ever decided to leave Aransas Pass, Charline and I would love to have him work with us. I told him that I knew he would be a valuable asset to our service department. Dad didn't say yes, but he didn't say no, either. I hung the phone up and thought that was probably the end of that.

Within two hours, however, I had a call from Dad's boss, Walter Boehnke, who had befriended me in many ways over the years. His opening line was, "Red, can I do anything to help you with your problems?" I was surprised and asked him why he thought I had any problems. He replied that Dad had come to his office and told him that I was having so many problems with my business that he had to move to San Antonio to help me out. Dad told Walter that he would stay in Port Aransas until Walter could find his replacement, but as soon as possible he had "to go help his boy." Charline's perception had been right on target. Dad would never have told me that he wanted to work for me.

Mr. Boehnke and I had a nice laugh about that, and I asked him to please keep our conversation just between us, which he did. A few weeks later, my parents moved to San Antonio, and Dad spent the rest of his life working for me. Every morning he would mosey by the office to say hello and give me a hug. We are a hugging family. I had one of the most devoted fathers of all time. Dad was very warm and soft-spoken and really believed that his children could do no wrong. My father had such confidence in all of us that if one of his kids shot the sheriff at high noon he would have said, "Well, there must have been a good reason."

Whenever I got the chance, I dropped by Dad's work area to visit with him. He liked that, but I liked it even more. To have an opportunity to work with your father for several years is an experience that most people don't get to share. It takes a special man, secure and humble and unselfish, to work for his son. My dad did it without hesitation, without demands, without conditions. All he wanted was to help, and to let his wife enjoy her granddaughters. Dad was fifty-six when he went to work for me. He had been working since he was nine years old, but I don't think financial rewards ever figured into my father's definition of success.

Dad's memory for detail was spectacular. He could remember people, events, times, dates, and circumstances. He was a slow reader, but he retained everything he read. He couldn't wait to read the technical manuals to see how the new technology worked. He was wonderful at dealing with people, and he thrived on fixing their problems. You had a very comfortable feeling in his presence, and when you left you felt better for having been there. No one could fake the concern he showed. That was a plus in our business, where you never hear this from a customer: "Good morning, my car is running perfectly, and I want to tell you what a great day it is."

After Dad had worked with us for a couple of years, Charline suggested that I talk to him about taking a month off for vacation instead of the usual two weeks. I had learned not to question Charline's insights. When I raised the idea with Dad, he sort of hesitated and said, "I don't know. You really need me here." But I could see in his eyes that he was receptive.

So we worked it out. Later we made the vacation two months instead of one. That was the schedule for the last five years before he retired.

Dad retired just before he turned sixty-five. We had a nice reception for him, and I read a telegram from Henry Ford II and a nice letter from President Johnson congratulating Dad on his retirement. Charline and I gave Mom and Dad a top-of-the-line motor home and a Texaco credit card as a going-away present. Dad was always loyal to the places where he had done business, and he wouldn't buy gasoline at any station but Texaco.

On a typical trip Mom and Dad would be gone for five or six weeks, then come home, stay a week, and take off in another direction. They became history buffs and traveled all over Alaska and the Northwest, meeting old friends and making new ones. Once, I got a call from a friend of mine in Seattle. He said I was wasting my money if I was spending any on public relations. He had just spent ten days in Hawaii, listening to my father, and he had never heard such puffery about my business.

Six years after retirement, Dad and Mom were camping out with a group in the Santa Fe National Forest in New Mexico. As they watched the sunset, Dad took out his Bible and read aloud from Psalm 24:

"The earth is the Lord's, and the fullness thereof; the world and they that dwell therein. For he hath founded it upon the seas, and established it upon the floods. Who shall ascend into the hill of the Lord? Or who shall stand in his holy place? He that hath clean hands and a pure heart; who hath not lifted up his soul unto vanity, nor sworn deceitfully. He shall receive the blessing from the Lord, and righteousness from the God of his salvation."

Mom and Dad played dominoes until about ten that night, kissed, and went to sleep. About two a.m. she heard him groan and utter three words: "Mother, I hurt." She saw him try to sit up and then fall back in his bed. He did not move again. When they called an ambulance, it was already too late. The date was August 28, 1974. He was seventy-one years old.

Willie Nathan McCombs was a loving and caring man who never pressured his children about what they should do. He was always a booster, a man of compliments and encouragement. He was extremely proud of what he did, never losing sight of the fact that fixing and repairing machinery was a true talent. In his mind, he probably felt people in management, such as myself, had the lesser role. He was probably right.

Gene McCombs

I have two sisters, Mildred, whom we call "Sissy," and LaWanda, who is the youngest of my siblings. For many years, Sissy was a medical researcher in New Orleans. She now lives in Round Rock, Texas. My other sister, LaWanda, was the ticket manager for the San Antonio Spurs. She still lives in San Antonio.

Of the kids, however, my brother Gene was the one who was more like my father than my sisters or me. Gene, who was an evangelist, was married for forty-nine years to the former Mary Broadway, a delightfully ironic name for one who walked beside her husband with God. Gene and Mary raised two children, built four churches, and recited the Twenty-third Psalm together every night of their marriage, in sickness and in health. The first time I ever heard Gene preach, just out of his teens, I predicted he would become an evangelist.

Gene preached across the South and had a good name, if not a big one, as the founder of the McCombs Evangelistic Ministries. He was sweet-tempered and rarely critical—qualities he inherited from our father. Gene was younger than me by three years, and we had a typical big brother–little brother relationship. My total admiration for him really came about when he was in the seminary training to be a Baptist preacher. He married before I did and had a beautiful daughter and son.

I shared my resources with him in a minimal way while he attended school. In his second year in the seminary, a mutual friend brought to my attention that Gene was living in absolute poverty. I was not aware of that, and I immediately went to Fort Worth, where I found a half-day's supply of food in his refrigerator. He had lost a part-time job and truly was in dire circumstances, which he had never mentioned. When I asked him what source of income he had other than the meager amount I was sending him, he said he had borrowed a hand mower and was mowing lawns. At that time he was the pastor of a church that paid him nothing, and he had the expense of buying gasoline to get there.

As a young car salesman, I wasn't exactly running around with hundred-dollar bills falling out of my pocket. Charline joined me in offering to share what we had. We all received more from Gene than we gave. I was so struck by his faith, and his insistence that he was fine and that everything would be okay, that I embraced him. I made a promise that, for the rest of his life, whatever my living circumstances were, I would commit to him that he would have the same. It was a privilege for Charline and me to be able to share our good fortune with Gene and Mary.

Although he was basically disabled for the last fifteen years of his life, Gene was a daily inspiration of faith and hope. Never once was there a negative thought. I was privileged all of my adult life to experience that kind of love from my parents and subsequently from Gene. I recognized that where God had called him to minister to the people, Gene had been faithful to that commitment in such a way that it was uplifting for me. From time to time, I found it easy to look at whatever situation I was in and never feel I had the bad end of anything. After Gene died, his impact on my life did not stop, because every day I refer back to some of his letters that lifted my spirit and continue to play a huge role in my life.

My financial aid to Gene had an unexpected consequence. There were times in his ministry when some of his parishioners would question how a poorly paid Baptist minister could live in a fine home, drive a new car, and travel to Europe. The church was paying him only $600 a month. This is a sad commentary, but fortunately not a common one.

Gene McCombs died in July 2000 after a painful twenty-year struggle with lupus. He was sixty-nine. The Memphis newspaper, the *Commercial Appeal,* referred in its obituary to his "purity, humility and integrity," adding that these were "not words that come to mind when you think of an evangelist." He not only was a brother but my rock, and I was his supporter. Having loving parents and siblings is a gift from angels.

Texas governor John Connally with Henry Ford II at the HemisFair in San Antonio, 1968. Courtesy San Antonio Light *Collection, Institute of Texan Cultures, UTSA, # L-7149-64-f7.*

Chapter Six

IACOCCA AND THE BIG THREE FOLLIES

TWO OF THE MOST INFLUENTIAL MEN IN MY LIFE DURING MY first fifteen years in the car business were Henry Ford II, the president of the Ford Company and grandson of the founder of the company, and Lee Iacocca, the brains behind many of the Ford Company's most successful cars.

Henry the Second and Iacocca

Young Henry Ford suffered from being in the giant shadow of his grandfather, whose name he bore. Anyone would have. Old Henry hand-built his first car in 1896, inspiring Will Rogers to later observe: "It will take a hundred years to tell whether he helped us or hurt us, but he certainly didn't leave us where he found us."

That verdict had been in long before I arrived. Just as I always wanted to be involved in the decision making in the towns where I lived, I lobbied and politicked my way onto the Ford Dealer Council. Every manufacturer has one. I was elected chairman of the national council in 1963, five years after I became a Ford dealer. At that level, you have access to the company's leadership, including Henry the Second. I know, it sounds like royalty, but in a sense the Ford family was.

A national chair represents six thousand Ford dealers around the country in expressing their views and complaints and problems to company management. In this position, I had contacts on an ongoing basis with Lee Iacocca, who at that time was vice president of the car and truck division. He became president of the company in 1970. Lee was the guy who developed and promoted the Mustang in 1964 and revived the Ford racing team. I found him to be everything that has been written about him: bright, extremely energetic, forceful, fun, and tough. We fought and laughed and had lots of battles. Obviously, Lee won most of them because he was the boss. The eighteen-hour workday was routine for him. He had a sort of Sicilian loyalty to his ideas and to his people, but this did not include Henry the Second.

From time to time, certain issues went all the way to Henry's desk. I loved the opportunity to push a program from the dealers' point of view, to act as their spokesman. Henry was totally aware of the goings-on in the company; he was very much hands-on. He did not mind giving you one of two answers, a "no" or a "hell, no."

The hot issues between the dealers and the company generally related to the warranty terms, pricing, car models, and options the competition offered but Ford did not. Those are issues that are more or less permanent. It is hard for people outside of the business to understand, but the relationship between the dealer and the manufacturer has never been an easy one. There has always been distrust and animosity.

Before Ross Perot sold his General Motors stock back to the company, he called one day from Dallas and asked if he could fly down and spend a couple of hours with me on what he called the "automotive" business. He wanted to know why this chasm between the company and the dealers existed. We had a lively discussion. Perot wanted to know how to change the culture at GM. I told him honestly that I didn't think anyone could.

Publicly, the dealers would say great things about the manufacturer. The car companies always stressed that they loved the dealers. But the fact is, the contentious atmosphere that generally exists is an inherent part of the structure. You learn to live with it, which requires a lot of give and take by both sides.

Lee Iacocca was a master at playing the give-and-take game with his dealers. Lee is down-to-earth, but he is also a very sophisticated man. He is always ready to go head to head with anyone on the issues. At times, he was sympathetic to the dealers' needs, although that rarely led to any positive results. Nevertheless, he was accessible. I was surprised to have as much access as I did to the man who headed the Ford Motor Division.

What sticks out in my mind is how competitive Lee was. He absolutely had to win. He is a take-no-prisoners kind of guy. Lee also had an "I'm down in the trenches with you" type of attitude, which was a quality that appealed to the dealers.

HemisFair

I generally got along well with Lee, but we did bump heads occasionally. Our most memorable conflict, which stemmed from the planning for the HemisFair in San Antonio in 1968, had little to do with the relationship between dealer and manufacturer. I was vice chairman of the HemisFair executive committee and therefore deeply involved in planning and promotion for the fair. We planned for twenty-six industrial exhibits and freestanding buildings that featured a theme. I knew it would be expensive, but I thought, for personal and marketing reasons, that I could count on Ford to sponsor one of those exhibits.

We attracted some major Texas corporations such as Humble Oil and Southwestern Bell as sponsors, but we were having no success with national corporations. The problem was that San Antonio was a city beloved by tourists, but it had a low per capita income and absolutely no entrée to corporate America. I asked Ford for a sponsorship, but the request was held up at corporate headquarters for almost twelve months.

John Connally, who was governor of Texas during this period, had been a major proponent of the fair. He called a meeting to see what could be done to attract some major national corporations. As a member of the sponsorship committee, I was asked to give one of the reports at the meeting with the governor. Early that morning before the meeting, I called Lee Iacocca and begged him to get Ford to sponsor a building. I reminded him that the proposal had been under consideration for a year. He replied flatly that the company was not going to do it. "This fair has no economic or *political* significance for the Ford Motor Company," Lee declared. The conversation actually escalated into a cussing fight on the phone. I remember just boiling when he referred to "that dusty little town of yours," concluding with, "Mr. Ford will be sending a personal emissary to Governor Connally to select an art object as our gift to the fair."

I knew when I hung up with him, however, that our problem was solved. John Connally was one of my heroes. He was a handsome, imposing figure who turned heads when he walked into a room. Connally was then the most popular governor Texas had ever had. He was respected across party lines, and he carried scars from wounds sustained in the assassination of President Kennedy.

After my talk with Iacocca, I called Governor Connally and complained, "Have I been stupid or what? The Ford Motor Company sees no economic or political significance in the HemisFair." Connally said, "Fine, you call Iacocca and tell him we won't be bothering him again. The president will be calling Mr. Ford to point out what this fair means to the southwest and to the countries of the Western Hemisphere." Of course, the president was Lyndon Johnson of Texas.

I called Lee Iacocca back. When I gave him Connally's message, I could hear the sudden change of interest in his voice. He did not want us to go over his head. But the last thing he wanted was for Lyndon Johnson to negotiate directly with Henry Ford. "Give me forty-eight hours," he said, "and let me talk to Governor Connally and see what we can work out." The record will show that when the HemisFair opened on April 6, 1968, Governor Connally and Lee Iacocca posed cheerfully for photographers in front of the grand and modern Ford Building.

Once we recognized that the key was to get President Johnson to call other corporate heads, our sponsorship problems vanished. The HemisFair literally put San Antonio on the international map. Many of the buildings, including a convention center and arena and the 750-foot-tall Tower of the Americas, were designed for permanent use. The arena served as the first home for the Spurs pro basketball team.

The Altercation

I had many other dealings with the LBJ White House. During LBJ's presidency, the White House press corps and the presidential staff were based in Austin whenever the president was out on his ranch near Johnson City. With a lot of help from a lot of people, we persuaded President Johnson to move his official Texas headquarters to San Antonio. At the time, I was head of the San Antonio Chamber of Commerce. When the press corps made its first trip to San Antonio, I gave the official welcome. I told the reporters that we were delighted to have them in San Antonio. "I want you to know," I said, "that I am here to help you to do your jobs." So I gave them my office and home telephone numbers and told them to call me if they wanted or needed anything. That was not a very smart thing to do, because I got some very unusual requests that were nearly impossible to fulfill.

Every time the president returned to Texas, the press corps came to San Antonio, and I welcomed them with a margarita party at their hotel. One particular time they were staying at the Tropicana Hotel, which was on the San Antonio River. The party was on the hotel patio right by the river. I came late to the party because of a business meeting. As I was approaching the patio, one of my friends, a chamber official, came up to me and said, "Red, I'm glad you're here. We have a problem at the patio bar with a couple of reporters who are having a loud argument."

I went to the bar and realized that I knew both of those guys, so I stepped between them trying to be the peacemaker. The next thing I knew, one of the guys took a swing at my face, which I blocked, and countered with my own punch. It landed and my adversary went down. Before he could stand up, a woman walked up and started beating me over the head with a purse and tried to jump on my back. By that time my adversary was on his feet, so I grabbed him and pushed him into the river. I quickly left the scene.

I was so embarrassed by what I had done that I called the editors of our local newspapers and informed them that, "I have made a perfect fool of myself this evening at the Tropicana Hotel." I told them what had happened and pleaded for them to treat me easily. Both newspapers showed me a great deal of respect by not printing a story about the incident. But I couldn't sleep that night because I was so ashamed of myself.

The next morning I called George Christian, who was President Johnson's press spokesman. I knew George well. I started to say something about what happened when George cut me short and said, "Red, you don't have to tell me about it. I heard about the fistfight." I told him that it really wasn't a fistfight, but a reporter did wind up in the San Antonio River. I asked him if I could come down and apologize to the members of the White House press corps for my behavior. "Red, that won't be necessary," George replied, "I'll take care of it. I think everyone understands why it happened." And then he said, "By the way, Lyndon says that if you have it in you, he knows another reporter that you might want to throw in the river."

Missed Opportunities

Inevitably, Lee Iacocca and Henry Ford II parted company in the only way they could, with Henry the Second firing the confrontational Lee in 1978. Iacocca went on to become president of Chrysler. He took that company through bankruptcy and a federal bailout and, in time, would return it to prosperity. A year after firing Iacocca, Henry Ford II stepped down as president, and in 1980 he resigned as chairman of the board, leaving the loyal and able Phil Caldwell to run the company. For the first time in its history, there was no member of the Ford family running the Ford Motor Company.

The intrigue at corporate headquarters had no direct impact on what was transpiring in San Antonio, or Texas, but I had my own quota of missed opportunities. I am not one who feels tempted to look back and say what I wished I had done or not done. But I will think about what I could have done bigger and what I could have done better. Ford had invited me, actually urged me, to enter the California markets at the start of the 1960s, offering Phoenix, Las Vegas, and Albuquerque as well. I declined, and those were all big-time mistakes. I didn't think I would have the ability or the capital to succeed out west; I now know I would have.

I am generally credited with being a far-thinker in this business, but I must admit there are serious indications that I was not. I did not understand that a small, odd-looking German car, the Volkswagen, would ever sell in the United States. I was wined and dined and offered the Volkswagen franchise for about half of Texas, with headquarters in Houston. They courted me very heavily because they knew I could sell cars and that I had access to capital, which we had to find on our own in those days. But I didn't believe that the little Volkswagen "bug" would have any appeal to Texans. To me it was like a little tub turned upside down with a washing machine for an engine. I didn't think it had a chance. I politely said thanks but no thanks.

Soon after my miss with Volkswagen, Japanese cars began to roll onto our docks. I also had major doubts that Americans would buy those Toyotas and Nissan's little green Datsuns. At first, they basically just dumped a bunch of junk on the market. The cars weren't much good at all. But little by little, the Japanese obviously became a factor in the market. I didn't think they would ever have a real place in the American drivers' mind. I was so totally wrong about the competitive threat from Japan that I almost missed the boat.

In 1963, when I was the national spokesman for Ford's dealers, I was invited along with some other car dealers and about a dozen bankers to a conference in Washington, D.C., sponsored by the U.S. Chamber of Commerce. The purpose of the conference was to discuss the issue of foreign manufacturers coming to the United States, whether or not they might be a competitive threat, and how we should respond if we decided they were going to be a problem.

The BigThree had their top people there. I'll never forget how arrogant they were. Their basic response was to be irritated that the question had even been raised. They basically asked why we were taking up their valuable time to come to Washington to discuss the issue. The guys from Detroit argued that the foreign car makers had an insignificant percentage of the market and that would always be the case. "The Europeans make these little bitty cars that we don't want to make anyway because we can't make any money on them," Detroit argued. "Those foreign cars won't last and they can't run on American highways."

I got a little bit ticked off. "Yes, right now they have 3 percent of the market," I pointed out. "That's not significant, but what makes you think that they can't make bigger cars? What makes you think that they can't make pickup trucks? What makes you think that they can't do the same thing in manufacturing as we do over here?" I was almost laughed out of the room by the Big Three representatives. They thought I had lost my mind. "The Europeans don't want to make bigger cars," they argued. The Japanese weren't on the horizon at that point and Mercedes Benz was showing no interest in the mass market in the United States. "We taught them everything they know. They're doing what they do best and that's to make little cheap stuff that the American people are never going to buy." The geniuses in Detroit thought we had invented cars in America and no one else could compete with us. Here the U.S. Chamber of Commerce was thinking this might be a problem and perhaps we should plan for it. Well, we didn't plan at all.

When some dealers realized that these imported cars were going to be more popular than Detroit would admit, they decided to get on the bandwagon and add foreign car brands to their existing dealership, but Detroit gave them a lot of trouble. They told their dealers they would not allow them to do it. Some of the dealers told Detroit that they couldn't tell them what to do. "We're independent," they argued. "We own our business and we represent you and we've got our share of the market." The Big Three got away with that behavior for a while, but my fellow dealers and I didn't like it. We finally prevailed, however.

The imports already had a foothold here before I finally realized what a force they would become in our industry, so I belatedly entered the field. My first experience was with the French-made Renault, which didn't do well over here. Renault gave me a big territory but it didn't matter. We couldn't attract enough buyers to make it worthwhile, so I dropped Renault. My next import dealership was with Subaru, which was a success. I was the distributor for Subaru in the five Rocky Mountain states, with headquarters in Denver. The Subaru was ahead of its competitors in having all-wheel traction. That car was a great seller in those mountain states with their icy road conditions. I had fifty-two dealers in the Subaru distributorship network for about twenty years. Since then I have had great success with other imports.

So when anyone tries to tell me how smart I am, and praise me as a man of vision, I am able to stay in radio contact with the planet Earth by reminding myself that I am the prophet who lost World War II. I blew it on Volkswagen and the Japanese compact cars.

Nevertheless, my venture into the car business seems to have turned out okay. The money that I've made from selling cars has been the basis of everything else that I've been able to do. I didn't have family money or any other sources of wealth to tap. I never lose sight of that fact. By the year 2000, I had the sixth-largest retail car dealership operation in the world. I had about sixty car dealerships scattered over a number of states. I never operated under my own name except in San Antonio because people like to buy from a local guy. In most of the locations outside of San Antonio we used local or abstract names like Premier and Universal and Prestige. After our peak year in 2000, we sold many of our dealerships. At about that time, the onset of publicly owned national corporations such as Auto Nation altered the nature of the retail car business. It also gave us a lucrative buyer for many of our dealerships. The selling of those dealerships provided additional capital to expand my other business enterprises, as well as to make it possible to start new ventures.

Before I conclude this bit about my life in the car business, I should share my thoughts about the current state of affairs in Detroit. One of the lessons I learned from decades of dealing with the Ford Motor Company was that CEOs of big companies are quite capable of making mistakes. And I don't mean little mistakes. I'm referring to their habit of making enormous mistakes. I've already talked about how as a young man I was fascinated about business and different types of businesses and how they worked. I really thought until I was into my late teens that businessmen didn't make big mistakes. I thought that what they did was always right, and had to be, or they couldn't have stayed in business. I learned, as I got older, that businesspeople actually make a lot of mistakes. That was really a revelation to me. I had to get my mind adjusted because I had put them on a pedestal that they really didn't automatically deserve. But it was the business leadership of the Big Three who really brought that home to me.

Corporate Thinking

I've already discussed Ford's problem with the Edsel, but there have been many other examples of corporate fuzzy thinking and a basic inability of management at the highest levels to get a firm grip on reality. For example, for a long time Detroit couldn't see the market for a factory-installed car air conditioner. They believed an air conditioner would be too expensive for most consumers, which meant that only a few cars would actually have them. And that meant it would not be cost effective because it would take forever to recover the costs of development. My fellow southwestern car dealers and I really pushed Ford to get an air conditioner in our cars. We sold little add-on air conditioners, but they weren't very effective. We finally persuaded Ford to install air conditioners at the factory. When they finally came out, our customers grabbed as many as we could get from Detroit. To Ford's surprise, air conditioning was a huge hit. Within three years, 95 percent of our customers were requesting air conditioned cars.

Unfortunately, the first models, which came out in 1957, were not reliable. In the heat that we have in Texas and in places such as Arizona and Nevada, the air conditioner pulled too much power out of the car's engine, which made the car underperform. At the same time, the air conditioner didn't really cool that well. That generated complaints from our customers. They had every good reason to complain because they had been promised by Ford's advertising campaign that they would get a comfortable, air conditioned, car. But that wasn't what they got. The manufacturer's warranty on new cars in the late 1950s was three thousand miles or ninety days, whichever came first. So as dealers, we had to face our customers every day knowing that the car really wasn't performing well because the engineering for the air conditioner was flawed.

The air conditioner problem lasted much longer than it should have. As the dealers liaison with the Ford Company in 1963, I was the person who had to scream and holler at the company to get the company to fix this problem. Ford eventually granted me a hearing in Dearborn, where I heard the engineers present their case as to why the air conditioners were just fine the way they were. They had a slideshow with charts and graphs from tests they had conducted with these air conditioners in the Arizona desert. They had thermometers on the visors, under the rear seats, and along the window ridges of the car that "proved" the problem didn't exist.

I went to Dearborn well armed with information about how our customers brought their cars back to us over and over again to repair these malfunctioning air conditioners. I explained what we had tried to do to fix the air conditioners at our shops, but it was basically an engineering flaw. As dealers, we did not engineer or manufacture those cars and we could not fix that problem.

They listened to my pitch, but I could tell it wasn't working. I thought there was no way that I was going to persuade these guys to solve our problem. Ford's general sales manager, an elderly guy from Georgia, was at the meeting. After the engineers had their say, the sales manager declared, "Well, boys that was a good show. Red, let me see if I can sum up our meeting before we decide what to do. The boys in engineering have proved that our air conditioner properly cools under the seat in the back of the car, on the sun visor above the windshield, and along the side of the door openings. So what you're saying is that you don't really care about that. What you want is an air conditioner that cools your ass!"

I said, "Yes sir, you summed up accurately." So the general sales manager turned to the engineers and said, "You guys have thirty days to come up with a solution that we can apply to our existing cars, whether it's new compressors or whatever." It was a great win for the dealers and for our customers, because they did develop a solution. But war had to be waged to get management's attention.

Consumer financing was another important opportunity that Detroit ignored for many years. Throughout the 1950s the dealers pleaded with Detroit to get into the financing business, but it wasn't until the mid-1960s that we had factory-financed companies such as GMAC, Ford Motor Credit, and Chrysler Credit to loan money to car buyers. Now it's customary and they all generally make more money out of the financial arm of their business than they do the manufacturing arm. So they weren't too smart in that area either. They had to be shoved into the loan business, which is now a highly lucrative profit center.

There are many more examples of Big Three blindness that I could cite, but I don't want this book's printer to have to cut down the forest of trees necessary to make enough paper to discuss them all. Suffice it to say, I cannot believe that I am a part of and have lived through the basic destruction of the greatest industrial complex in the world for over seventy years, basically because of bad corporate management decisions. The Big Three's leadership had the choice to do things differently, but they didn't. Detroit lost its way. It got to the point where their boards didn't do their duty; they just rubber-stamped management's bad decisions.

The worst mistake Detroit made was in not understanding that at the end of the day the customer was the one making the decisions and that Detroit auto makers were dependent on customer loyalty. Customer loyalty began to erode back in the late 1960s. Before that, your grandfather drove a Ford, your father drove a Ford, and you drove a Ford. We had families that had a multigenerational tradition of buying from only one car company. When I was a young man, people bragged about being a Ford family or a Chevrolet family.

But when these European and Japanese cars came along, Detroit wouldn't accept that these foreign companies might be offering a better product. On an objective basis, you can argue about whether it's a better product or not, but at the end of the day the customer is going to make the final decision about what car they will buy. And a significant number of customers decided they would buy foreign cars. The Big Three in Detroit failed to understand it, and their directors let management take them over the cliff. It's that basic.

Every morning when most people in business get out of bed, they have to realize that if they are not attentive to the customer's needs and desires, then somebody else is going to be selling to that customer. And I don't see anything wrong with that. That's how our capitalistic system is supposed to work. It allows a guy like me from a little place that nobody's ever heard of to come in and become a big player in a great industry. And guys like Michael Dell and Sam Walton were able do the same thing. Who could believe that a hillbilly like Sam Walton from Arkansas could change retail standards for the entire world? He did it because he paid attention to his customer's needs and desires. Despite all the unwarranted criticism of Walton, no one forces anyone to purchase anything from Walmart. They have customers because they offer a competitive product, and their customers know it. This is one of the basic laws of good business practice, and it should be the focus of every course in the schools and colleges of business on every campus in this country.

I don't want to end on a sour note, no matter how easy that would be, because, believe it or not, I'm sincerely optimistic about the future of the U.S. car manufacturing business. As this is being written, Ford, my original car family, has just reported a large profit. And Ford was the only one of the Big Three that did not need a huge infusion of federal money to keep from closing the company's doors. Ford's management has actually figured out a few things about the need to offer a competitive product.

It appears that General Motors may not be far behind Ford in that regard. I'm especially optimistic about General Motors because of my strong faith in its new CEO, my old friend from San Antonio, Ed Whitacre, who is the former head of AT&T. Ed is the ideal person for the job. If he can't turn General Motors around, I'm not certain anyone can. I've heard a few grumbles about Ed not having a car manufacturing background, but that's irrelevant in this case. What's the car business anyway? The car business is taking a bunch of pieces and putting them together and offering them to the public in a way that they will like. For about forty-four years, Ed Whitacre spent his life with one company, Southwestern Bell. When the federal government, in its lack of wisdom, broke up AT&T into all the Baby Bell telephone companies, Southwestern Bell was the smallest. It should have had the most difficult future, but what happened? Ed decided that you can't stay little and stay alive in that business. You have to get big, and you have to consolidate, and that's just what he did. His management was masterful, and it resulted in the creation of the new AT&T, one of the real success stories in U.S. business today. I'm confident that he'll show the same skill at GM.

Let's not forget that our automobile industry isn't starting from scratch. We are blessed with magnificent industrial plants, and we have a large pool of highly skilled labor to work in those plants. We have everything it takes to make it work. But we can't rescue the car industry with the government running it. That's a disaster. There's nothing the government does that is cost effective. The federal government needs to get out of the way. Now that we have weeded most of the clowns out of management and the board of directors at GM, the company is now in position to move forward, rehire many of its skilled workers, and get competitive products on the market.

Those running the auto industry will be hungry instead of fat and arrogant like they were when they sat on mountains of cash, and that's great. Hunger makes you tougher, it clears the mind, and it makes you more aggressive. I've always said to the managers of all my businesses, don't worry about building up a bunch of cash in your operation because I'm going to suck it out of there. Too much cash makes people silly. It makes them lazy, and then they get arrogant. And that's what happened to Detroit.

Red McCombs with the mascot for the San Antonio Spurs basketball team, 1973. Courtesy of the McCombs family.

Chapter Seven

SPURS AND NUGGETS, 1973–1985

I'VE HAD THE OPPORTUNITY TO OWN AND ENGAGE IN A LOT OF different types of businesses in my life. Knowing how diverse my business interests have been, people often asked me which one was most fun. My usual answer is that my favorite business is whatever I'm doing today. Well, that's an easy answer, and it's partially true, but it's not the whole truth. My favorite business far and away, without any question, is the sports business. I say that because sports make my adrenaline flow faster than anything else. Yes, my adrenaline flows if I hit a good oil well or if I've got a business that is outperforming expectations—but not really. What really causes me to jump out of my chair is a sporting event in which I have a personal stake.

It all started with my ownership of that Corpus Christi Class B baseball team when I was twenty-five years old. I enjoyed it extremely. There is such a thrill that comes with making decisions about who is going to be on your team's roster and who is going to be coaching the team. It is a thrill that comes with knowing that you're in such a unique business and so few people are in it that in essence it's you against the world and you beat them. There is no greater thrill.

Leasing a Professional Basketball Team

My friend Angelo Drossos was responsible for getting me involved in my first big-league professional sports venture. Angelo was dark-haired, fast-talking, very handsome, and personable. I met him when he was operating a bar in San Antonio called the Dragon Lady. He also owned a pair of chili-dog parlors and managed some boxers and promoted their fights. A car accident left him with a shattered arm and a limp, but he wasn't lacking in confidence. When he wanted a regular job, I gave him one, and for five years he was one of my top car salesmen and managers. We became close, lifelong friends. I was the best man at his wedding.

In 1973 Angelo told me that the Dallas Chapparals, a team in the American Basketball Association (ABA), was for sale and looking for a home. Angelo knew that I had long felt that if San Antonio was ever going to join the ranks of big-time cities, it needed major league professional sports franchises in baseball, football, and basketball. Angelo believed that the Chapparals gave us a real opportunity to make that dream possible.

Angelo wanted to assemble a group of local businessmen to help him purchase the Dallas team. He asked me to be the lead investor. This deal was a long way from being a slam-dunk because it carried significant financial risk. The Chapparals were losing about $800,000 a year. The ABA, which had been founded in 1967 as a rival to the National Basketball Association (NBA), was barely breathing. Some of its original franchises had gone bankrupt. Nevertheless, it did have a few successful teams featuring some exciting stars, including the great Julius "Dr. J" Erving.

Angelo and I eventually figured out a way to get the deal done. We assembled thirty-four additional investors from the San Antonio business community, including John Schaefer, Marshall Steves, Joe Straus, Linton Weems, and Art Burdick, which made our financial risk more tolerable. With the exception of Weems and Burdick, I doubt there was a real basketball fan in the whole group. I certainly wasn't. I was a baseball and football guy. But I wasn't nearly as bad as Marshall Steves, who was a member of one of the city's pioneer families. "You can count me in," Marshall told me. "But as far as pro basketball goes, I'd rather watch water drip from a faucet."

I agreed to serve as president. Schaefer, a San Antonio real estate developer, and I each agreed to cover 25 percent of the losses for the first year, with our partners slicing up the rest. In addition, instead of buying the team, we leased it for $200,000. We reserved the right to purchase the franchise during the term of our lease. A lease limited our investment losses if we failed to find a fan base for pro basketball in San Antonio that first season. If the team succeeded, we could purchase it outright, which we did at the end of the first season for an additional $600,000.

At the last minute before we closed the deal, I started to get cold feet. I couldn't find anybody in San Antonio who was excited about basketball except Angelo. He came to my house to talk me into staying on board. In the end, he and Charline kept me from bailing out. She had no interest in the sport whatsoever, but she had heard me talk about this great need to have a major sports franchise in San Antonio. I had been talking about it for years. We had learned during the HemisFair that San Antonio was not on the radar of any Fortune 500 company. San Antonio didn't have a bad image; it had no image. We needed a major professional sports team to get on the radar. How could I cut and run when one was finally, literally, on our doorstep? The hope that this team would put San Antonio on the national map was much more motivation for me and my partners than any expectation that we would make money. Except for Angelo, we all doubted that this would be a profit-making enterprise.

Angelo agreed to learn the basketball business and operate the club on a day-to-day basis. In the beginning, he didn't draw a salary. He believed the good times were coming, even when I was unsure. We swallowed hard and closed the deal, knowing we could always cancel the lease and cut our losses. In our desire to spread the risk we may have gone a little overboard. Our deal was creative by any standard. We might not be able to lead the ABA in the standings, but we certainly led the league in partners. Once we closed the deal, we renamed the team the Spurs. We dropped the team name Chapparals to signify a new beginning for what had been a problem franchise. The team badly needed a new brand.

Involvement in the Spurs required a McCombs family makeover. Neither Charline nor I had ever seen much in the way of basketball games—high school, college, or pro. When Charline discovered the Spurs would play forty-five home games, she made it indelibly clear that I should not expect her to see a majority of those. She would pick and choose.

I could and did accept her terms. There was an unforeseen turn of events, however. After the third game, she was hooked. By the middle of the season, she was suffering from a stomach disorder. She had trouble sleeping, saw several doctors, and took all sorts of tests. Once we eliminated the serious stuff, her physicians concluded that her problems were caused by nervous tension—too many close games, too many winning or losing shots at the buzzer. How do you fix that? She took a little medicine, a lot of deep breaths, and occasional glasses of milk. I was concerned about her, but once she knew the source the pains began to fade. Even as intense as I would get, screaming and hollering, I never had that feeling in my stomach of having swallowed a grapefruit wrapped in barbed wire. Well, maybe once or twice.

Angelo and I knew very little about basketball, but we were both picking the brains of people who did know the sport and we were eager to learn. Bob Bass, our general manager, who had coached three different ABA teams before we hired him, was a huge help to us both. Bob knew the game at every level. He did a great job from day one, as he did in all the different roles I asked him to undertake during my time with the Spurs. He was, in the best sense of the phrase, the ultimate organization man—loyal, unselfish, and always available. On Bob's recommendation, we hired Tom Nissalke from the Seattle SuperSonics to serve as our first head coach. Before moving to Seattle, Tom had coached the team in Dallas. Tom was smart and eager, with the eye of a teacher. I liked and respected him very much.

It's hard to remember now, because the team is such an integral part of San Antonio, but the Spurs were not exactly an instant sensation in the Alamo City. Our first game, which was played in the old HemisFair arena on October 10, 1973, against San Diego, drew less than six thousand fans. On top of that, we lost! That set the pattern for our first seven games as we won one game and lost six. Only two thousand fans were present to see the one game we won. To say that fan interest was minimal is an understatement.

Swen and the Iceman

We realized that something had to be done or we were headed straight to oblivion. That's when Earl Foreman, the owner of the financially troubled Virginia Squires, helped us out. Actually, Earl wasn't really interested in helping us out. He needed cash to keep his franchise in business. Angelo and I realized that Earl's situation presented us with an opportunity to buy two of his players, Swen Nater and George Gervin, who would make huge contributions to our team. We bought them in two different transactions.

In November 1973, we paid Earl Foreman $300,000 in cash and gave up a first-round draft pick for Nater, a seven-foot-tall center out of UCLA. Swen was a sensation in San Antonio. He had an outstanding season. A few games after he joined the team we sold out the HemsiFair Arena and we began to breathe a little easier. Swen also drew close to our family. He had been orphaned as a boy in the Netherlands and was not reunited with his mother until many years later. He married his sweetheart, Maureen, in San Antonio. In the summer after the first season, we all vacationed together in California, drawing the friendship even closer. Swen was popular with all the fans, and Charline adored him and his wife.

Swen Nater was our immediate lifesaver, but the second player we bought from the Squires, George Gervin, would turn out to be the most crucial acquisition we made in our first ten years. Gervin had been dismissed from his team at Eastern Michigan University after one season because of a fight with a player on an opposing team. A six-foot, eight-inch guard, George was playing under the pro basketball radar with a semipro team in Michigan when a scout for the Squires signed him. I had never seen an athlete suited up to play a game as skinny as George Gervin—even in high school. But he moved like a line of poetry. The first time I saw him play for the Squires, I told Angelo "We ought to see if we can get this kid on our team."

There was a meltdown in the ABA almost every week. We were at a league meeting in New York and Mike Storen, the commissioner, had announced there would be no more trades, cash or otherwise, with the Virginia Squires. The league was trying to sell the franchise, and if the player ranks were depleted any further the only assets would be their ugly red, white, and blue uniforms.

Just before the owners' meeting with the commissioner, Angelo and I talked to Earl Foreman about buying Gervin, who was one of his remaining stars. During the meeting we slipped notes back and forth about how to do the deal. Storen soon spotted this exchange, grew visibly annoyed, and called a recess. He gave us all a big league ass-chewing, having assumed, correctly, that the notes involved a player transaction. We had been forewarned that the commissioner would not approve it.

Nevertheless, before the day was over—January 30, 1974—we had agreed on a cash price of $300,000 for Gervin. Knowing that we faced a problem with the commissioner, Drossos began working on the details of the deal. My job was to call the Frost Bank back in San Antonio to tell them to wire us $300,000—we had bought another player. An officer of the bank, Clyde Crews, could not resist asking, "Do you guys know what you're doing?" I assured him we were now experts. We sent the information in for league approval, and Storen went through the ceiling. "Not only will this transaction not be approved," he roared, "but if Gervin attempts to play for the Spurs, every game will be forfeited."

We laid low for a few days. Angelo made arrangements for Gervin to hide out in a San Antonio motel. After several days of negotiating with

Storen, we knew there was no hope of changing his opinion. Angelo and I asked the federal court for an injunction to restrain the league from enforcing this rule. Judge Adrian Spears enjoined the league and set a quick date for the hearing, clearing the way for us to bring Gervin out of hiding so he could play. Our fans didn't realize, nor did we, that he was going to be the linchpin of our franchise. He went on to play in eleven straight All-Star games.

Our fans rallied around us, in effect, for taking the bull by the tail and looking the situation right in the face. The fans love it when you stand up to authority. Still, it was a terribly cheesy thing to do. We had taken advantage of the Squires and their fire sale, and we had defied the commissioner. The judge ruled in our favor and gave us a permanent restraining order. Although Storen and I actually remained friendly, it was not a good decision, and I was in no mood to gloat. You teach your kids to play by the rules. We had violated them with gusto. The results were fine, but the means were less than honorable. I resolved that if the league had any future problems with the Spurs, we would deal with them outside the courtroom.

By the end of the season, you could see the team begin to jell. We finished our first season in HemisFair Arena with a 45-39 record, and Swen Nater was named the ABA's rookie of the year. It also soon became clear that Gervin, who had the nickname of "The Iceman," had more talent than most of us would ever see again, which is why he is in the Basketball Hall of Fame, and one of the NBA's all-time "Top 50" players. Gervin also was a wonderful person. Always, without hesitation, he made whatever personal appearances we asked of him. He was a joy to be around, always outgoing, gentle with kids, and generous with the media. His active involvement in the community played a critical role in making the Spurs San Antonio's team.

Prior to the Spurs' first season, we drafted as our first pick George Karl out of North Carolina. We were able to sign him and he turned out to be a hard-nosed player who really had his head in the game. He was almost a 100 percent basketball animal, and he battled for playing time that first year. In the ABA, we had a maximum of eight teams, sometimes seven, and we played each other enough times to build up fierce rivalries. George Karl became known as the guy on our club who would take a charge from anybody. He had some classic collisions with George McGinnis, a power forward and a bone crusher. Karl had a following in San Antonio and made friends there for life. He later became the head coach of the Seattle SuperSonics and Denver Nuggets.

During our second season, in early December 1974, Bob Bass fired our head coach, Tom Nissalke. Tom's style was structured and sound but short on excitement. I didn't see us playing the run-and-shoot game the other ABA teams used. The ABA had pioneered a more wide-open style of flashy offense, and its players popularized the dunk. We desperately needed to attract fans, and a fast-paced, high-scoring game was what the fans wanted. Bob loved the run-and-gun game, so he took over the coaching duties. The team finished with fifty-one wins and second place in the Western Division.

To realize how deeply attached the fans become to a team, all an owner has to do is trade away one of the team's most popular players. After our second season, we lost to Indiana in the first round of the playoffs, four games to two. Bass thought we needed to make a change. In June 1975 he came to Angelo and me and said, "There's a deal out there right now that might not come along again. It would be a chance to strengthen this team."

He said that the New York Nets (the Nets were not yet in New Jersey) had always coveted Swen Nater. My response was, "Who wouldn't? He's a seven-footer, blond, just coming into his own." Bob said, "Swen is a good player, but not great. He will never be better than he is now. I think you should consider trading him. I think we can get two starters." I agreed, but reluctantly.

In a matter of days, Bob had structured a deal that sent Swen to the Nets for Larry Kenon, an outstanding six-foot-nine forward, and Billy Paultz, a six-foot-eleven forward. We also acquired Mike Gale, a six-foot-four guard, for cash. The trade was completed with no leaks. No one locally knew about it except Angelo Drossos, Bob Bass, and me. The deal was completed late at night, and we had to wait for a conference call with the league office the next morning to confirm the terms. Still, it was a done deal.

That night I went home, sat down to dinner, and realized I had a problem. Charline said, "You can't imagine what happened to me at the beauty shop today. A woman said, 'What do you think about your favorite player being traded?' I said, 'Well, that's wrong. Not only will Swen not be traded, his jersey will be retired here and hang from the rafters.'" Ironically, the woman who told her this wasn't even a fan. I was choking on every bite of food. Charline and our three girls went to bed, and I stumbled into the library.

I was up early the next morning and called Charline from the office. "Sweetheart," I said, "there is going to be a press conference at ten. I regret to tell you that your friend was right. We've traded Swen to the Nets." Charline started sobbing on the phone. "If you're going to do things like this," she said, "I think you ought to get out of the business. The players become your friends and you can't treat them that way."

At three o'clock she called me back, unable to contain the excitement in her voice. "Honey, can you come home right away?" she asked. After what had happened, I didn't want to ask her why. I said I would be there in fifteen minutes. I walked onto the patio, and there was Charline with Swen and his wife, Maureen. Charline embraced me and said, "You can't imagine what this sweet guy has done." She turned to Nater, and he was literally too choked up to talk. "Honey," Charline went on, "he's willing to take any kind of pay cut you want to give him. Money isn't that important to him."

All I could do, short of finding a hole to crawl into, was say, "Let's sit down and talk about what happened." I explained that it wasn't a question of money. The deal was done. When you're traded, you have to go where the trail takes you. I felt like a dog, and and the three of them were crying when I left. That was the intensity level Nater had. I don't know of anyone who gets any pleasure out of shipping somebody out, or giving out a pink slip. But we felt that it had to be done to keep us competitive.

Our trades really paid off for us during the 1975–1976 season, and we made the playoffs, losing to Julius Erving ("Dr. J") and the New York Nets. We also placed four players on the ABA All-Star team: Gervin, James Silas, Paultz, and Kenon. I should add that Kenon's making the All-Star team was very helpful to me at home!

In June 1976, the four surviving ABA teams—Denver, Indiana, the Nets, and us—finally merged with the NBA. When we joined the NBA in 1976, we realized that it was the right time to retool, and Bob Bass stepped aside as our coach. Doug Moe was the new coach, with Bass showing his class by serving as Doug's assistant. Doug Moe had been a favorite of mine as a player. He was a happy-go-lucky type who loved the wide-open game and believed that it was acceptable for coaches to laugh and have fun.

Our debut in the NBA was in Philadelphia on October 22, 1976, against the 76ers. We drew a crowd of more than seventeen thousand fans, who watched the Spurs beat the 76ers, who had acquired Julius Erving as a result of the league merger. The Spurs went to the playoffs that first year, but we lost in the first round. Nevertheless, with the ABA-NBA merger a reality and with a winning team led by the exciting George "Iceman" Gervin, professional basketball was now firmly established in San Antonio. Except for the 1979–1980 season, when we won as many as we lost, the Spurs enjoyed winning seasons the first seven years we were in the NBA. We also won five division titles with a high-scoring, entertaining team. It was an exciting and very satisfying time for Charline and me.

The Denver Nuggets

In June 1982, just after the Denver Nuggets had been eliminated from the NBA playoffs, I got a call from Carl Scheer, the general manager of the Denver Nuggets. Scheer explained that the club was in desperate financial shape and badly in need of cash to take care of its debt. The owners had decided to sell the team. They asked Scheer to seek out a buyer. My friend Doug Moe, who had coached the Spurs in the 1970s and was now the coach of the Nuggets, urged Scheer to call me.

By 1982, Charline and I owned a ranch in the Cuchara Valley in Southern Colorado, and we were spending a lot of time there, especially during the summer. I also owned a Subaru auto distributorship in Denver and had other business interests in the city. Charline and I both love Colorado, so Scheer's call got my immediate attention. I told him that I was strongly interested in the deal and would go to Denver to begin the negotiations.

I was attracted to the Nuggets franchise not only because of my Colorado interests, but also because of my desire to be the sole owner of a professional team. I wasn't unhappy with my partners in San Antonio, and the success of the Spurs was deeply gratifying. As I have mentioned, I originally got involved with the Spurs because I knew that a professional team in San Antonio was essential to our goal of getting the city some badly needed national visibility. That had been accomplished.

I went to Denver and worked out a deal to acquire the team. I agreed to assume the club's debt and to provide a limited amount of cash as needed to support operations. The total of debt and cash amounted to about $10 million. I also agreed to keep the team in Denver. When I bought the team I was able to negotiate steep discounts in its debt load. After all was said and done, the total purchase was $5.5 million. I sold my 20 percent interest in the Spurs to Angelo, who by this time had increased the number of partners from the original thirty-five to sixty-three.

Cash trades, which are no longer in vogue, were still significant when I bought the Denver club. During the early part of the 1983–1984 season, I fell in love with the soft, outside jump shot of center Danny Schayes, who was in his rookie year with the Utah Jazz. Danny's dad, Dolph, had been one of the greats in the early postwar years of the NBA. We had a center nearing the end of his career, Rich Kelley, so I thought a Kelley-for-Schayes swap would really improve our team. Our coach, Doug Moe, hated the idea. He told me point-blank to "forget it."

Well, I didn't forget it. I knew that Utah was strapped for cash. I contacted Frank Layden, the coach and general manager in Utah. At first, Layden said he had no interest in trading Danny, a player he had just drafted. But Layden's cash-flow problems soon worsened, and he was back on the telephone with me. "I will trade you Schayes for Rich Kelley and $300,000 in cash," he said, "but I want to tell you as a friend, I don't think you're going to help your club. Even though Danny is younger and will be in the league longer, you need Kelley's toughness. I don't think Doug Moe will let you do this."

It was a hard sell. When I repeated the terms to Moe, he snapped at me: "If you want to throw some money around, give some to me and Big Jane (his wife). We can use it. You want to pay me peanuts, and then throw away your dough on that big stiff." I kept moving the idea along and, finally, Moe agreed. Danny went on to play for the Nuggets for eight seasons. Although he never became a "star," he gave the team depth and was a major contributor to our successful efforts to reach the playoffs. As far as I'm aware, that was the last transaction in the NBA where cash played the major role.

Doug Moe and I had a relationship that can only be characterized as "candid." As a Texas "Bubba," that is the kind of relationship I relish. One time when the Nuggets didn't get a shot off in the final seconds of a game that we lost by a basket, I assumed it was because the casual Coach Moe had failed to call a play during the timeout. So I scolded him about it after the game. Doug informed me that he had called a play, but the players forgot it. Then Doug said, "Red, I do believe that you are the dumbest SOB in basketball." That taught me a lesson about coaching from the stands. It also is a typical example of Doug Moe's style.

During my first season as owner of the Nuggets, our team returned to the playoffs, and Danny Schayes played an important role in making that happen. This time we won the first round. Our opponent in the second round was none other than the San Antonio Spurs. Naturally, I usually root for my home team, but not this time. I'm a fierce competitor, and losing isn't in my vocabulary, so I had a burning desire to take it to the Spurs. Unfortunately for me, the Spurs took it to us instead. Once again, the Nuggets had failed to get to the NBA championship series.

After the loss to the Spurs in the playoffs, I decided to make some changes in the Nuggets' management. Although we had a great offensive team, we weren't physical enough on defense, so I also decided to push for a trade to get us a different mix of players. I had been fortunate that Carl Scheer was the general manager of the Nuggets when I purchased the team. I had worked with Carl in the ABA. He was one of the most creative people in the league. But I wanted him to concentrate on marketing the team to our fans. I have always been impressed with Vince Boryla's talents as a basketball man. During his coaching days, he had a nice touch with the players, even with a doomed Salt Lake City team. Vince now lived in Denver and had become wealthy in private business. He had been associated with the first professional basketball team in Denver back in the late 1940s.

Immediately after the end of the 1983–1984 season, I convinced Vince to join us as president and general manager to run the basketball side. I switched Carl to the marketing side. I held a press conference at McNichols Arena, where the Nuggets played their home games, to announce the management change. After the press conference, Vince drove me to the airport, and on the way I dropped a little bombshell. "Vince, let me give you your first assignment," I said. "We need some new players who will toughen us up on defense. I think we need to make a trade. We have only three players anyone would want, Kiki Vandeweghe, Alex English, and Dan Issel, who is near the end of his career." The previous owners had traded away most of our draft choices. I told him to get something done that summer.

We had pulled right up to my private plane, and, as I was getting out of the car, I told Vince that he had full authority to make any deal he wanted. "Tell me about it when it's over," I said. "I have real strong opinions, and I'd rather trust your judgment than mine." Vince asked what would happen if he made a deal and I didn't like it? "Then you won't last long," I said, flashing him a big smile. "But I don't expect that to happen."

In June, Vince called to tell me that he and our head coach, Doug Moe, had traded Kiki Vandeweghe to Portland for forward Calvin Natt, center Wayne Cooper, and guard Fat Lever. I was stunned. "You got three players for Kiki?" Vince answered, "No, we got three players, and their first and second draft picks." We ended up with four starters.

That deal paid off immediately. We won twelve of our first fifteen games in the 1984–1985 season, eventually finishing as the Midwest Division champs. We again faced San Antonio in the first round of the playoffs, but this time it was the Spurs who were ousted from the playoffs. We easily prevailed in the next round against the Utah Jazz to advance to the Western Conference Finals against the Los Angeles Lakers. I thought we had an excellent chance of winning, but, after five closely fought games, the Lakers came out on top.

Charline and I liked everything about Denver. We didn't move there, but we made a lot of good friends and had a great time when we were in town. The team was competitive and entertaining. Charline loved Doug Moe and his wife and became a devoted Nuggets fan. I certainly had no plan to sell the club anytime soon.

Everything was going well until May 1985, when I made one of the biggest blunders of my life. I sold the Nuggets to Sidney Schlenker, a friend from Houston, in a phone conversation that lasted less than twenty minutes. Sidney owned 10 percent of the Houston Rockets, but he wanted his own franchise. He called and said he wanted mine. We were winning. He liked our organization. I told him I wasn't interested in selling. "Any chance you'd ever be?" he asked. "Maybe three years or so down the line," I answered.

Sidney asked what I would sell the Nuggets for whenever I did decide to put the club on the market. I tossed out $20 million, a figure that I thought was outrageous. "I'll give you that right now," he said. I thought about it for a heartbeat or two and then said, "I'll take it." It was a major error on my part. We didn't need the money. There was no pressure to sell. But most of all, I had done it again to Charline. I didn't realize, again, what an emotional blow this would be to her, or how attached she had become to the town, to Doug Moe and his wife, Janey, and to our general manager, Vince Boryla.

I couldn't make it up to her. When the genie is out of the bottle, it's gone. I get over hurts, and I put the deal behind me, but it takes Charline longer. I'm not sure she ever did get over this one.

If the reader will permit me, this is my chance for some serious groveling. I've always said that I've never owned anything. I'm a salesman. I've only signed one lifetime contract, and that was with Charline. So far, I'm pleased to say, she hasn't tried to renegotiate it.

San Antonio businessman Angelo Drossos, partner with Red McCombs in many business ventures. Courtesy San Antonio Express-News *Collection, Institute of Texan Cultures, UTSA, # E-015-137-A, and the Hearst Corporation.*

Chapter Eight

HOORAY FOR HOLLYWOOD

I WOULD GUESS THAT ONE OF MY LESS-KNOWN BUSINESS ENDEAVORS was my foray into the world of Hollywood. As glittering as Hollywood may be, however, it was not the glitter that attracted me. My relationship with the motion picture industry was all about business. I have absolutely no interest in the Hollywood celebrity scene. I'm not even a movie fan.

Sam and Irv

My trip to the world of movies came out of my involvement in professional basketball. During my first fling with the Spurs in the 1970s, my dear friend Angelo Drossos and I became friends with fellow basketball team owners Sam Schulman and Irving Levin. Sam owned the Seattle SuperSonics and Irv was the majority investor in the Boston Celtics, the premiere basketball franchise of the time. Irv earned lasting fame by trading the best professional basketball franchise for the worst.

Following the Celtics' 1976 championship season, Irv swapped his interests in the team to John Y. Brown in exchange for ownership of Brown's struggling Buffalo Braves. Irv renamed the Braves the Clippers and moved the team to San Diego, where they immediately became one of the biggest losers in professional basketball. That had to be one of the worst stock trades in history. Irv endured a lot of good-natured ribbing about it over the years. "San Diego is in my backyard," Irv explained to me. "I can't go back and forth to Boston all the time and enjoy this the way I'd like to." That made sense to me.

Like Irv Levin, Sam Schulman was a breed apart. In those days the league only had seventeen teams. Whenever the owners voted on league business, the votes were usually sixteen to one against whatever Sam proposed. He was the only owner I ever heard of who wanted to do away with the reserve clause, which kept players tied to one team for life. It was Sam Schulman who stole the great Spencer Haywood from the ABA, escalating a conflict that almost wrecked professional basketball. His fellow owners stopped talking to him and took him to court. When the ABA and the NBA merged, the suit was dropped. But Sam was widely regarded as a bomb thrower. Sam's strongly stated opinion was that if a guy in any sport doesn't want to play for Seattle, or Los Angeles, or any other team, why should he be made to do so because the owners have decided that the reserve clause is good for the game?

"In other businesses of mine," Sam once said, "I sign people to contracts of maybe five years. At the end of that time, they are free to stay or move elsewhere. And life goes on. It should be no different in sports." This is the way it is today, of course, although I doubt even a visionary like Sam Schulman could imagine how crazily the contracts would escalate.

Sam's and Irv's primary careers had been in the movie industry. I was drawn to them because they were interesting people and they had spent many years operating successfully in various facets of Hollywood. Regrettably, both are now gone. Irv died in 1996, and Sam died in 2003. They were fun people, and I liked them a lot. Occasionally, they came up with business opportunities that I invested in. Of course, some paid off, and some didn't.

Although Irv Levin and Sam Schulman both had experience working in Hollywood, Irv was much better known, and he had the most contacts inside the industry. Irv was an authentic war hero. He flew more than thirty missions over Germany in World War II and was decorated with a Distinguished Flying Cross and Bronze Stars. After the war, Irv got involved in the business of producing movies, mainly the kind of low-budget independent films that wound up in drive-in theaters. In the early 1960s, he was one of the entrepreneurs who started the National General Corp (NGC), which owned and operated a chain of movie theaters. Irv also produced a number of bigger-budget films including *Divorce American Style* (1967) and *The Cheyenne Social Club* (1970). In the late 1960s, he teamed with promoter Freddie Fields and actors Sidney Poitier, Paul Newman, Steve McQueen, and Barbara Streisand to create the First Artists motion picture company. They produced several films including *The Getaway* and *A Star is Born*. So Irv was a guy with an excellent track record, who definitely had his movie studio connections.

SLM

In the late 1970s, Irv and Sam developed a creative way to finance motion pictures. Their plan was to buy an interest or a percentage of the distribution cost of movies already completed. The major studios were eager for investors in the distribution side of the business. The idea was that Irv and Sam, with their solid experience, would negotiate a purchase price to buy an interest ranging from 10 to 50 percent in a finished but not yet released movie. Investing in a movie after it is "in the can" reduces the investors' exposure to the cost overruns that frequently occur during filming. In 1981, Irv and Sam invited Angelo and me to participate in this business plan as investors. I liked the idea.

So I joined Angelo, Sam Schulman, and Irv Levin to form a company that we called SLM (Schulman, Levin, and McCombs). Irv had just sold the San Diego Clippers, and he used his profit to help fund the company. Angelo, Sam, and I invested a substantial amount of cash, but we also relied on borrowed and leveraged capital.

Some people, who obviously didn't know me, assumed that I got involved in SLM because of the glamour of Hollywood. As I said earlier, my involvement had nothing to do with the glamour of it. The truth is that I was very interested in the deal structure, not the movies. Charline and I were invited to all the premieres, of course, but I don't think we went to more than a couple during all that time. I was invited to the sets when they were making movies, but I'd rather take an aspirin than have to go watch someone make a movie. I had zero interest in that.

I was attracted to the SLM deal because it would let me work on the inside of an industry with well-connected movie people who weren't getting a free ride. Irv and Sam put up the same amount of money as Angelo and I put up. I liked the idea that I could access a big-dollar industry with very knowledgeable partners and not pay a premium for getting in. I thought we were inside the table with an advantage in an industry that was a big industry. I've done a lot of things like that. It was an interesting investment, and I just looked at it as a moneymaking opportunity. I thought that we would do well with it and would build up a pretty serious company.

I had nothing to do with the daily management of SLM, and I had little to do with selecting the films. I was hardly ever involved in those meetings because I really had no knowledge of what made a good movie and what didn't. I didn't see that as my expertise. How am I going to judge whether one film was going to do better than another before it was released? Angelo was more active in SLM, and he helped Irv and Sam raise money, but I was just an investor.

We had an investment limit based on the cost of each individual film. Whether we spent fifty million dollars on a package or whether we spent twenty million dollars didn't matter to me. Our concern was with the cost of each individual film in the package. We discovered from experience that the rule of thumb was that the more it cost to make a film, the harder it was to make any money from it. It just took too much money to get any money back. That didn't work in our little model. So I told my partners: "Hey, let's just don't take those expensive films. Let's take the less expensive films." I thought we had a firm agreement on that strategy, but eventually it didn't turn out that way.

SLM operated throughout the decade of the 1980s. During that time, our group bought distribution interests involving multimillions of dollars in dozens of movies at the major studios, primarily at MGM and 20th Century Fox. Typically the studio would offer one package that included several movies. At any one time we might have anywhere from a 10 to 50 percent interest in four or five films that were in theaters. We had some pictures that were winners, and we had many that weren't, but we did a lot of business.

Rhinestone

The fortunes of the company ran hot and cold. One of the hot successes was *The Verdict*, with Paul Newman, which was released in 1982. Another winner was a 1984 release, *Romancing the Stone*, which starred Michael Douglas, Kathleen Turner, and Danny DeVito. No one expected that film to be as successful as it was, but we made about $25 million on it. We also ran cold in 1984 by investing in an artistic and commercial flop called *Rhinestone*.

It was the *Rhinestone* deal that caused me to think that it might be time to get off the SLM train at the next station. I happened to be in Los Angeles on other business when the deal was made to invest in *Rhinestone*. While in town, I attended a meeting with my partners at 20th Century Fox. SLM was buying an interest in four films. I was just kind of like a fly on the wall because they had already pretty well cut the deal. After we got to the studio I sat quietly by myself and looked over the details of the deal while they discussed some minor points. I soon realized that we had a problem, so I interrupted the discussion to ask for clarification. I asked if the basis of this deal was an investment in one movie in the package that cost much more than what I had thought our limit had been. That expensive movie was *Rhinestone*.

Angelo said, "Well, Red, yes, it is." I pointed out that we had decided that we weren't going to buy an interest in movies that cost more than our agreed-upon limit. At this point, the guy from 20th Century Fox said, "I talked them into this one, Red, because if the other three movies for whatever reason don't work, *Rhinestone* is absolutely guaranteed to be a hit." The studio guy said it couldn't miss because of the stars: Dolly Parton and Sylvester Stallone. They both were really hot numbers at the time. The studio guy said that everyone was certain that if the movie didn't track well, Parton and Stallone would still carry it. People would rush to the theater just to see those two stars paired together.

I replied that I was not questioning whether Parton and Stallone would carry the film or not. It was the cost that concerned me. I told my partners that we should take *Rhinestone* out of that investment package and replace it with a less expensive film. I just knew that we hadn't done well with films that had cost over a certain amount. Anyway, I thought that my partners and I had agreed on that point. That made Angelo very unhappy. He burst out, "Well, Red, can't you see that they've made us a special deal on this? They weren't even going to let us in on this deal." I answered, "Well that's good. That means they won't mind us getting out of it."

This heated discussion went on for a while. Finally the executive with 20th Century Fox, a nice guy whose name I can't recall, said, "Look, Red, I'll tell you what, I'll make it more palatable. If you guys leave *Rhinestone* in the package, we can do a deal where you just pay us half price if the film is a bust. And if it does do well, then you've really made your money." Angelo quickly said that was an even better deal, "Let's do it, draw the contract that way." Irv and Sam also insisted that this was a good business move, mainly because they considered this movie to be a sure-fire blockbuster. *Rhinestone*, the movie, was an attempt to exploit the commercial success of the song "Rhinestone Cowboy," which was a huge hit for Glen Campbell.

I was put off by the idea that my partners wanted to veer away from our original plan. I didn't like it one bit, but I wasn't going to stop the deal. They had already agreed to it in principle. *Rhinestone* turned out to be as big a loser as the song was a winner. In fact, some film critics have argued that it was one of the worst movies ever made. It was a turkey, and the whole deal was a turkey. That movie caused us unbelievable stress and money and everything else.

Goodbye to Hollywood

Our partnership continued for a while despite the *Rhinestone* incident, but the bloom was off the rose for me. It became more difficult to attract other investors, so the investment load fell mainly on the four of us. I realized that we had been to bat enough times, and the hits were scarce. We never did really make good money. Fortunately, we made just enough to keep the company going, but it was pretty much a break-even situation overall. I realized that if this deal was ever going to work, we would have already found that out. I decided to get out of SLM as soon as it made financial sense. We had a bank debt of about twenty million dollars and I wanted to take care of that before I left the company.

In 1985, Irv and Sam settled a distribution dispute with 20th Century Fox. As a result, we got a twenty-five-million-dollar payday, which would pay off our twenty-million-dollar bank debt and leave about $1.25 million for each of us. So when I heard about the settlement, I called Sam and Irv and complimented them. I said that I couldn't wait until we could get together, and I would buy the champagne, even though I didn't drink. "Fine," they replied, "we look forward to it."

A few days passed and I hadn't received my money, so I called Angelo to see what had happened. Angelo said, "Well, Red, you're ruining a big surprise. Sam and Irv want to surprise you by coming to San Antonio and bringing the money to you." I replied that was wonderful, but they really could surprise me more by putting the money in my bank. Angelo replied, "No, Red, just wait. I'm going to talk to them this afternoon and we'll set a time."

Two or three days later Sam and Irv flew to San Antonio. They and Angelo came by the house and took me to a restaurant for dinner. At the restaurant, Irv reached inside his coat pocket, pulled out an envelope, and handed it to me. It was a check for $1.25 million. I thanked Irv and Sam and told them how great it was to get this payout. After we ordered our meals, Angelo said, "Well, you think this payout is good, Red Man? I want Irv to tell you about something even better."

Irv said that there was a package of movie prints available for distribution that we could get for about ten million bucks. There was a group of investors being assembled that would buy the package from us for something like thirty million dollars. The only catch was that we would have to hold on to the movie package for about ninety days. To get this deal done, we each needed to put back in the pot the money that we had just been paid and sign a note for the remainder, which was about six million dollars. "Sounds like a great deal," I replied, "and I want you guys to enjoy it, but I am finished."

My response didn't seem to surprise Schulman or Levin, but Angelo almost went berserk. "What do you mean you're finished?" Angelo shouted. "Is this a joke? Is this more of your bull?" I answered, "No, you guys, we've had a good roll. We've been in this for several years. We have had a lot of opportunities, and we still have a few assets in the company, but I'm opting out." Angelo asked me about my shares in the company. He said that it wasn't fair for me to keep my shares and let them stay in and bankroll the company. I replied that I would be happy to sell my shares to him, Irv, and Sam.

Angelo pointed out that the value of our shares was about one dollar and eighty-five cents a share. "You dump all of your shares on the market," Angelo argued, "and you probably couldn't get over seventy-five cents a share." I replied that I would sell them to the group for seventy-five cents a share. Angelo was stunned. "What has happened to you?" he asked. "I have loved my friendship with you three guys," I replied. "We've had a good run. But you still see something in the company that I don't see. So you can have my shares at that reduced price." Sam and Irv accepted my decision, but Angelo didn't. We went ahead and ate our dinner, punctuated with nothing more than small talk. They drove us home, but it was a little bit cold in the car. As I got out of the car, I told Sam and Irv that I would take them to the airport the next morning.

The next morning about seven o'clock, Angelo called me at the house and asked if I could be at his office at eight thirty. He said Sam and Irv are coming over. I said, "Sure, but Angelo I'm not going to revisit that deal." He replied, "Don't ask me what I want to do, Red, you just come. You owe it to us." When I arrived at his office, Angelo started to resell the deal to me. He told me about how they had let me do anything with the company that I wanted to do and that I owed this to them. Besides that, he argued, "We're partners, and we've been in this thing together. We came in as partners; we need to stay as partners." I realized that he wanted me to sign that six-million-dollar note.

I told Angelo that we had settled this last night, but Angelo continued to argue with me. It made Sam and Irv a little bit nervous because they didn't want to be in the middle of it. I said, "Angelo, it is settled. If you don't want to accept my decision that's your business, but it's done. I am no longer in the movie business." I told Irv and Sam how pleased I was that they had made us some money. I was selling them my shares for virtually nothing. I said, "I hope you guys do your deal and get rich." That was the end of our partnership. I was out.

I'm sorry to say that they went ahead and got the deal done somehow. And, as it turned out, they were unable to resell the package, which tied up their money. This bad deal, coupled with the losses from *Rhinestone*, actually took the company down. So the venture ended with my getting out at the right time. They all ended up with a terrible loss. I'm truly sorry that they did.

When I was involved with SLM, a couple of my friends in San Antonio asked me if I had any worries about investing in the movie business because of the bad reputation the studios had when it came to proper financial accounting. I told them that I had no concerns because we had those two guys, Irv and Sam, who were in the business, and I was confident that they knew all the tricks. We never had any issues there. For one thing, we didn't have to worry about what it actually cost to make the movies because we weren't involved in that part. Our investment was in the finished films, and at our end of the deal there was no debt. All we had to worry about was distribution of the money that comes back from the ticket sales. And frankly, as I looked at it, in the years I was in it, I don't think there was any messing around with the accounting. I think the idea that such actions are common in the entertainment industry is a myth.

Overall, SLM was a wash for me. I made some money and lost some. I don't have any regrets about it. You know, a lot of people think that I get involved in a lot deals like SLM or professional sports because of the glamour or the uniqueness of doing it. But the reality is that if I don't have more than a good shot at getting a financial return, I don't do anything, because I'm not in love with any of that stuff.

Red McCombs in his office with one of the saddles he has collected, 1999.
Photo by J. D. Talasek. Courtesy of the McCombs family.

Chapter Nine

LLOYD'S OF LONDON

THE WORLD-FAMOUS AND LEGENDARY LLOYD'S OF LONDON has insured everything from the *Titanic* to Betty Grable's legs to Dolly Parton's bosom. Captains and kings and ordinary people have thought and talked about Lloyd's since the seventeenth century. In 1980, I happened to read a book about the company, and I was fascinated by the history of it. In brief, the story line is this: Three hundred years ago, merchants in England sold their goods to merchants in Venice, but pirates controlled the seas. In 1668, a conversation took place in Earl Lloyd's coffee shop that changed the way the world did business. One merchant happened to mention that he had received a very nice order from Venice, but it was payable only on delivery. Since he could not guarantee that it would ever arrive, he lamented, how could he accept the risk of filling the order? A gentleman spoke up and asked, "How much would you pay me if I guaranteed that order?"

So that began a regular practice. A statement of a ship's cargo would be read aloud. Among the coffeehouse patrons, those who were willing to share the loss if the cargo disappeared signed their names below the list. From that small conversation grew one of society's most revered institutions, one that we take for granted today. Although at risk for billions of dollars, Lloyd's had a business plan that did not include capital that would come anywhere close to covering potential losses. From the day it was founded in a London coffee shop, the company essentially has used as its capital the honor and good name of its shareholders, who are called members, as if they belonged to a very privileged club, which indeed they do.

I was more or less smitten by the idea that this company everyone knows, that had played such a huge role in building worldwide commerce, was in the early 1980s still underwritten by the pledge of each member to surrender his entire net worth if called upon to do so. I was fascinated by that idea, and I thought, "Hey, I want to be a part of that."

A Name of Lloyd's

The story so intrigued me that I contacted Lloyd's of London and spoke with David Coles, who was the representative of several underwriters. Lloyd's had been accepting non-UK citizens for just a few years. We began the process of my becoming a member, or as one is sometimes referred to, a "name" of Lloyd's. As I casually mentioned this possibility to my associates, I could not contain my enthusiasm. In turn, they looked at me with disbelief and said, "You are begging to be a part of a company where you commit your total net worth?" I said, yes, that is the element that excites me. Of course, I understand why this impulse makes lawyers and accountants nervous.

I can no more explain why I need this sort of stimulation than others can describe the allure of climbing a mountain. Frostbite? Avalanche? Snow-blindness? Let's go! You bring the beer. I don't do mountains. But in my lifetime, I have occasionally found it hard to resist a proposition that gives me a chance to go broke.

After two years of submitting records and processing papers, I received the phone call I had been waiting for like a lovesick teenager. "Mr. McCombs," I was told, "you will now select from the following dates to meet with the committee that makes the final decision." At the time, Lloyd's consisted of 270 syndicates, insuring hundreds of different types of programs. I had applied to be part of a program that insured workers' comp, the airlines, and maritime losses. The schedules of the syndicates are as varied as life itself.

My investment was a minimal amount of capital for a share in the annual profits. As a return on cash, historically, it was phenomenal. That was not my primary motivation, although I did not ignore it. The real advantage to me was belonging to a unique society, the only one whose balance sheet was to a large extent the honor and bond and word of its members.

Yet when David Coles called, I could not resist trying a bit of gamesmanship, even though I knew in advance what his answer would be. I decided to pull one of my Red McCombs "push-it-to-the-limits" ploys. I explained to Mr. Coles that my wife, Charline, would come with me to the meeting. In a superior, aristocratic, tone of voice, he responded, "Mr. McCombs, no one goes before the committee except the candidate." I explained to him that Texas was a community-property state. I was testing him, of course. As I expected, his reaction was totally negative. "David," I said, one good old boy to another, "everyone has a boss. You go talk to yours because this is a deal-breaker." It really wasn't a deal-breaker, but he agreed to consult his boss, although he was clearly not happy about it.

When Coles called back, he said that the policy was as he stated and he regretted that both parties had spent two years in this process in vain. He would be returning my materials and documents promptly. He sounded sincere when he said he was sorry it had not worked out. "Oh, well," I responded. "If they're going to be ornery about it, I'll just give in and make the trip anyway." I don't know what I would have done if they had said, "Sure, bring your wife." I just wanted to see if I could bend a rule. The last thing Charline wanted was to sit through one more committee meeting when she could be enjoying London.

Lloyd's on Lime Street

In 1982, Charline and I flew to London, took in the sights, and then toured the historic Lloyd's building on Lime Street, where the exhibits reflect an unending admiration and debt to the Royal Navy, especially Lord Nelson and the other naval heroes of long ago who ultimately defeated the pirates. I soaked it all in—the magnificent paintings, the use of the big ledger, the storied bell that rang in the event of a calamity. Even in this day of modern technology, if a calamity occurs it is entered into the ledger by hand with a quill pen dipped in an inkwell. No one surpasses the British at carrying on a tradition.

We were treated to a private luncheon with the leaders of Lloyd's and the committee that would judge me. At lunch, I realized I was short on cash, and we were leaving the next day to spend a couple of weeks traveling in Europe. I turned to David Coles, mentioned that I needed $5,000, and said Charline would write them a check while I was going before the committee.

While there was a nodding of heads, and nothing was said about that request, I sensed that something was askew. When I left to go with my sponsor, there was a noticeable amount of whispering and ducking in and out of rooms. Finally, I was told that the banks were closed, and Lloyd's doesn't keep cash. I found that comical. Doesn't keep cash. They were able to get a bank to open, and Charline cashed the check.

The board room was at least ninety feet long, with two conference tables, ten chairs on one side, and a single chair for the candidate on the other. The scene was quite imposing, but it was a very simple interview. The interview committee had three members. Quickly, they asked if I understood that I was signing over my net worth according to English law, forfeiting any rights I might have under U.S. law. The underwriter would have the authority to bind me to any kind of insurance program he saw fit, with absolutely no input from me.

I had already accepted these conditions in a lawyer's office, but they wanted to confirm that I had a full understanding of these terms. My advance to them was something like $150,000, but I was agreeing to bind my potential loss to my entire net worth. They asked me if I had any reservations about this obligation.

I believe they were surprised by my reaction. I was clearly enjoying myself. I asked them if any candidate had ever gone to this level and decided not to proceed. They said, yes, very rarely, but it did happen, usually because of heirs becoming members and the liability being passed on.

My second question was, "Do you have women who are members?" The answer was yes. It had been a men's club for two or three centuries, but had grown more tolerant in recent years. They had not admitted members from outside the United Kingdom until 1968. I knew all I needed to know. With the stroke of a pen, I bound over my entire net worth to the good judgment of Lloyd's of London.

The excitement I felt personally from this decision overwhelmed any concerns I might have had. The reality of losing one's wealth had not been a significant item in the history of Lloyd's. Sadly, it is now. Lawsuits that were initiated by U.S. members wiped out family fortunes here and among some of the grand names of England and Europe. Some had been members for three hundred years. Lloyd's has suffered losses beyond anything they had forecast.

Asbestos and Torts: Time to Leave

So how did I fare in what I still regard as the deal with the most class of any I ever made? I was lucky to get in and lucky to get out. While I was in Denver on business related to my ownership of the Nuggets, I was in my room at the Brown Palace Hotel reading the morning paper when I noticed a small item on the business page. A court in California ruled that the Johns Manville Company, which had its corporate offices in Denver, was liable for a man's health problems attributed to the use of asbestos in ships that were built in California in 1940 and 1941. It was a small story that escalated into a huge story with grave consequences. Johns Manville was among the first of several large manufacturers to declare bankruptcy.

At the time, I don't recall that the asbestos story received much attention across the country. But my intuition kicked in. If a hunch turns out to be right, this is referred to as having "vision." A man had been awarded millions in damages because of a product used forty years earlier. That was a red flag. Unrealistic tort claims were probably going to become the order of the day in the United States.

At that point, I called my office and told them to submit my resignation to Lloyd's immediately. You are allowed to resign from Lloyd's, but your obligation continues for another three years. In my case, it turned out to be eight because of lawsuits filed in the United States attacking the unlimited liability of the standard agreement. A lot of those who sued did get some recourse and did not lose their entire estate. But there were staggering losses, particularly in the United Kingdom, where members saw their income stream shut off, and many had their property foreclosed to pay off debts.

I am not making a judgment on those who sued. What comes to mind is the old line about life being like Las Vegas. You're up. You're down. In the end, the house always wins. That doesn't mean you didn't have fun. From a bottom-line viewpoint, it was a very lucrative venture, because I earned about 30 percent on my original investment. I also had the personal fulfillment and pride of knowing I had been involved in the most unusual business concept in the world. And I had the good luck, or foresight, to not overstay my visit.

The Collector

Out of that trip to London came another of life's pleasures: an exposure to the marvels of Europe. Beginning in the early 1970s, we began to vacation there from time to time. Among other things, the trips fed my passion for collecting. As a collector, I rank somewhere between avid and obsessed.

Over the years, I have gone from antique ivory to precious silver to Texana, western Americana, Indian artifacts, and antique guns. I have all but jumped out of my boots when I got a call from a broker saying he had a piece dated 1690, or finding a general store ledger that reported General Custer had purchased supplies for his troops before leaving in a week on a patrol that would take them to Little Big Horn. I spent fifteen years chasing a Gatling gun with its full encasement, platform, and carriage, then bought not one but two. I would have bought a dozen. The thrill is in realizing that the prize has been worth the chase.

I don't consider myself an expert on anything I collect. My system is to look at an item and decide what my level of interest is. If that exceeds the price, then I buy. My purchases are not always prudent, but I never intend to sell them anyway. There is one duty that I believe strongly applies to collectibles: you should share them with the public when opportunities arise, which I try to do.

When I first started to collect silver, we were nearing the end of a two-week family driving tour of Ireland. Charline and myself and our daughters Lynda and Connie ended up in Dublin one afternoon, and the girls had plans that didn't include me. With time on my hands, I wandered into the hotel lobby to buy a fine cigar to smoke in the park. I was paying for my cigar when I noticed a paperback on the joys of collecting antique Irish silver. I sat down and began to leaf through the book. According to the author, Irish silversmiths were not considered superior to others in their time. There were so few of them, and such little demand in such a poor country, that all of this had converged to make Irish silver relatively rare.

I was intrigued by this, and asked the concierge for directions to the nearest shop. They had several pieces, among them two beautifully matched soup tureens. I had no knowledge of what a fair price would be—a distinct disadvantage in such matters. So befuddled, but intrigued, I found myself going back to the shop and trying to barter with the owner. I made some headway, then I ran into a dead end. He wanted about $8,000 for the set and would not budge. There was no more headway to be gained.

The four of us were in the car with our driver, ready to leave Dublin, and I was still complaining about the high-priced antique Irish silver, and what a rip-off I thought it was. My daughter Connie, who was sixteen years old at the time, interrupted me. "Daddy," she said, wearily, "you must be the most stupid man who ever lived." Sixteen-year-olds can do that.

My self-esteem has taken an occasional dip, but I thought this assessment might be a trifle harsh. I said, "Well, Connie, share your thoughts with me." She continued, "For two days you have bored us to tears with how much you loved those two stupid soup tureens. Why didn't you just buy them and spare us all this misery?" My answer was, "I thought the price was too high." And in my daughter's eyes I could read the message: "Here is a man who can afford to buy something he wants, and he doesn't like the price given him by a person who does this as a profession."

I told the driver to turn the car around, went back to the shop, and bought the two soup tureens. We still have them. And, in case you were thinking this story would come full circle, it doesn't. I insure my collectibles with a company in San Antonio.

Red and Charline McCombs at their ranch in Johnson City, 1980. Photo by Bill West. Courtesy of the McCombs family.

Chapter Ten

THE TEST

DARRELL ROYAL WAS THE MOST SUCCESSFUL FOOTBALL COACH in the history of the University of Texas. Mental toughness, common sense, and wit are the Royal trademarks, and he has shared them with his friends. Darrell once found himself pondering a statement by Oliver Wendell Holmes. The late chief justice of the Supreme Court had been quoted as saying that if he discovered a secret formula for avoiding the afflictions and misery and grief of everyday life, he would not reveal it because people need to be tested to overcome adversity. "That struck me as profound," said Royal, "and I gave it a lot of thought. What I finally concluded was, piss on Oliver Wendell Holmes."

I understand how Darrell feels. He is one of the least selfish people I have ever met. But the truth is most of us do get tested. I know I did.

My Battle with Alcohol

In my forty-eighth year, I realized I had a problem with alcohol. I've had people ask me how you can tell when you need to stop drinking, and my answer is a simple one. You know you have a problem when you can't get through the day without it. I didn't drink at all until I was twenty. Up to then I had been trying to develop as an athlete, but even so I was not your typical twenty-year-old. I began to drink socially, at a fairly steady clip, from the time I was twenty-five. Gradually, my drinking became a little bit more of a necessity. The need sneaks up on you, which is one of the reasons why this illness can be so hard to confront. Another reason is the fact that drinking is traditionally a kind of American sport, legal, acceptable, and all too available.

When I was around forty-eight, I began to challenge myself to see if I could go several days at a time without a drink. I found that it was virtually impossible to do so, and that bothered me greatly—although not enough to stop, or even cut back. An addiction to chemicals is hard for anyone to fully understand if they haven't been through one. Most of the people I have known who were addicted to booze were able to hide it pretty well. But they had to become liars and sneaks to live with their habit. In my vernacular, instead of becoming falling down drunk, they stayed half drunk all the time.

But the damage to your health catches up with you, even if the problem never reaches the proportions of Ray Milland in the movie *Lost Weekend,* with bottles hidden in the light fixtures. I don't think I ever became mean or unruly or passed out with my head in a spittoon. I had enough discipline to build and maintain a multimillion-dollar enterprise. I didn't like the way I felt. My system had to be fed. It was like feeding a python.

In 1977, about the time that I was becoming aware of my drinking problem, but doing nothing about it, the Houston Astros major league baseball team came on the market. Judge Roy Hofheinz, the visionary who built the Astrodome, the world's first indoor stadium, had suffered a stroke and had gradually lost the ball club and other properties to his creditors, the Ford and General Electric credit companies. Everyone was eager for a sale. It is rare when players and fans feel any warmth toward an owner. It is impossible to hug a credit company.

The franchise and the real estate could have been bought for a price below the market, but no local buyers were clamoring to take on the judge's faded empire. The Astros were a last-place team, and the Astrodome was in a state of some disrepair.

Owning our minor league baseball club in Corpus Christi had been one of the best times of my life, so I was very interested in this unexpected opportunity to get back into baseball. God, however, had other plans for me. One morning at home I went into a convulsive state. Charline thought I was having a stroke. In fact, I had experienced an attack of hepatitis, magnified by my overuse of alcohol. I also had been taking medications that don't mix with alcohol. I don't remember the ambulance ride to the hospital in San Antonio. I was unconscious and unaware for several days, and the doctors were unable to diagnose my illness, so Charline made the decision to move me to Methodist Hospital in Houston. Within an hour, the doctors in Houston determined that I had alcohol-related hepatitis. They didn't know if I would make it.

After my hepatitis had been diagnosed, the doctors asked Charline if I had a drinking problem. She replied, quite honestly, no, she didn't think so, "but he does drink a lot." The first few days, Charline was told bluntly that the odds were against my survival. Then they told her a miracle was happening. I would survive, but I would be dependent on a dialysis machine. Then they said I was facing a long period of recovery, but I would not be on dialysis. "There are complications," they said, in a message intended for me. "He has a surprisingly healthy liver."

Once I was conscious, and praying constantly, I began to come out of the fog. After eight days in the hospital, my mind had cleared and I no longer had a craving for alcohol. That may sound glib, too quick or too easy, but it was true. My body had been detoxed. I asked a doctor the best way to be sure I could quit drinking. He said different people try different cures. Some join Alcoholics Anonymous. Others check into clinics and go through rehab. Still others withdraw from their friends and society. None of the ways are easy.

My hospital stay, which lasted for six weeks, and the physical crisis I survived, had carried me through the hard part. This was a last-resort treatment. I don't recommend it. There are better programs than a near-death experience. When I got in the car with Charline after I checked out of the hospital, I looked at her and said, "I will never, ever, have another drop of alcohol." And I haven't. I just stopped. I went through the process without joining a twelve-step program. I follow the twelve steps and strongly believe in them. But my recovery came in a different way.

I thanked God for delivering me, and with His help I have been sober for more than thirty-two years. I have not had a drink since November 12, 1977, and I don't plan on ever having another. I would rather blow my brains out. But I do know it is a day-to-day issue. What I want to stress is that anyone in the same fix that I found myself in cannot get out of that fix without help. My doctors verified this for me after my release, when I came back for a series of weekly tests. I was told that they had treated many patients who had died from conditions not as severe as mine. They attributed my recovery to three factors: excellent medical technology, a highly motivated patient, and a power greater than any of us. I was blessed by that power and consider it an absolute truth. I can't say this any plainer: God intended for me to do other things.

All of the above explains, in part, why I didn't jump when the Houston Astros were being shopped in 1977 and 1978. During part of that time, I was too busy to chase the deal. I was in a hospital trying real hard not to die. Over the next eighteen months, the Astros were still on the block. My interest in the deal began to pick up, and my health and energy had been restored. Just as everything might have come together, a doctor discovered a complication with one of my kidneys, unrelated to my earlier ordeal. The surgery involved an incision that went from the belly button to the backbone, and while the convalescence was not a long one I had begun to get that picked-on feeling.

Gary Woods

When I went through my hospital stay and my illness with hepatitis, my dear friend and partner in the communications business, Lowry Mays (about whom I have much more to say later in this book) started scolding me almost the moment he realized I wasn't going to die. I had missed a chance to purchase the Houston Astros, an amusement park, and a string of hotels because I was incapacitated.

This was, he pointed out, not a good thing for one who insisted on being a one-man band, as I had been with all of my most important business ventures. Lowry was concerned that I didn't have a right-hand man who worked with me as an overseer of the various entities in which I was involved. Basically, the management line went directly from me to the foot soldiers. I had no chief of staff.

Lowry spent a serious amount of time telling me I needed someone in such a role because of the scare we had endured because of my illness. It was not good business practice for me or my family or anyone else not to have a person under me who would be a conduit to all my ventures. I listened, and I understood his concerns. But I really did not plan to follow his advice. I felt that I had been successful the way I had always done it, and I really couldn't see bringing in someone at such a high level. I had started my businesses out of my hip pocket and let one thing lead to another. That had always worked.

Lowry called me a few weeks later and said, "Red, you have to be the luckiest SOB in the world. I just had a call from a fellow I know in Houston, and he wants to go to work for you." Lowry said that he felt strongly that this guy would be perfect in the role of president of my holding company. He would report directly to me. I really wasn't interested, but within a few days I received a nice letter with a resume enclosed. It was from Gary Woods, the guy Lowry had recommended to me. At the time Gary was the chief financial officer and director of a public company. He was a young man with an impressive record, from his educational background (he had a doctorate) up to his executive position with an oil company.

After reading the resume, I placed it over on the right-hand corner of my desk. People who know me well recognize that this is not a good sign. That corner historically has been a Bermuda Triangle for documents and proposals that just disappear. I didn't think much more about it, until Lowry called and asked me what I thought of Gary Woods's credentials. I told him that they were as impressive as I had ever seen. Lowry asked me if I had responded to him. I told him no, I hadn't done anything about it. His voice was hesitant. He said, "Don't tell me you put it over on the right-hand corner of your desk?" I replied that, as a matter of fact, that's exactly what I had done. Lowry pleaded with me to talk to Gary. I agreed, but basically just to get Lowry off my back. I had no intention of hiring anyone.

When Gary called, he quickly sensed my total lack of interest. Somehow he succeeded in getting me to agree to meet with him at my office in San Antonio. Later, when we had our face-to-face meeting, I was still in no frame of mind to hire him. Eventually, I suggested to Gary, in a nice way, that he was more than qualified for my world, but I really didn't feel I needed anyone in that role, and with his background he would have no difficulty finding exactly what he wanted. His response was: "I'm not looking for a job. I thought I made that clear to Lowry. I have a great job. I have offers of other jobs, including company presidents, but I want to go to work with you."

I was kind of stunned. I asked the obvious question: Why me? "Well, I'm a native of Lockhart [near Austin]," Gary replied, "and I've followed your career. I've been impressed with your programs as an entrepreneur. I have a very disciplined background in finance, and I think I can learn a lot from you. And I hope I can offer something to you. But I'm interested in working with Red McCombs. I'm not looking for a job."

Frankly, I was pleased by what I heard, so I asked Gary how much money he was making, and he told me. I said, "If you want to come to work for me for half that much, we will start whenever you want. Since I don't have anyone in a role like this, I don't have any criteria for what the job should be. And I can't tell you if there will be any bonus or not, and that will be at my sole discretion." Gary replied that my offer sounded rather "harsh," but he would accept it.

I decided on the spot that this guy was sincere and wanted to work for me. When I asked him where he wanted to start, he said, "Well, I know you don't want to spend your time bringing me up to date. Why don't I just take files and start going through them? As I come to questions I will learn as I go." Gary went to work learning all of our investments just by taking my income tax returns and going through them. I knew after the first week that we were going to be a great combination. Gary doesn't waste words and doesn't spend time jaw-boning, as I am apt to do all the time. He gets to the root of the matter quickly. His skills are monumental. By the end of the first year, I was so impressed by what he had done that I saw to it he was compensated many times over from the salary with which he started.

Fortunately for me, career-wise, I think the arrangement has been satisfactory for Gary Woods. Since the end of that first year, I have always indicated to him that he can have a piece of any of my businesses. He selects only the ones he chooses to be involved in. His batting average on choosing good deals is much better than mine. Gary had his own resources when he came to me. The ventures of mine that he has taken an interest in all have been with him paying for his shares up front.

Gary is more than a partner—he has become a part of our family. There is no possible way I could have done half the things I've done since Gary joined me, if he had not been there. In the economic downturns of the late 1980s and early 1990s, I don't believe my skills alone would have helped us survive without Gary's expertise. At times, he has advised me against some of the ventures I chose. I will say that his advice has proved correct about 90 percent of the time. However, he is such a great team player that when I take on an investment he opposes, he gives his all trying to make it work. Even when it doesn't work, he has never said, "I told you so."

The Ranches and Longhorn Cattle

I was in and out of the hospital in late July, and Charline thought I needed a change of scenery. She suggested that we fly to Aspen on our Learjet. The doctors said I could set my own pace, and after a few days in Aspen I began to get antsy. I started to think about buying another ranch.

From the time we married, Charline had indicated to me many times that she would like to own a small ranch in the Texas Hill Country, west of Austin. Now, I need to explain that her image of a ranch had no close connection to what a ranch really is. Hers was a Hollywood image, the Ponderosa with a large garden. I had grown up in ranch country and knew that running one was hard, grueling work, accompanied by occasional heartache. But while I was recovering from my bout with hepatitis in 1978, Charline took me on drives through the Hill Country. Very shortly, we didn't have a little ranch. We owned a 5,000-acre spread north of Johnson City.

I now had the ranching fever. I decided that two ranches would be better than just one. I chartered a small plane to fly all over the western United States to look for a ranch from the air. When I saw a promising place, we would land, and a real estate broker would meet the plane and take me on a tour. Charline thought I had lost my mind. But it was a great way to see the American West, the Rocky Mountains, the Painted Desert, and the Badlands. I spent a month traveling across Colorado, Wyoming, Utah, Montana, and some of the Dakotas. We fell in love with an area of Colorado, where we now have a ranch that plays a meaningful role in our lives. This is what is known as the Law of Unintended Consequences. I am not certain we would have wound up in the cattle business, at all, if I had not twice felt a need to relax and rebuild my strength. In addition, the twists and turns in my health also prevented me from making a play on the Astros. New Jersey businessman John McMullen bought the team in 1979.

My plan for the ranch near Johnson City was to stock it with longhorn cattle and start a business buying and selling longhorns. Although I was looking at raising longhorns as a potentially lucrative business, my interest in Texas history is what initially got me interested. Longhorns played a key role in the story of Texas. The Spanish brought longhorn cattle to the New World only one year after Columbus had made his first landing. Eventually, the Spanish spread longhorns all over Mexico and Texas. In the middle of the nineteenth century, the longhorn became the basis of the Texas cattle industry. The golden era of the Texas cowboy, which stretched from the end of the Civil War until the early 1900s, was marked by the famous longhorn cattle drives from Texas to Kansas. The longhorn has an almost mythical place in American culture as a symbol of that romantic period in our history.

I knew that Charlie Schreiner, of the legendary YO Ranch, and Happy Shahan, in Brackettville, had longhorn herds. I went to Charlie for advice about how to get started. Charlie turned me over to his son, Walter, who became one of my closest friends. What I found out very quickly was how narrow the price spread was between the best cattle and the ones graded as merely good. But no one wanted to sell their best cattle, which made it difficult to start your own herd. I had hit a brick wall. Suddenly, while flying over ranches all day, a light came on and I knew what I needed to do. If the top cattle were so hard to buy, why didn't I create a market? All I had to do was overpay and build up my own herd.

It was possible to buy a mediocre pair of longhorns, a cow and a calf, for $750. I started making offers of $1,500 and $2,000 a pair, and the ranchers started selling to me. I fell in love with this idea of creating a market. I teamed up with a young man named Alan Sparger, whose father owned a large herd at Hondo. Alan, who owned a smaller one, was like a living encyclopedia of Texas longhorn cattle. He knew every breed.

If I was going to create a market, I wanted to do it with a big splash. In 1978, I decided to stage a large sale and bring in people from all over the country. Alan tried mightily to discourage me. The idea was frivolous, he said. I had been in the business for less than eight months. I would be known as a trader, not a true cattleman, which was roughly the difference between a pimp and an art collector.

I respected Alan's thinking, but marketing is something I know a little bit about. So we proceeded with the sale. We sold 150 cattle, losing money on many of them. But when it was over, I had in one day created a new market and attracted buyers from sixteen states.

I staged two auctions a year for twelve years. I copyrighted the phrase "The Texas Legacy Sale," and started the first Tux and Boots Cattle Sale in Houston. In the ballroom of the fancy Westin Galleria Hotel, we staged a sale of Texas longhorn cattle, covered by the national media, including the *New York Times* and the *Los Angeles Times.* We charged a hundred dollars a head just to get in the door, sold out every affair, and gave that money to charity. The longhorns not only were back as a breed—they were back with a vengeance. By 1990, I had raised a bull named Redmac Beau Butler and syndicated him to twenty different breeders for one million dollars. We did it in one day, and the syndication was oversold.

Some people have claimed that my work with longhorn cattle is a hobby. I had a big argument with a reporter who was writing a story for *Sports Illustrated* about the sports owner who owns this longhorn cattle ranch. He argued that my ranch had to be classified as a hobby. I told him that it's not a hobby at all. "Okay," he replied, "then it's a toy." I told him that my toys cost two bucks. My idea of a toy isn't a ten-million-dollar ranch with a bunch of longhorns. The ranch is a moneymaking venture.

I am not prepared to say that breeding and selling cattle provided me with a kind of therapy, but my life took a definite turn after my two hospital stays. I became much more sensitive about putting limits on what I could or could not do.

Red McCombs with longtime business associate Gary Woods, 1999.
Courtesy of the McCombs family.

Chapter Eleven

WHEELING AND DEALING

As I said at the beginning of this book, I plead guilty to the charge that I have been a wheeler-dealer almost my entire life, stretching all the way back to my childhood when I set up that deal to peddle nickel bags of peanuts. As far as I'm concerned, "wheeler-dealer" is just another name for an entrepreneur with attention deficit disorder! But I guess my real definition of a wheeler-dealer is a business person who transforms under-performing assets into high-performing assets. Or, as they say on Wall Street, we "buy low and sell high." However you want to define wheeler-dealer, the fact is that the satisfaction I get out of doing deals is one of the things that pushes me out of bed every morning.

I have another characteristic that many wheeler-dealers have. I'm a master planner's nightmare. The truth is I never have had a long-range plan to help guide me in business. I'm a *today* person. I don't even make a plan for the week. My business "plan" has simply been to take advantage of any opportunity that might come my way, wherever and whenever that may be. Which means that over the years there has been a large element of serendipity in my business dealings. I'm a pretty energetic guy who gets out and around and who likes to be involved, which has brought me face to face with a lot of opportunities.

But it's not enough just to have a bunch of opportunities. A lot of people have opportunities thrown at them. You need to know it's an opportunity when you see it. And fortunately, I seem to have been hard wired to perceive value in things that others don't. The essential characteristics necessary for a successful wheeler-dealer include the vision to recognize opportunities and the ability to manage those opportunities intelligently. You also need to have the guts to take a plunge without wasting time navel gazing. Success in the world of the wheeler-dealer really is a combination of luck, vision, and sheer guts.

As a wheeler-dealer, I've spent most of my career buying underperforming assets. I've never been interested in start-ups. I try to improve on businesses that already have a customer base. From car dealerships to radio stations and sports teams, I have found new ways to revive a variety of dying ventures. Some of my business ventures have failed or have been off-loaded to others who could make them work. If a deal isn't working, I quickly jettison it, and I never look back. It's almost as if the deal didn't happen.

Although my life has been filled with more deals than I can possibly remember, one that I recall well was my acquisition and subsequent sale of a chain of convenience stores in San Antonio. Although it wasn't the biggest, most exciting, or most important deal I've ever done, it's a good example of how I have operated as a wheeler-dealer. The deal involved that mix of luck, intuition, opportunism, and intestinal fortitude that are typical ingredients in any wheeler-dealer's success.

The Mister M Stores

For many years my San Antonio office was next to my showroom at my car lot down on San Pedro Street. When you walked in the front door, if you didn't stop you walked straight into my office. I always had the door open. Suzy Thomas, my longtime assistant, had a little desk sitting right out in front. That easy access brought me a lot of business, but not much privacy.

An old friend ambled in one morning, just out of the blue. Fred was a used car wholesaler. In our industry there are a lot of pretty knowledgeable people that buy trade-ins from dealers and sell to other dealers. We call them used car wholesalers. It's a common practice in the business and this guy was one of those. We did a lot of business with him. So it wasn't unusual for this wholesaler to come by. I asked him if he saw anything out there he liked. "No," Fred replied, "but I do have a question. Considering the way you like to buy and sell things, why weren't you interested in buying the Mister M Food Stores?" That was a chain of drive-in convenience stores. The "M" stood for "Metzger," which was the name of the family that owned the chain. They also owned a dairy products company.

I knew the Stackey family, who operated the stores in San Antonio. It was no secret that Mr. Stackey, who was probably in his early fifties, was very ill. But frankly I didn't know that the chain was for sale. I was very interested. If it had not been for this used car wholesaler dropping by, I would not have known about this opportunity until after someone else snatched it away. Charline has always said that I have a very strange assortment of friends. My response to Charline's comment has always been that "You never know when one of them is going to bring you something."

I told Fred that I didn't know anything about the stores being for sale. It turned out that Fred's wife was a paralegal at Cox, Smith, which was a leading law firm in San Antonio that was involved in the sale negotiations. Fred said the buyers were the 7-Eleven people in Dallas. I just replied that his news was interesting and just dropped the subject. Fred soon left. As soon as he did, I grabbed the telephone and called Jack Guenther, a CPA and lawyer who was a partner at the Cox, Smith law firm.

I knew Jack very well. His dad was our auditor. I said "Jack, I want to get in and look at those Mister M books and I'd like to do it about two o'clock this afternoon." He said what are you talking about? "Well, it's no secret," I said. "Everybody in town knows that they're selling the company and everybody knows that 7-Eleven is interested." I told him I wanted to take a shot at it myself. There was a long pause. Finally, Jack said, "That's not going to work, Red. These people are about to go to contract. We've spent a lot of time with them." I didn't pull my old friendship routine this time, but I did say, "Jack, do I need to remind you that you've got a fiduciary responsibility to your client?"

"I don't need you to tell me how to practice law," Jack replied. I answered, "Well, then get it right." Jack said that he would call me back. When he did, Jack was not happy. He told me to come to his office at two o'clock that afternoon. He said he would clear everyone out of the room where they had the Mister M records and that I could have the room until six. I thanked him and went to his office.

I really didn't know what I was looking for exactly. I already knew Mister M had great locations around San Antonio. I also knew from selling them trucks that they were very tough to deal with. I was almost certain that they had often bought the property on which they had built their stores. I wanted to verify that. I didn't have any idea about how to run those stores, but I knew those properties. I brought my auditor with me. Within an hour we determined which properties they owned and which properties they were renting. It turned out that they owned about

80 percent of the stores and about 20 percent were on leased ground. The ones they didn't own had leases that were about two hundred dollars a month. I could not believe it. Those stores were on great locations worth five to ten times the rent they were paying.

We also looked at their tax returns for the three previous years, which is the easiest way to see what any business is actually doing. It was obvious from those tax returns that they had a pretty nice little business. They had more convenience stores in San Antonio than 7-Eleven or any of the other biggies. They also had about thirty-five stores in Austin and about seventy-five stores in Houston. Some of the stores had gas stations, some didn't.

I sent my auditor back to our dealership office and asked Jack Guenther to come back into the conference room. I asked him what form they wanted me to fill out to make my offer. "Red," he said, "we've pretty well got a deal with these other people." I answered that they had an obligation to look at my offer. I didn't have any idea what price the 7-Eleven folks were offering, but I figured out that I didn't have to estimate a value for the company at all. The real estate was what was really valuable, and that would be easy to determine.

I told Jack that I was going to make an offer to buy all of the assets of the company. He told me to just write the offer on a piece of paper. Deciding that I'd go for broke and see what happened, I put down a number for all the assets, including the inventory, which was something no one else would do because an offer price is usually stated as "plus inventory to be determined later."

"There's my number," I said. Jack looked at it and asked me for a closing date. I told him fifteen days with one hundred thousand dollars in earnest money. "I think that's a little light," Jack said. "Okay," I countered, "then let's make it two hundred thousand." I could tell by Jack's body language that my bid was better than the 7-Eleven bid.

I decided not to depend entirely on the bidding process, however. So I went directly to the owners, the Stackey family, who lived in San Antonio. I pointed out that I was a local guy and that I was sure they had a good offer from 7-Eleven. "I don't know what it is like to sell to a big national chain like that," I said, "but you also have an opportunity to sell it to a San Antonio boy. I just hope you give me a chance." I promised to leave the name the same and not change anything at the stores. "We'll have a local owner," I said, "and it'll be smooth." The Stackeys were very gracious to me. They liked what I had said.

I returned to my office and immediately began to wonder, "Where am I going to get the money?" Jack called me a little later and said, "Okay, Red, you've got a deal." I thanked him and then stressed that there were a number of details that needed to be worked out before we could complete the deal. I didn't mention that the main detail was where the money was going to come from.

The next morning, Jere Thompson, the CEO of Southland Corporation, which owned 7-Eleven, called me. I knew Jere casually through our mutual interest in the University of Texas. "Hey Red, what are you doing? You have screwed us up all the way around." I asked him what he meant. "You may be a good car jockey," Thompson replied, "but you don't know anything about the grocery business." He said that Southland had spent a lot of time and effort looking at those Mister M stores and had tried to buy them for years. "Now you go down there and put in an offer that trumps what we were going to pay. And the family is taking your offer because you're a local guy." I told him that they were doing the right thing by keeping the ownership local.

Thompson offered to buy the purchase contract from me. "We'll pay you a bonus for it," he said. "Will you sell us your contract?" I told him that I would be willing to look at an offer. Thompson said Southland would give me a bonus of fifty thousand dollars and pay off the contract. "You're getting close Jere. You can add one million in front of that and you can have it." Thompson sputtered, "You are full of it. Nobody is going to pay you that." I told him that Southland would be foolish if it didn't buy it on those terms, because they were in this business and I wasn't. "We're not about to do that," he responded. "I'll tell you another thing. You hold us up like that and I'll put a giant store across the corner from every one of your stores and I'll break your ass." I said that I guessed he was going to get that opportunity because the deal was not happening unless he paid me one million dollars for it. The truth is, I would have sold the stores to him for half of that, but I wasn't going to give them to him.

So that ended the negotiation with Jere Thompson, but then I had to go find the money. I went to my friends at Frost Bank. Naturally, they asked what I knew about running convenience stores. I told them that I knew everything about it. "It's just milk and cigarettes and gasoline. What is so hard about that? Anybody walking on the street would know how to run that business." That must have worked, because they loaned me the money.

Of course, I never had any intention of managing those stores. I knew the general manager, Jim Allen, who was a graduate of St. Mary's University and a very nice guy. He had done a great job managing the company, and he knew the business inside out. So, I just retained Jim as the general manager, and we got along fine.

Not long after I bought the stores, Jim counseled me that the convenience store business was very competitive. "Our business is tied very closely to gasoline sales," he explained. "We generate a lot of our food business from people who stop to fill up their car's gas tank." He said that if the store across the street was selling gas for a couple of cents less than our price we would lose half of our total business. In those days, gasoline price wars were fairly common. Jim wanted to know how he should respond whenever that occurred. I asked him how he handled it in the past. "Well," he replied, "I always asked the previous owners for direction and approval before I did anything." I answered, "Jim, you don't need to go to anybody because I'm giving you the authority. If our competitors drop the price of gasoline, you just drop our price a penny below their price." I told him that he had the authority to make those kinds of decisions. He appreciated that, and it worked well for both of us.

I also suggested to Jim that we immediately lower our prices on cigarettes and milk. Jim protested, arguing that the profit margins on those items were so thin that we couldn't make any money if we lowered the prices. I responded that we would take care of that problem by raising the price by at least 5 percent on everything in the store except milk and cigarettes. "Red, that's not going to work," Jim said. "Our customers are going to realize that a jar of pickles or a can of beans at our store is more expensive than they are at a grocery store. They won't buy that stuff from us if we raise the price too high." I replied that our milk and cigarette products would be loss leaders bringing more customers into our stores. "A guy who buys a jar of pickles at our store doesn't know whether the jar is a dollar ten or a dollar twenty at the grocery store," I argued. "But he knows exactly how much cigarettes and milk cost because he buys those every day." Jim remained skeptical until he saw how much money we were making with that strategy.

Jere Thompson doesn't make idle threats, by the way. He did open 7-Eleven stores across the street from many of our stores. And he did give us trouble. Every six months he would start a rumor with a food distributor that we were going broke and would not be able to pay our bills. It was a harassing tactic. I called Jere several times to complain. His answer was always the same. He wouldn't stop until we sold our stores to Southland.

And so Jim Allen and I rocked along for about four or five years with our Mister M stores. We were making money, and the real estate was appreciating in value. Frankly, I wasn't in any hurry to sell the business. In the meantime, we built a few stores, and it was working pretty well.

Out of the blue one day in 1981, I got a call from a guy named Pete Van Horn, who was the president of National Convenience Stores in Houston. NCS owned an extensive network of convenience stores, most of them operated under the name "Stop 'n Go." The company was founded in San Antonio in 1959, but it moved its headquarters to Houston in 1965. They owned about eight hundred convenience stores in several states. Van Horn said that he had heard that I had sold the Mister M stores to 7-Eleven. I told him that was not the case. "That's just some of the harassment I get from those guys," I said. "They spread these rumors about every six months."

"I see," Van Horn responded. "Well, will you sell them to us?" I immediately replied, "yes." I was so quick and direct that it sort of took him by surprise. We didn't even discuss the price. After a long pause, Van Horn said "Okay, I would like to meet you in San Antonio as soon as possible." I believe this was on a Thursday or Friday, so we made an appointment for him to come to my office at the car dealership the next Monday morning.

Van Horn showed up at my office on Monday as scheduled. After we exchanged a few pleasantries, he asked me what I wanted for the stores. I gave him a number, plus inventory. His response was that my price was about 25 percent too high. I asked Van Horn how he judged that. He said that he knew the current market value for the stores because they owned stores just like them all over the United States. I said, "Well then, I've offered them to you too cheap because I thought I was selling them for about 40 percent more than what the market is." He replied, "Well, no, the price you named is about 25 percent more than current market value." We looked at each other for a few moments in silence, then he said, "Nevertheless, we would be willing to pay that much for the stores. Are you agreeable to doing that?" I agreed. He pulled a contract out of his briefcase and filled in the numbers. I said, "Now wait a minute. Since we have never seen each other until about fifteen minutes ago, how do I know you have the authority legally to bind National Convenience Stores to this deal?"

He replied that his board of directors had met at his house the day before, which was a Sunday. He handed me a statement that his board had passed and signed granting him the authority to buy the Mister M stores. That was good enough for me. We made the deal. The whole thing didn't take more than thirty minutes. I didn't even have the time to warn Jim Allen that we were going to sell out.

A few hours later I got a call from Jere Thompson. He said "Red, I'm sure this is just a rumor, but I hear that you sold Mister M to National Convenience Stores." I answered, "Well, Jere, it's not a rumor; I did sell them." Thompson said, "Red, you know I've been trying to buy those stores." I reminded him that he could have bought those stores on any day during the past few years that I had owned them. I told him that instead, all he had done was create problems for me. "Frankly, Jere, I would have sold them to you, but you've been such a jerk that I'm glad I didn't." He replied, "Well, Red, thanks a lot." I said, "You're welcome."

Now before you start pushing pins into little dolls that look like Jere Thompson, I must point out that Jere actually is a very good guy. I still see him at University of Texas functions. He and his family have been strong and generous benefactors of the university, and they deserve much praise for what they have done for the university and a number of other good causes. The Joe C. Thompson Conference Center on the university campus is named for Jere's father. The reality is that there was nothing particularly unusual in the way he handled the competitive situation with us. Most companies play hardball; they have to do that to compete. Despite the tone of our conversations, I never really thought it was personal. It was just business. The wheeler-dealer world isn't for the faint of heart.

Coors Beer

Another example of my wheeling and dealing was when I became involved in a Coors Beer distributorship in San Antonio in 1981. I also got into that deal by accident, which has often happened to me. A friend of mine in Houston, Jack Criswell, with whom I had partnered in some other ventures, coveted a Coors Beer distributorship. Eventually one of the three distributors in San Antonio put their distributorship up for sale. Coors had been in this market about five years. Although the brand was doing extremely well, San Antonio really wasn't a big enough market to sustain three distributors. In those days, Coors often made a mistake by sticking too many operators in a lot of places. It made it hard for any of the distributors to make money. But Jack saw this as his opportunity to finally get into the beer business.

Jack had never been a beer distributor. So the next thing I knew he asked me to go to the Coors headquarters in Golden, Colorado, to meet with Coors executives. They wanted at least two people in the distributorship deal, and Jack wanted me to be one of them. Coors had the right to accept or not accept the partners in their distributorships.

At the time, Charline and I were at our ranch in southern Colorado. Jack flew over from Houston in his airplane and then took us up to Golden to meet with the Coors people, including Pete Coors, the CEO and grandson of Adolph Coors, the founder of the Coors company. I had met Pete before, but I did not know him well. We exchanged hellos and such and then sat down to talk. The Coors executives interviewed Jack, and then they asked me some questions about Jack. During this interview session, I sensed that something odd was going on. I could tell by their body language and the questions that they were asking that they were not really too excited about some of Jack's answers.

After the interview, we all flew back to southern Colorado, and Jack went on to Houston. After Charline and I got off the plane and started driving up the mountain to our place, Charline observed that it seemed to her that everything had gone very well. I said, "Honey, I'm afraid it didn't. Do you know what happened there today? Coors is going to turn Jack down and then offer the distributorship to me." Charline said, "Oh, they wouldn't do that." I told her to wait and see.

About two days later I got a call from a Coors executive. He said that he didn't want to go into any details, but Coors was going to reject Jack's application for a distributorship. "However," he said, "you live in San Antonio and if you want the franchise, we will approve that." I called Jack, who was very disappointed and surprised by this news. I said, "Look, Jack, here's what I think we ought to do. I'll go ahead and buy the distributorship. I'll keep it two or three years and then I'm going to sell it to you." I told him that I would front the deal and run the distributorship and that everything would be open and aboveboard. I said, "In the meantime, Jack, you're going to have to get in Coors's good graces so that I can sell it to you."

Immediately after I bought the distributorship, Pete Coors called and said that he wanted to come to San Antonio to have a dinner and a ribbon-cutting ceremony in honor of my joining the Coors business family. "I want you to invite twenty-five to thirty-five businesspeople," Pete said, "and we will host a little dinner the night before we have the ribbon-cutting ceremony." I told him that was great and asked him if I could do anything else. He laughed and said, "Yeah, I wish you could get your Catholic Archbishop Patrick Flores to come to the dinner. We offered him a nice public service award recently but he declined." Archbishop Flores had told Coors that he couldn't accept an award from them because of a labor union boycott against Coors in Boston.

I'm not a Catholic, but I had done a lot of things for Archbishop Flores and thought the world of him. He was a gentle and kind soul. I called and told him that I had bought a Coors distributorship. He said "Yes, congratulations Red. I saw that in the newspaper." I told him that the Coors executives were coming to town and that they were having a little dinner for my friends and me. I told the archbishop that Pete Coors had asked me to invite him to the dinner. "Pete said you probably wouldn't come because you had declined their public service award as a result of the boycott in Boston." Archbishop Flores replied, "Oh, yes. I'm not directly involved in the boycott but my Catholic brothers in Boston have a problem with Coors. I declined the award as an act of solidarity with them. I hope I didn't offend Mr. Coors."

I replied, "Well look, why don't you come to the dinner. We'll have you say the blessings and you can still get the award. Can you do that for me?" "I'd do it for you Red," he replied. So I called Pete back. "Pete you can bring that check and your trophy or whatever else you have for the archbishop," I said. "Archbishop Flores will be attending the dinner and he also will make a little statement welcoming you and the brewery and he will do a prayer." Pete said that he couldn't believe Flores would do that. "Well, he happens to be my buddy, not your buddy," I replied. "He's doing it for me." And typical of the archbishop, he came and gave a beautiful blessing. You would never have known that he had any issues with Pete Coors whatsoever.

So I became a Coors Beer distributor, even though I never intended to be one. That kind of thing has happened over and over again in my career. It's a good example of why I'm not a big fan of master planning. There are too many opportunities in the world that you don't know about until they knock on your door. I kept the distributorship for about eighteen months. It was not extremely lucrative, but it did make money. Nothing really earthshaking happened while I owned the distributorship. It was just another part of my stable for a while. In the meantime, my friend Jack Criswell had some business reversals, and he wound up not being able to buy the distributorship from me, so I sold it to a third party in August 1983—for a profit.

Win Some, Lose Some

I don't want to give anyone the impression that I'm the redheaded boy genius who never made a bad deal. I've made dozens of deals that I wish I hadn't done. Two were manufacturing enterprises where I had great products, but I could never make them work. One was a floor tile product and the other was a food product.

The food product was made of poultry, but it had the taste and appearance of beef and pork. Because it was poultry we thought we could make it cheaply, but it never worked that way. The food market is just so difficult to penetrate. We couldn't find our niche. We also made some mistakes with the manufacturing process. I stayed in that deal longer than I normally would because I fell in love with my management, which is always a mistake. They kept telling me that they had found the answers to our problems, but they never did. I stayed in it three years, but I should have jumped ship in nine months. The tile product never took off either. The competition was just too fierce. Because of those two particular experiences I have no interest in ever getting involved in a manufacturing business again.

Another less-than-successful venture was my involvement in a business to bring television to hotels and apartment complexes. It was called Multiple Directional Systems (MDS), which was a forerunner of cable. MDS had a license from the Federal Communications Commission that allowed you to bring special television program service to multiple units like motels. The system had a limited product, and it lost its competitive position when cable became available. But that venture turned out not to be successful, and I got out as fast as I could.

Before it was evident, however, that the business wasn't going to work, I nearly partnered with Clint Murchison, the owner of the Dallas Cowboys. Clint had the license for a major slice of the West Coast, including most of Northern California. It was MDS's biggest territory. Clint heard that I'd received licenses for Phoenix and other places, so he called me and said that he was thinking about adding a partner for his MDS license for the West Coast. I agreed to be his partner because the San Francisco Bay Area had the population density that looked, at least on paper, like it would really work there. I was excited about the opportunity. I crunched the numbers and did the diligence and all of that, and it looked really great.

I decided that I wanted another partner for my side of the deal with Clint, so I invited Lloyd Brinkman, another wheeler-dealer who, among other diverse enterprises owned the Mr. Gatti's pizza chain. Lloyd and I went to Dallas to close the deal. We were meeting with Clint in his boardroom going over some of the details and getting ready to sign the papers when one of Clint's assistants came in and whispered something in his ear. Clint smiled and said, "Red, the guy that I've been telling you about who is going to operate this enterprise for us is in the outside office. I'll bring him in to give you and Lloyd a chance to meet him."

We hadn't signed the contracts yet, but the lawyers had them spread out on the table. And in comes Dr. So and So, an academic who was quite full of himself. I don't recall his name. He began to pontificate about what he was going to do and how this would work. The longer he went on, the more nervous I got. So I asked him some questions. The bottom line was that he was a professor of some sort, and he had done a lot of work with air broadcast spectrums and such. It was pretty esoteric stuff that meant nothing to our deal. I sat there listening to this for about fifteen minutes. He really got carried away.

Dr. So and So continued with the lecture until I finally interrupted him and said, "Okay, Clint, I think I understand. Maybe we can go ahead with our business." Clint was just the nicest guy in the world. He said, "Well, Doctor So and So, thank you. Why don't you wait out in the outer office? I'm going to finish these contracts with Red and I'll be back with you." I said, "Clint we need a five-minute break." I grabbed Brinkman, and he and I went to the restroom, where I stood with my back to the door so nobody could come in. I said "Lloyd, did anything about that operator's presentation bother you?" Lloyd said, "Not really, Red. The truth is I couldn't understand the son of a bitch."

I said, "Lloyd, I don't want to embarrass you, but I'm not doing this deal, but you should go ahead if you want." Lloyd answered, "Well that's bull, I'm only in this because you asked me. If you're out I'm sure not hanging around." I said, "Well, this is not going to go down well with Clint, because there's been a lot of work to get this far down the road." I told him that if Clint was willing to pay an arm and a leg to this blowhard who didn't know a thing about managing any business, much less a start-up, I didn't have a lot of confidence in Clint's judgment. "I don't care how many Ph.D's this guy has," I argued. "It ain't gonna work. I just wanted to see how you felt about it before I jump overboard."

We went back in to Clint's office. I didn't want to tell him that I was killing the deal because of this guy he had brought in. That would give Clint the option of saying, "Well, we'll find somebody else." So I said, "Clint, this is hard for me to do because I don't have any tangible reason for it, but I'm not doing this deal. I've just made a mistake." I told him that I realized that I wouldn't be a good partner for him. Clint said, "Red, I've always wanted to be a partner with you on a deal." I replied that I didn't like the deal and I that I had tried hard to sell myself on it, but it wasn't working. It was awkward, but I just wanted to get out of there. So Lloyd and I left and took a taxi to the airport. On the way Lloyd said, "Well, Red, every time I'm around you something spectacular happens. But I sure didn't expect this." I told Lloyd that I could be totally wrong, but that was the way I saw it. This thing was not going to work. And Lloyd said, "If that's the way you see it, I'm with you." In any event, that deal ultimately played a big role in Clint's financial ruin. And that was a sad thing because Clint Murchison was a good guy.

More recently, I've had some interesting opportunities to make McCombs Enterprises a player on the international stage. A few of those opportunities didn't work out either. Three of them, one in the Dominican Republic, one in China, and the third in Iraq, are especially noteworthy because they developed in unusual circumstances.

Importation of Kia Vehicles

In 1984, the South Korean car company Kia gave me the opportunity to import and distribute their product in Mexico, Central America, South America, and the Caribbean. This was a very attractive offer because I had gained so much experience importing foreign cars as a Subaru importer and distributor. My Subaru business had become one of my largest and most profitable companies, with corporate and warehouse operations in Denver and port facilities in Oakland. I distributed Subaru vehicles to approximately sixty dealerships in the Rocky Mountain states. In my meetings with the Kia representatives, they implied that if I had success with the distributorship deal they were offering me in Mexico and the other areas south of the U.S. border, Kia would let me distribute their cars in the United States, which they planned to do no later than 1995.

I thought that was a very promising deal, so we signed the papers with Kia and created a separate company to manage the business. We selected Santo Domingo in the Dominican Republic as the location for the company headquarters. We quickly hired management and staff to run the corporate office and to manage the warehouse and vehicle storage facilities in Santo Domingo. Everything was working smoothly until early 1985, when we tried to establish Kia dealerships in Panama and in Caracas, Venezuela, which had great potential as lucrative markets. We soon discovered, however, that Kia had already given the distributor rights in Panama and Venezuela to other parties without telling us.

That was an unhappy discovery, but I just chalked it up to a communication problem between the South Koreans and us. We worked out that problem and proceeded to appoint dealers in the regions we were allocated. A few months later, however, when we received our first shipment of some 1,000 vehicles, we found that many of the cars were damaged, lacked important components, and were generally not the models and body styles that we had ordered. In addition, we had ordered 1985 models, but many of the cars that arrived were 1984 models. That was bad enough, but we also learned that we couldn't obtain spare parts for the vehicles.

Throughout the last half of 1985, we held numerous meetings with Kia representatives trying to correct these rather severe problems, but they were all to no avail. I consulted my attorneys to determine how we could recover our investment in the Kia cars we now owned, but they weren't optimistic about our chances. After an unsuccessful attempt to get Washington to put diplomatic pressure on South Korea, I realized that the only way I was going to salvage the situation was to find someone to buy my Kia import company and its inventory of cars. After several false starts, I found a capable purchaser who was based in the Dominican Republic. Gary Woods, who was handling the negotiations for me, made several trips to Santo Domingo to get the deal done.

In the beginning, Gary's meetings with the potential purchaser followed the normal sequence of steps that are taken in the sale of a business: fact-finding, due diligence, and tentative negotiations. As time passed, however, the meetings took on a contentious tone as the buyer sensed our urgency to close the deal. Late one evening in early July 1986, Gary traveled to Santo Domingo in my Learjet for an early morning meeting with the buyer. When he arrived at the meeting place, no one was there. After Gary made several telephone calls to the buyer's office, two of his "assistants" finally showed up. They told Gary that their boss would not be available until two o'clock that afternoon. Gary noted that these guys were acting in a hostile and intimidating manner. At the designated meeting time, no one appeared. After another hour passed and no one appeared, Gary called the buyer's attorney and told him he would return to Texas at five o'clock if no one had showed up by then. By five o'clock, no one had appeared. The situation was getting very uncomfortable, so Gary told his driver to rush him to the airport and not to stop for any reason. Gary later told me that he kept looking out the rear window of the car for the twenty-minute ride to the airport. As he boarded my jet, he told the pilots the same thing, "Don't stop for anyone." He didn't feel safe until he was airborne.

Early in the morning the day after Gary returned to the office in San Antonio, the buyer's attorney called him. He said that he and the buyer would fly to Houston that afternoon for a meeting to close the deal. Taking a chance, Gary flew to Houston and he finally made the deal. Although we were under pressure and were very motivated sellers, in the end we had a negotiating advantage. The buyer didn't speak English, so his attorney was also his interpreter. Gary knew enough Spanish to understand the discussion the buyer and his attorney had in front of him about what terms, conditions, and prices they were willing to accept. They had no idea that he could follow their conversation.

In late July 1986, we signed the papers and sold the company and car inventory to the Dominican businessman. But we weren't out of the woods yet. The sale occurred only a few days prior to a presidential election in the Dominican Republic. The buyer quickly turned around and sold the entire inventory to the Dominican government for what we understood to be a significant profit. His associate, the incumbent president, lost the election. Shortly thereafter our buyer was convicted of some crime and was sent to a Dominican prison. His jailing apparently was the result of his friend, the former president, losing the election. Although we received most of the purchase price at the closing, a small amount was payable in installments. With our buyer locked away in a foreign prison and his presidential ally now out of office, we weren't optimistic about getting the rest of our money. To our great surprise, however, all of the installments eventually were paid in full. Not long after the buyer was imprisoned, Gary expressed his sympathy to his attorney for the buyer's misfortune. The Dominican attorney replied, "You do not understand our country. This year he is in prison, next year he could be president."

That was the end of the relationship with our friends in South Korea. When Kia finally introduced their cars to the United States in the mid-1990s, you will not be surprised to learn that I had no interest in reviving that relationship.

A "Deal of a Lifetime" in China

Over the years I have been asked to become a U.S. dealer for two or three brands of Chinese cars that different businessmen were hoping to import for sale in the United States. After I saw the prototype cars and studied the business plans, however, I decided the products weren't viable for this country. In late 2007, Marc Ganis, a friend of mine from the world of professional sports who is the founder of Sportscorp, contacted me about a potential investment in a Chinese automotive manufacturer. Marc and a young Chinese businessman, Kenny Wang, who was living in New York City at the time, wanted to bring Mr. Wu Xiao An, the chairman of Brilliance Automotive, to meet with me in my office in San Antonio. Chairman Wu earned his MBA at Fordham University and spoke excellent English. He had two officials from Brilliance traveling with him.

Brilliance manufactures several models of Chinese cars and vans. The vans use styling and technology licensed by Toyota, but the cars are purely Chinese products. Brilliance also has an exclusive license to build BMW 3 and 5 Series cars in China. Chairman Wu was looking for someone to lead the process of importing Chinese cars into the United States, to build a dealer network to sell these cars, and to invest in Brilliance. In addition, Chairman Wu wanted to learn about the used car business and wanted me to develop a plan to introduce used car sales to Brilliance's network of over nine hundred dealers in China.

Chairman Wu offered what every knowledgeable American entrepreneur wants: an invitation to do business in China! Our first meeting lasted for several hours. Before any actual business could be done, we had to follow the Chinese custom of exchanging gifts and engaging in long conversations about everything except the business at hand. We all sat in the conference room of my office building and talked, listened, and exchanged ideas. A translator accompanied the Chinese executives who were traveling with Chairman Wu. I soon realized that I had to make brief statements because they were more easily translated. At one point, I launched into a rather long story about my experiences selling used cars. About halfway into the story, the translator stopped taking notes. At the completion of my story, the translator looked at the Chinese guys, smiled, shrugged his shoulders, and said nothing. Apparently not everything I said could be translated well.

After my meeting with Chairman Wu, I decided to send my daughter Marsha, my oldest grandson Carson, and Gary Woods to China to evaluate Brilliance and their car dealerships. They flew to Hong Kong, where Brilliance has its headquarters. Marc Ganis and Kenny Wang met them at the airport and took them to Chairman Wu's office. Kenny knew everyone, knew how to get everywhere, and was a most gracious host for my daughter, grandson, and Gary. They traveled to Shenyang the next day and toured Brilliance's manufacturing plant, where they watched Brilliance's workers assemble minivans and cars. They also toured the company's BMW plant. They met with the entire board of directors of Brilliance and exchanged so many business cards that they had none left to offer after the second day. They even drove Brilliance's Chinese cars. The final day, they visited Beijing, attended two more meetings, and then returned to the United States.

After Marsha, Gary, and Carson returned to San Antonio, they gave me a full report, which was enthusiastic and positive. Based on their observations and other information, I developed a preliminary business plan for implementing used car sales in Brilliance's new car dealerships in China. My plan included the idea of adding a finance and insurance department to enhance the dealers' profitability. The basic idea of the plan was to create a joint venture with Brilliance that would establish McCombs Enterprises as the gatekeeper through which we could bring other U.S. companies into China. I thought it had the potential to be the biggest deal of my career, but I realized there were problems.

The most significant problem was engineering. The Brilliance cars were attractive, drove well, and had good fit and finish, but the cars would have to go through several engineering changes to bring them up to U.S. standards for emissions and crash protection. After a closer study of the engineering issues, I determined the Chinese car importation plan was not ready for prime time. I advised Chairman Wu that the time was not right to set up a network of U.S. dealers and begin the arduous task of importing new Chinese cars into the United States. But we continued our talks about implementing a used car program in China, as well as pursuing other opportunities.

In May 2008, my daughter Marsha and her daughter, Anna Shields, returned to China to continue our evaluation of the potential for a used car business. After they returned to San Antonio, we realized that the financial numbers weren't adding up in a way we thought would be profitable quickly. The reason the used car deal looked so good was because there was no established used car business in China other than a few consignment-sale businesses for luxury cars. But there was a cultural reason why there was no used car market in China. The Chinese people did not understand the concept of trading in a used car and buying a new car. So while we could easily teach the structure and procedure of used car sales in a dealership, we could not change the culture of the people. Their tradition was to purchase a vehicle with cash and keep it in the family until it could no longer be used. By the time a car reaches that stage, of course, it has no value.

We finally decided that my deal of a lifetime was not going to happen. As it turned out, we were smart to jump ship. Our entry into China would have required a joint venture with Brilliance and a significant monetary investment. The economic downturn in 2009 hit Brilliance and all Chinese automakers very hard, and Brilliance's stock performance since that time has been poor. The Chinese government owns 50 percent of the company, and it controls the leadership. Chairman Wu is an insightful, well-educated, smart businessman, but our relationship was with him, and the Chinese government could remove him from his chairmanship at any time for any reason. The reality is that investing in a company in a country that doesn't operate like ours is very risky. I think the Chinese people will eventually begin to understand the value of used cars, but that day is in the future. In the meantime, I'm keeping my eyes open. If the cultural change occurs during my watch, I'll be eager to go back to the largest market in the world.

I've done other deals that didn't work. Here's what I do with a deal that doesn't work—I take it and give it my best shot, but I don't hang around. If I can't get a cash flow within a reasonable time I'm out. To me cash flow is the mother's milk of success. Without it you're dead in the water. Everything I do business-wise revolves around cash flow. I'm gone if I can't get a company's cash flowing almost overnight. Very highly paid business consultants will tell you that's an unrealistic strategy. It may be. But I don't buy into this "burn rate" idea that we're going to take so much time and that we've got so much capital that we can just burn money for another ninety days or so. I don't buy that. While you're developing a company to do what it ultimately will do you should have some other ancillaries that can give you some cash flow while the main company develops. If not, adios, I'm out of here. I've sold out of deals and lost money. I don't even give it a second thought except that I'm happy to be out. It's just sayonara and goodbye. I'm on to the next thing.

Lowry and Peggy Mays with Red McCombs at the McCombs Ranch in Johnson City, 1978. Courtesy of the McCombs family.

Chapter Twelve

CLEAR CHANNEL

IN 1970, I TRIED TO PURCHASE SAN ANTONIO'S WOAI-AM FROM THE AVCO corporation. WOAI is a fifty-thousand-watt clear channel radio station with a signal that can be heard throughout the southwest during the day and throughout North America and Mexico at night. A clear channel station broadcasts on an AM frequency that no other station in the United States is allowed to use. WOAI was a landmark pioneering radio station with a fascinating history. By 1970, however, the station had abandoned its traditional format and gone downhill as a result.

I wanted to buy WOAI because, in the several years prior to 1970, many of the locally owned broadcast companies had sold out to big corporations with headquarters out of state. I was worried that San Antonio was not going to have a local media voice of significance. That was a major concern. But I also was interested in the radio business because of my own success at using radio commercials to attract customers to my car dealerships. I could see that the radio industry had some intrinsic value as an investment. I was attracted to radio because it is a powerful medium, the capital expense of setting up a radio station is minimal, and you have no inventory. You have twenty-four hours a day available on your spectrum number.

AVCO wanted to sell WOAI, but we couldn't agree on a price. The station wasn't doing well, but my reason for wanting to buy it was really not because of the value. Although the deal fell through, I remained interested in that industry, and I never gave up on the idea of eventually owning WOAI.

Lowry Mays

Sometime in 1972, Lowry Mays, who at that time was an investment banker, stopped by my office to talk about a radio station he was trying to unload. I had known Lowry since the 1960s, and I had invested with him in a number of joint ventures and limited partnerships. Lowry grew up in Highland Park in Dallas. He was a Texas Aggie with a degree in petroleum engineering. After serving in the military, Lowry went to Harvard for his MBA degree. He's eight years younger than I am. I don't remember exactly where or how we were introduced, but we developed a very strong personal relationship. We did some real estate and oil deals together, and we became very close friends. We both liked doing deals.

Lowry found himself owning an FM radio station almost by accident. Acting as a business broker, Lowry had sold the station to a mutual friend of ours and for whatever reason the mutual friend didn't want to close the deal. The station, KEEZ-FM, had a rock-and-roll format, but it had poor ratings and no cash flow. The main problem was that FM radio was a very marginal business in those days. Most automobiles had radios that could only receive AM broadcasts. That would soon change, however, and FM would eventually dominate over AM. But I didn't see that coming. Aware of my strong interest in WOAI, Lowry offered to sell KEEZ-FM to me for $125,000, which was the amount of money he had in the station.

I explained to Lowry that there was a night and day difference between WOAI and KEEZ. I told him I had no interest in KEEZ, but if the seller only wanted $125,000 for it I felt that was a minimal amount of money to risk. I proposed that if he would commit to me that he would really get serious and try to buy WOAI and some other stations, we could go into business together. I didn't think we could make any money from the FM station, but I suspected that if we someday could get WOAI, maybe we could make a few bucks.

Lowry told me that he was not in a position financially to buy any radio stations, he knew nothing about operating a radio station, and he really wasn't interested in owning one. I assured Lowry that I did know how to run a radio business. Today, Lowry loves to tell people that he found out later that I really didn't know anything about how a radio station operated. But the truth is that I did. It is a fairly simple business. Not easy, but it's fairly simple. I assured him that I had bought a lot of radio advertising and that it had made me some money. I felt certain that we could figure it out, especially if we hired a top-notch general manager with solid radio experience to run the broadcast operation. The guy I had in mind was Doug McCall, the general manager of KTSA, the top-rated AM station in San Antonio.

I also told Lowry that we would not have to put any of our personal money into the purchase of KEEZ. Instead, we borrowed the $125,000 from Frost Bank. I don't recall the conversation lasting very long, but we decided to do the deal ourselves, and Lowry would try to buy a few other radio stations. Lowry and I created a business entity we called San Antonio Broadcasting to serve as our ownership company. We were able to bring McCall over to be our general manager. He did an outstanding job, but we continued to lose money. I urged Lowry to go after WOAI, but another deal in Oklahoma came up first.

Lowry heard that an advertising firm that owned two stations in Tulsa was interested in selling them. One of the stations was an AM; the other was an FM. Lowry went to Tulsa to check them out. The AM station had potential, but the FM station was less promising. The seller, however, required that both stations had to be in the deal, so Lowry and I bought the stations for $750,000. We figured out a creative way to finance the purchase. We sold the land on which the transmitting tower sat for a lot more money than we paid for the radio stations.

WOAI and Clear Channel

We now owned three radio stations that were losing money, which was not part of my normal business plan! Fortunately for us, however, the station I had long wanted, WOAI, once again came up for sale. Lowry and I jumped at the opportunity to acquire the station, but it took us more than a year to put the deal together. After we made the purchase in 1975, Lowry and I brought in John Barger to run the radio end of the business. John was a veteran broadcaster who had been the manager of KRLD-AM in Dallas. At Barger's suggestion, we changed the name of our company to Clear Channel because we now owned a clear channel station. We had plans to buy a few stations outside of San Antonio, so we needed a name that didn't tie us to one city.

We recruited Barger not only because of his deep overall experience in the industry but also because he had converted KRLD-AM into a successful 24/7 news talk format station, which is what we wanted to do with WOAI. Barger offered to sign a contract that gave him 10 percent of the station's net operating profit. That was an offer we couldn't refuse because WOAI *had no net profit* at the time. That was definitely an incentive deal, but it paid off for everyone, including Barger, who had us operating in the black in one month.

By 1978, WOAI was generating a nice profit, thanks to Barger and Stan Webb, whom Barger recruited from another San Antonio station to be our sales manager. Webb also turned our Tulsa stations into moneymakers. We soon acquired additional stations in El Paso, Port Arthur, and Austin.

During the first two or three years, Lowry kept his day job as an investment banker. After we found success with another half-dozen stations, Lowry looked at the industry and decided he wanted to delve more deeply into the business than we had planned. I was delighted with that decision, because Lowry is an extremely talented guy. This was the first real indication I had that we might build a fairly good-sized regional company. Until then, there was no thought in my mind that we would ever become a huge, international company. My thinking was along familiar lines: do the one deal, buy some assets, increase their value, and then sell. But on a clear day, I didn't see forever. Lowry did—and I give him all the credit for that.

Lowry and his wife, Peggy, a San Antonio girl, have four children, and sons Mark and Randall took leadership positions in the company. Lowry has served on the Texas A&M University Board of Regents, as chair of the Chamber of Commerce and the United Way, and he is a past chairman of the National Association of Broadcasters. He is a member of the Texas Business Hall of Fame and has been recognized by his peers multiple times. He served as the chairman of the board and CEO of Clear Channel.

In those early years, Lowry and I talked about the stations every day. I was very much hands-on. I was not a paid employee, but I was involved in every decision of any significance that Clear Channel ever made. It was not my role, however, to run the business on a day-to-day basis. I'm not a radio broadcaster, and I don't flatter myself as having any talent at selecting entertainment content. I was a principal in at least twenty different businesses, and radio was just one of them.

Lowry and John Barger ran the day-to-day business very well. I did tell Lowry what I thought he needed to do about overall business strategy because I found it fascinating. Here is a business that gives you twenty-four hours of airtime, and all you have to do is put on programming that is good enough so people will listen and advertisers will buy commercials. You don't have any inventory, and you don't have to worry about manufacturers seeing your product on shelves—everything was on the airwaves.

Lowry's style was a little different than mine, but we never had any problems. Of all the years that we were together in that ownership, we never had any differences that caused ill feelings. However, we did have differences in strategy from time to time, particularly on the growth side. I was very much a bull on growth, and Lowry was more conservative. And all of those little differences were rationalized and resolved as we went through purchase by purchase by purchase.

We never had any plan to build Clear Channel any larger than we could operate profitably. What we wanted to do was get up to the ownership limit established by the federal government, which was a maximum of seven stations, get some cash flow, and then sell them. There was never any plan to make it a big company—not ever. But then other opportunities came along, and as those opportunities came to us we began to expand, although we had no idea at the time where this was going to take us.

Lowry was diligent from the day we started about informing his directors what the plans were, what changes he wanted to make, and what the future might bring. He is not an "I Did It My Way" kind of guy. In 1985, for example, Lowry asked me to fly to Kentucky with him to take a look at two stations for sale in Louisville. I believe the price he mentioned was $20 million. My response was, "Lowry, you're not talking about radio. You must be talking about television stations." He said no, these were radio stations, but they represented a large portion of a very good market. They had been owned by the Bingham family, publisher of the *Louisville Courier-Journal*, since their inception.

I went to Louisville with him, and we closed the deal. One of the properties, WHAS-AM, first went on the air in 1922 and had a place in the history of the radio industry. The station was the first to do a live broadcast of the Kentucky Derby. It's also a clear channel station that broadcasts at the 840 frequency. It was rated number one in the market. The other, WAMZ-FM, was recognized nationally as one of the top country-and-western stations. That turned out to be a very profitable deal.

We continued to grow throughout the 1980s. We took Clear Channel Communications public in 1984, and then we brought in Alan Feld, Ted Strauss, and John Williams to serve on our board. They were all friends of Lowry's from his Highland Park High School days. In addition, in 1984 the federal government raised its ownership limits from seven to twelve, and the growth kicked into a higher gear. We expanded into the television business in 1988 by buying WPMI, Channel 15, in Mobile-

Pensacola. Lowry's son Mark earned his MBA at Columbia University and joined the company in 1989 to help on the financial management side of things.

Clear Channel was a major player in the broadcast industry nationally by the mid-1990s, but it was Congress's passage of the Federal Telecommunications Act in 1996, which essentially deregulated the industry, that really opened the door for us to eventually become a dominant player nationally. The sky was now the limit. We had anticipated that the Telecom Act would pass two years prior to its passing, so we were well prepared to expand. Lowry handled almost all of our lobbying in Washington in support of the Telecom Act, and he was very good at it.

We also went international, with properties in Asia, Australia, and Europe. We acquired several media companies, including Jacor Communications, which owned 230 radio stations in fifty-five markets. That was a $4.4 billion deal. In 2000, we purchased SFX Entertainment, which was the largest owner and operator of venues for live entertainment in the United States. That was a $3.3 billion deal. But the biggest deal was our merger in 2000 with AMFM, the radio giant owned by Dallas investor Tom Hicks. That was a $23.5 billion deal. The federal government required us to sell off nearly one hundred radio stations before it would approve that merger. Clear Channel also became number one in the United States in outdoor amphitheaters and second in billboards.

No question, Clear Channel is one of the great business success stories of the last twenty-five years. Clear Channel, at last report, was the largest operator of radio stations in the world, with over 1,200. At one point we owned twenty-eight television stations. Not surprisingly, the sheer size and reach of our business attracted a number of critics who spread nonsense about how we had killed the "golden era" of Top 40 radio with such broadcasting strategies as "voice-tracking." Our critics also charged us with political censorship, which was absolutely untrue.

The reason why we got so much bad press to me was very simple. First, we were so much better than the other companies in the radio business. Some of our competitors did a good job of making us look like bad guys, which we weren't. Also, people who were concerned about public policy suddenly realized that on any given day, half the people in the United States might be listening to a Clear Channel radio station. That's quite a huge audience, and nothing like that had ever happened before. So that seemed to be a threat from some kind of political standpoint, even though we had no official or unofficial political position. Rather than admit that they were getting beat in the marketplace, it made them feel better to say, "I got beat because these guys are just gorillas, and I'm just a little guy." The fact is, all of our stations were little guys, too. We operated 1,200 stations about the same as someone else would run one or two. They are all individual stations. We had to prove again and again that we were primarily committed to the communities in which we operated. I believe that we made a lot of progress in that area before we sold the company.

In 2008, we sold Clear Channel Radio for $28 billion to a private equity group. Before we sold it, we broke the company into three parts. One part was the entertainment group that is now called Live Nation, which is the entity that owns the entertainment theaters and arenas. Another group is Clear Channel Outdoor, which involves all the outdoor billboards in the United States and internationally in about sixty countries. The third part was our radio company, which is what the equity firm purchased.

I have no direct involvement with these companies now, but my daughter, Connie McCombs McNab, is on the board of Live Nation and another daughter, Marsha McCombs Shields, sits on the board of Clear Channel Outdoor. Occasionally I'll ask one of my daughters about some issue involving those companies, and they'll say, "Dad, that'd be a conflict of interest, I can't tell you." I never would have dreamed that I would have a meaningful role in creating a business that would spread worldwide and become number one in the world at what it was doing. Clear Channel has thousands of employees and operates in sixty-two countries.

When you list the significant things in my business life, Clear Channel would have to be at the top. It isn't something that I dreamed about doing. I would never have thought that I could ever have had the chance to do something like a Clear Channel. That's why I don't really believe in long-term plans. There was no way I could have ever planned Clear Channel. When you see a chance, take it.

Spurs owner Red McCombs and Angelo Drossos congratulate David Robinson for being named to the NBA All-Star Game, 1990. Photo by Jim Blaylock/ San Antonio Express-News/ *ZumaPress.com*.

Chapter Thirteen

SPURS REDUX

DURING THE FIVE YEARS THAT I OWNED THE NUGGETS, THE Spurs fell on hard times, with four losing seasons and one break-even season. Fan interest and attendance dwindled along with the win column. Spurs management made a major mistake during these years that did nothing to help the situation. They traded George Gervin to Chicago in 1985. It didn't work for anyone, not George, the Spurs, or the Bulls. Gervin was the face of the franchise in San Antonio. He was an icon who attracted fans to the games just to see him play. Trading him made no sense, even in his declining years. Can you imagine the Yankees trading Joe DiMaggio or the Red Sox trading Ted Williams as they neared retirement? The Spurs management finally woke up in December 1987. They held a celebration at the HemisFair Arena to retire George Gervin's jersey and to recognize his critical contributions to the success of the franchise.

Problem for the Spurs

As attendance fell and community interest faded, there was widespread talk around the NBA and in the national sports media about the Spurs being a prime candidate to relocate to another city. Spurs management seemed clueless about how to resurrect their fortunes. In addition, my friend Angelo Drossos, who owned about one-third of the team's stock, was ill, although I didn't realize it at the time, and it had an adverse affect on his decision making.

The Spurs had drafted the United States Naval Academy's star center, David Robinson, in the first round of the draft in 1987. In a sense, the Spurs were just waiting for David Robinson to finish his two-year navy tour of duty and then come to their rescue. I was seriously disturbed by the prospect of San Antonio losing the Spurs after all that we had done to build the franchise and raise the city's national visibility in turn. Losing the Spurs would be a disaster for San Antonio's civic image and its prospects for corporate development.

By this time in 1988, I was deeply involved in our Clear Channel Communications enterprise, which was going great guns. Unfortunately, nothing else was doing that well. At the time, I had my own cash shortage, the result of what was referred to in Texas as the financial holocaust. Oil prices had crashed, the real estate market collapsed, and banks and savings and loans had gone belly-up. I had plenty of assets, but not much that was liquid. After I sold the Denver Nuggets in 1985, I bought a one-third interest in the Spurs with some of my profit, but that did not give me the control I needed to turn things around.

To prevent the Spurs from being moved out of town, I called Angelo in May 1988 and proposed that I acquire control of the club, despite my own cash issues. I told Angelo that I would place a value on the Spurs at \$47 million and purchase his and the other shareholders' stock on that basis. If they didn't want to sell, they could buy my stock, which was one-third of the ownership, on a value basis of \$44 million. I offered them more money than I would take myself if they decided to buy rather than sell. I did that to get their attention. I told Angelo that if they wanted to buy, then they had to pay me quickly. If they wanted to sell, I would pay them quickly. I said, "Angelo, I know you don't have to do anything and I understand that, but I don't think that would be the right thing to do for you, for me, or for the club."

Angelo asked me how long he had to make a decision. "Until noon," I replied. I didn't want Angelo massaging the offer and coming back with a lot of issues that distracted from the real heart of the deal. I wanted to get in or get out. It was that simple. I do a lot of business deals like that. If it goes one way that's fine; if it goes the other way, that's okay with me, but let's get it over with. There's not any point to haggling about it endlessly. About a quarter of noon, Angelo called me and said, "I've talked to my partners and we all agree to accept your offer of \$47 million."

So the deal was done. I now owned the Spurs, except this time I owned nearly 98 percent of the stock, and I had total control over the club. One of the first things I did after buying the team was to bring George Gervin back to San Antonio to work in our community relations operation. We needed to get our old fans back, and George was important to that effort. He had struggled with drug addiction and recognized how destructive it was. He was unable to break his addiction until he went to John Lucas's center in Houston. George got sober and stayed that way and has been a contributor ever since. I'm not much for climbing on a soapbox, but I believe addiction is an illness. Still, not everyone is a victim. Some are just bad apples.

The next thing I did after acquiring the Spurs was to hire a new head coach. Just before I bought the team, Angelo had fired Cotton Fitzsimmons and replaced him with Bob Weiss, a good and studious man but an uninspiring coach. I knew we had to make a change. We needed a coach of the first rank who had a national reputation.

Larry Brown

As Bob Bass and I began to look for a new coach, the news flashed that Larry Brown, the head coach at the University of Kansas, had accepted and then rejected an offer from UCLA. Brown's Kansas team had just won the NCAA national championship. Larry Brown played and got his coaching start under Dean Smith at North Carolina. He is as demanding of himself as he is of his players. He has won wherever he has coached, and that is a high compliment, because few coaches have moved around as much as Larry Brown. Guys who sell stock in phony uranium mines don't move around as much.

When I heard the news that he was returning to Kansas, I allowed my imagination to take a leap. I had to think hard about Larry Brown's nervous feet, but the Spurs were at a crossroads. We had the lowest attendance in the league, the lowest ticket prices, the lowest everything. Hiring Larry Brown would cure our credibility problems. I knew we were not going to win until David Robinson completed his service in the navy and then had time to develop as a professional.

I decided that we had to have Brown, his ability, his record, and his name. I believed that he was our best chance of keeping the Spurs in town. It really didn't seem logical that Larry would walk away from UCLA and a job that was pure gold, go back to Kansas, then walk away again to come to San Antonio. But I knew that logic doesn't always prevail in these matters.

I had $47 million on the line, and that investment had stretched me big-time, but I wanted Larry Brown as my coach. He agreed to talk. When we had our meeting, I talked for a solid hour, barely taking a breath. In the end, he asked me one question: "Who will make the basketball decisions?" I told him that I would reserve the right to approve the big decisions, but that it would be highly unlikely that I would veto anything he wanted to do. As an added assurance, I agreed to make him player personnel director as well as head coach. Bob Bass would become my assistant.

We had a deal. Money and terms never came up in our talk with Larry, and I was in no mood to drag it out with Joe Glass, his agent. Joe asked for a base salary of $400,000 and incentives worth about $275,000. I got tired of hearing his agent recite his list, and so I asked him to come up quickly with a total. "It's about $675,000," he said. I responded: "Okay, then I'll just make it $700,000, total, guaranteed." We signed a contract for five years worth a total of $3.5 million.

We won only twenty-one games in Larry's first season, which was the worst season in Spurs history. But our marketing and sales of tickets and suites went through the roof. Larry's presence was a huge attraction. In addition, David Robinson would be joining us in time for the next season. I knew we were on our way.

By the time the 1989–1990 season rolled around, David Robinson had shed his sailor suit, joined the team, and led us in nearly every category. David enjoyed one of the best rookie seasons for a center in the history of the NBA. Although we had waited two years for David, his parents moved to San Antonio after he graduated from the naval academy. During that time, David flew into San Antonio whenever he could to visit his parents. While he was in town, he spoke to school assemblies and rode buses all over South Texas, helping to sell our program. He never had that superstar mindset. I can say with certainty that the Spurs are still in San Antonio because of two players, in different decades: George Gervin and David Robinson.

Early in Robinson's career, Dave Checketts, the president of the New York Knicks, offered to trade his star center, Patrick Ewing, and $10 million, for Robinson. This was when money was extremely tight and my investment in the Spurs had severely reduced my liquidity. I told Dave that $10 million wouldn't help me in terms of my needs, but $25 million would. For $25 million in cash I was willing to take the heat in San Antonio that was certain to come after the buildup we had given Robinson. Checketts couldn't do it, so the deal didn't happen.

Patrick Ewing and David Robinson were probably equal in ability, but Robinson was the kind of player I wanted to build a team around, a perfect fit for San Antonio. His contract had a burdensome provision—every three years he would get the average of the league's top two salaries—but we were counting on him to save the franchise. It's hard to put a price on that. In retrospect, the $25 million in cash would have untied a few knots in my belly, but as I have always known, tough times never last, tough people do. We worked our way out of it, and Robinson became a franchise icon.

Prior to the start of the 1989–1990 season, we traded Alvin Robertson, a great defensive player, to the Milwaukee Bucks for six-foot-nine forward Terry Cummings. We also had an outstanding rookie, Sean Elliott, who was our first-round draft pick. We finished with a 56-26 record, the biggest turnaround in NBA history. In the only discordant note, we lost in the semifinal playoffs to Portland in seven games. Nevertheless, the Spurs were definitely back in business after suffering through a long series of bad seasons. There was no more talk about moving the club to another city.

The 1990–1991 season was almost a copy of the previous season. Larry coached the team to fifty-five victories and the Midwest Division championship. We lost to Golden State in the first round, however. The NBA championship remained just beyond our reach, but I was certain that we were at the cusp. I had high hopes that Larry Brown would coach the team into the championship game the next season.

The first part of the 1991–1992 season did not go as well as I had expected. By January, we had a 21-17 record, which was not bad, but the team had been inconsistent and had not played up to their talent. We lost three out of four on the road—to Golden State, Chicago, and Boston, games Larry felt we should have won. No one takes defeat any harder than Larry Brown. Losses leave Larry depressed. He reacts to them like a death in the family. But I wasn't terribly worried about the situation. I had every expectation that we would improve and head into the playoffs.

After the bad road trip, we had a home game with the Clippers. Before the game, Larry took me aside and said, "Red, you need to get another coach. These guys are not going to respond to me. There is more talent here than I'm getting out of them." I could see how downcast he was, but I found his words upsetting. There are two kinds of momentum in sports. One carries you along on wings of eagles. The other drops you like a rock down a drainpipe. Players take their cue from the coach. I said, "That's dangerous, Larry. You need to quit talking that way." Larry responded that he needed to quit, "or you need to fire me."

"Okay, I'll fire you, but first you need to go back to your room and think about it." I quickly found Gregg Popovich, his assistant coach, and told him what had happened. I had no intention of firing Larry. I said, "Go get him and pull him back together." All Gregg could say was, "Oh, shit!" When Gregg called, he said he thought Larry would be okay. He called again after practice and said everything was fine.

I had a business meeting downtown the next day. A waiter slipped me a note: "Call Joe Glass immediately." That was Larry's agent—not a good sign. "Red, we need to talk about this," he said. It was clear that Larry had worked himself into a torment. He wanted out. I scheduled a meeting with Larry for nine the next morning, but he failed to show up. When Bob Bass called him to see what had happened, Larry said that he wanted me to fire him.

My attitude was basic: You have not been fired when an owner is trying to talk you into staying. Larry Brown could have coached for me as long as he wanted. As I told the media when I announced his departure on January 21, 1992, "Larry asked me to make it clear that he was not resigning, that he was being terminated. It's a very unusual situation to ask to be terminated." What propels Larry isn't clear, but he moves fast and in an orbit all his own.

So Larry Brown was gone. He immediately became head coach of the Los Angeles Clippers. Since leaving the Clippers, he has coached five other NBA teams. At the time of this writing, Larry is the head coach of the Charlotte Bobcats.

I asked the ever steady and dependable Bob Bass to come back for the fourth time and coach the team the rest of the year. We finished with a 47-35 record and second place in the Midwest, but Phoenix swept us in the first round of the playoffs.

Tark the Shark

A day or two after the wire services spread the news of Larry Brown leaving, I received a phone call from Jerry Tarkanian, former basketball coach of the University of Nevada, Las Vegas. Jerry and I had never met. Calling from Las Vegas, Jerry said straight out, "Red, I see Larry Brown has left and I want that job." I was impressed with his directness and how easy it was to talk to him. "Have you got anybody in mind to replace Larry?" he asked. "No. I don't plan to replace him until the off season." I told him, truthfully, that it was very unlikely that I would hire a college coach. He asked, "Would you mind if I called from time to time?" I said not at all. We became telephone pals.

Tark called two or three times a week, and I grew more and more impressed. I mentioned this to Bob Bass, who put his head in his hands and said, "Oh, no, Red. No matter how great a coach he is, we need to stay with the pros."

Near the end of the season, the Spurs flew to Los Angeles to face the Lakers, and Jerry and I made arrangements to meet for the first time. We had been talking on the phone for about a month. I made the arrangements, and the CIA could not have been more discreet. We planned to meet in the morning at a place I picked, fifteen miles from the hotel, not known as a sports hangout.

Charline and my daughter Lynda rode out with me on the team bus to the Forum, as we always liked to do. While the players were getting dressed, I went to the floor to kill time, visiting with the broadcasters and people who worked for the Lakers. Charline and Lynda dropped by the Forum Club. The doors of the Forum were not even open yet to the general public. The Spurs had left the locker room and were going through their shoot-around. I took a seat in the fourth row and, like locusts, here came a swarm of reporters from every direction. As they descended on me, I thought, Good Lord, what's happened?

They peppered me with questions: "Have you already hired Tarkanian? What exactly is the deal?" I looked at them and was pleased that I could say quite honestly, "I have not only NOT hired Jerry Tarkanian, I have never met him. Never seen him." No one asked if we had talked. They were shaking their heads, wondering where such rumors come from, how they get started.

I learned later what had happened. As any basketball fan knows, Tarkanian has a very recognizable profile with his bullet-shaped head and dark, hooded, mournful eyes. Charline and Lynda were in the Forum Club when he walked in. They knew of our phone calls, and I had never told them I was keeping our talks a secret. They walked over, introduced themselves, and joined him for a drink. Charline and Lynda were tickled when they rejoined me just before the tip-off. "You'll never guess who we just met," they said. Oh, yes, I could.

After the game, I was walking to the visitors' dressing room, and passed by the door to the Lakers' quarters. There was Tarkanian, with a crowd of people around him, including some reporters. I couldn't avoid him. I held out my hand and said, "Coach, I'm Red McCombs of the San Antonio Spurs." He said, "Oh, so nice to meet you." I went inside our locker room, having effectively killed the story—for the time being.

I did not offer Jerry the job at breakfast the next morning. But in the cab going back to our hotel, I told Bob Bass, "I'm going to hire him." Bob said, "No, Red, please. At least wait until the season is over before you decide." I agreed, but I told Bob that I wanted Tark and the turbulence he brought with him.

Jerry Tarkanian had won a national championship at UNLV and just missed another. He also made the Running Rebels the most hunted team in the history of college basketball, unfairly I thought. And the courts later agreed. He engaged in an endless series of battles with the NCAA. Sworn to bring him to justice, all the NCAA's agents really did was make him take his act out of town. In the end they were found guilty of conspiracy and had to pay him millions to settle the lawsuit.

As soon as the season was over, I slipped Jerry into town without leaking the news. I even hid him in a room next to the press conference without his being seen. My excitement led me into one of my more embarrassing boo-boos. The reporters gasped when I brought him in, setting up his appearance with the words, "I want to introduce you to the new coach of the San Antonio Spurs, Jerry Tarkington." I said it twice. Still, in spite of that slip of the lip, I was happy. I knew he was a winner, and he would bring new life to the team and the city.

Of course, the transition from college to pro is not a sure thing in coaching. The critics asked how he would fare in a league where no one cares what anybody did more than twenty-four seconds ago. Would he lose whatever edge he had in Las Vegas, where the Rebels were not exactly a shining example to the youth of America? After they won the national title in 1990, a reserve forward named Moses Scurry was asked how they did it. "We a well-in-shape team," he replied. But I was confident that the colorful variety of players Jerry recruited in Las Vegas would help him deal with the pro temperament.

But Tarkanian was a different person in the pros than he was in the collegiate game. Ten or twenty years ago, he might have slam-dunked the league. But he did the one thing he could ill afford to do—he did not trust his own instincts. Just as Jerry got my attention by using the phone, he loved to get opinions from people all over the league. It didn't occur to him that they might have their own agenda. His sources told him he didn't have a point guard; this guy is overrated; that one lacks grit. All I asked him to do was use his own judgment and do the things that worked for him before. The floor was the same size as the one in the college game. So was the basket.

I have no doubt that he could have been a great coach in the NBA, but he let other people poison his mind. So his pro career lasted twenty games, eleven of them losses, and you could see the pain on Tark's face—the fear that the season would never end. This is not an uncommon feeling among NBA coaches, but none of the others carried the burden of Tarkanian's success in the college game.

The day he got fired, December 18, 1992, I hadn't even planned to visit with him. I had a speech to make for the United Way. Meanwhile, Bob Bass and Gary Woods were huddling in the Spurs office, working on the team's budget. I stopped by and was going over a few points, when Tarkanian suddenly appeared. We had lost a game in Houston the previous night in the last few seconds. In the dressing room, Tark thought he was having a heart attack, but it turned out he was simply dehydrated. They held the plane for him.

Tark heard I was in the office talking to Bob and Gary. He was concerned about his symptoms and what was causing them, namely, the team. "I've got to talk to you," he said. "I can't," I told him. "I have a speech to make to the United Way and I'm just leaving." Jerry insisted, "I've got to talk to you, NOW."

We didn't plow any new ground, but Tark got very emotional about the lack of talent. He told me that with the players he had, the team could not play .500 ball. This attitude startled me. I had expected a period of adjustment. The slow start had not rattled me. I tried to turn Jerry's attention to the team's history. I had been in the league, off and on, since the mid-1970s. I told him this team would not only play .500 ball, it would contend for the Western Conference title.

He shook his head. "You misled me," he said, "on the ability of these players." While Tark was venting, I decided he was through. I said, "Coach, excuse me a minute. I've been here longer than I thought. I've got to make a call. You need a Coke or anything?" I ducked into Bass's office and said, "Bob, see if you can get John Lucas on the phone." Lucas had founded the drug rehab center in Houston that had helped George Gervin, and was back there after coaching a team in the Continental League.

"Ask Luke if he wants to coach the Spurs," I said. "If the answer is yes, ask him to do an evaluation of our roster, just two sentences on each player. Then tell him I may be calling and to stand by the phone."

I picked up a Coke and went back in to see Coach Tarkanian. I needed to buy a little time while Bass tried to locate Lucas. So I said, "Coach, let's go over this again." And Jerry jumped on my invitation, unloading all over again the flaws and failings of our players. In a few minutes, I excused myself to go to the restroom. Bass was waiting for me, nervously. Luke was standing by the phone. The answers were yes and yes, and here's his evaluation.

I was so hyper I couldn't read Bob's handwriting, but the analysis was basically very positive. He thought the team had the potential to win 70 percent of its remaining games. I took a deep breath and said, "Okay, Bob, call Luke and tell him here's what his contract is going to be, and it's not negotiable. If he wants to do it, tell him to book a seat on the Southwest Airlines flight at five. You can pick him up."

Bass asked me not to do it. I asked him why. "Too much trauma," Bob replied. "This team can't take all this." I reminded Bob that I had been talking for years about finding a place in the Spurs organization for Lucas. "This is it," I said. "You call John and see if we have a deal."

I had to go back to Tarkanian and do some more double-talk. Tark was still ranting about how bad the team was. I excused myself again. Bob told me that Lucas was coming, he would fly in on the five o'clock plane. "Get with our PR people," I said, "and set up a press conference. Don't say who the coach is. The press conference is only to say that Jerry Tarkanian has been fired." I went back to Jerry. "Coach," I said, "you were my friend when you walked in this door and I want you to be my friend when you walk out. But as of this moment, you are no longer the coach of the Spurs. The reason is, your expectation level is so low compared to mine, they are never going to mesh."

His jaw dropped. "I didn't mean to get you so upset," he said. In fact, I was now completely calm. "I'm not upset," I said, "but it's over." "Well, let's wait a minute," said Tark. "No, it's over," I said. "You're not coaching tonight." Tark protested. "It's four o'clock," he said, his forehead wrinkling, "and I'm not coaching tonight? Who is going to coach?" I said, "Rex Hughes," who was one of his assistants. Jerry left without another word. I felt a strong sympathy for Tarkanian, the Shark. He was a great guy and a great coach, but in San Antonio he had been a fish out of water.

In between parting ways with Tarkanian and the start of the press conference, I squeezed in a call to Charline. I said, "Honey, you better turn on the news. There's a press conference at five." She said, "I don't have to watch the news. You fired him, didn't you?" I asked her how she could know that. "I could see it coming," she said, "from the way he was talking." Had I said anything at home about him? "That's just it. You weren't saying anything."

I was in for another surprise. Charline asked me when I was going to announce the new coach. I told her after the game. "Well, is Luke here?" she asked. I nearly dropped the phone. "How did you know that?" I asked. She was doing an Agatha Christie number on me. "It wasn't hard," she said. "You've always wanted to give Luke a chance to coach. The new man had to be available and he had to be someone you had no doubts about. And if he was much more than an hour away by air, he couldn't get here in time."

An hour or so later I held the press conference to announce that Tark was out. Bob Neal of ESPN was in town, so our press conference was covered nationally. I wanted to get two bangs for my buck and announce that Lucas was the new coach. But I also was moving with caution. I wasn't counting my chickens until Lucas was on the ground in San Antonio and we had a signed contract. So I decided to wait until after the game to make the announcement.

I hurried over to the locker room to inform the assistant coaches. They were stunned. They had no idea and, of course, there was no way they could have known because I hadn't intended to fire Jerry Tarkanian. Rex Hughes would take over the team for the night. Then I told the players the events of the day. It was hard to read them. I said, "When you go out to warm up, I don't want you talking to any reporters. You can talk to them tomorrow. We have a game tonight." I walked out, the room eerily silent behind me.

John Lucas

John Lucas had played for the Spurs in 1983 and 1984, after breaking into the league with the Houston Rockets in 1976. He was the first pick in the NBA draft that year as a point guard out of Maryland. And it was there, in Houston, where his story almost ended, ten years later. Lucas woke up from a night he could not remember, wandering through the downtown streets, his shoes missing, his clothing soiled, unable to find his car. He missed practice that morning and failed a drug test later that day. He had insisted, up to the moment the test results were returned, that he was clean. Bill Fitch, then the coach in Houston, forced him to seek help by kicking him off the team and out of the game he loved. This was in March of 1986, and his decline seemed irreversible.

The tragedy was this: nothing in John's life that he held dear—not his family, his career, his teammates, his reputation, not even money—would rank ahead of the moment of pleasure he enjoyed from drugs. If a bright, attractive, talented, savvy fellow like John Lucas couldn't figure it out, who could? He was no high school dropout, but the product of a stable home, the son of two educators, good enough at tennis to play the game for a living. There was nothing to dislike about the fellow who, as a basketball player, had been dubbed "Cool Hand Luke."

We had watched John hit bottom and bounce back from the wreckage of drug addiction. Whatever else he may have accomplished, he has to be given a ton of credit for rescuing his life and for helping so many others. Charline loved him. We all did. I knew at least in part how the media was going to play the news: Red McCombs was giving an ex-junkie a chance to coach in the NBA. It would have been a major story, no matter who the characters were.

I conferred one more time with Bass. He said, "I'll pick up Luke, he gets in at six, just in time to talk to the players and coach the game tonight." I told Bob that he wasn't coaching that night. "But," Bob objected, "I told him he was." "Just tell him he ain't. He has to be incognito. But as soon as the game is over, I want him in the dressing room before the players shower. Put him in with the engineer, up in the Jumbotron." Bass didn't see the need for all the deception. "Luke comes to half our games," he pointed out. I said, "Yeah, but this is different. When I give the sign, you bring in Luke." I had drawn up a one-page contract. "When he steps off the plane, you get Luke to sign it."

In the arena, the buzz was everywhere. The crowd had heard the news in a stream of bits and pieces. It was like fireworks going off. Bob was seated ten rows below me, to my right, and I had told him to bring me the signed contract as soon as he had concealed Lucas. As the game got under way, he hadn't brought it. I made eye contact with him before the half.

Bass came to my aisle and whispered that Lucas hadn't signed the contract. "No problem," Bob explained, "he just has to tell his agent." I said, "I don't care if he tells his agent, but if I don't have a signed contract in my hand, he's a spectator. This has been too big a day to leave that big a loose end." A few minutes later, Bass handed me an envelope with three copies of the contract inside, all signed.

You never know how teams will react to disruption and confusion. But our guys were terrific, blowing out Dallas, 122-101. After the game, we followed our usual custom and went into the locker room. I was already inside when the players started filing in, high-fiving each other because they won. I congratulated Rex—he is undefeated as a head coach—and I worked the room, hoping that Bass had Lucas waiting outside. I opened the door a crack, and there they were. I said, "Just a second."

I raised my voice: "Listen up. Congratulations, guys. Now I want you to meet the new coach of the Spurs." You could hear a canary feather drop. I let it stay that way for maybe fifteen seconds, then I hit the door and Lucas walked in. "What, isn't there any excitement for the new coach?" I asked, and then the place exploded. I will never forget what Lucas said to the players: "Guys, you are the most out-of-shape team I have ever seen in professional basketball. And that goes for you, Mr. Robinson. I know we have a game to play, but we start two-a-day practices tomorrow. We're not going to take a month to get in shape. I'll see you tomorrow."

Then John walked out to face the press conference. The sad note was seeing Rex Hughes standing there. I hated that. His moment of fame had lasted for just about the fifteen minutes Andy Warhol had said everyone would have. Otherwise, no one could have written a better script. The reporters were not expecting a new coach to be announced. I sat down at the microphone and said, simply, "I want you to meet the new coach of the Spurs." Lucas slid into the seat beside me and fielded the questions. "I'm going to find out," he said, "if they have the will to win. Among those out there, who won't let you lose?"

There were two reactions that I had not expected from this decision. Neither of them was a part of my thought process, even though they have touched a big part of my life. The first was the reaction from the African American community, from CEOs to the workingman, who said: "Hey, you gave a guy a chance who already had two strikes against him." The other was from people who said, "You have shown that a person can have an addiction, overcome it, and contribute at the level of upper management." I had so many responses along that line; it was humbling. I received letters from people who said, "I have an addiction. Thank God,

I'm sober, but I have been blackballed from going up the ladder. You gave a chance to a guy who not only was addicted, but the whole country knew it."

The reaction was both beautiful and meaningful. Regardless of how many games John Lucas won for us, the results were overshadowed by the message sent to tens of thousands of people who shared his experiences. I didn't hire him out of any sense of nobility, but the example it set was by far the most important result of my decision.

Having said this, I ought to admit that it is part of my nature to give an edge to the underdog. Having been addicted to alcohol, which is so hard for people to understand, I know what a blessing it is once you get sober. You are so grateful for your second life. You realize that if you had stayed on the side of addiction, you were dead. So you rejoice in the new life. Sometimes, in spite of yourself, you look like a genius or a hero.

I had found myself in urgent need of a coach who could hold together the fragile psyches of a team in near disarray. The previous coach had shown little or no confidence in them. Lucas had a huge advantage. They knew him. He had been in the league. He had helped some of them with their personal problems.

So the team responded by winning twenty-four of their next twenty-eight games under John, a surge so unlikely in the NBA that you would compare it to catching lightning in a thimble. We finished with forty wins in our last sixty-six games, close to the 70 percent goal I had envisioned. It was a goal that did not intimidate Luke. The Spurs reached the Western Conference semifinals but lost to the Phoenix Suns. By then, however, I had sold the team.

John spent two seasons taking the Spurs to the playoffs, winning fifty-five games with a team that Tarkanian labeled a loser. One of the sad side effects of my selling the team was the inability of Lucas and the new owners to find a comfort level. He resigned during the 1993–1994 season and moved on to Philadelphia, but he made the mistake of doubling as coach and general manager, a task I regard as unworkable. A handful can do both, but most can't.

John Lucas didn't last in Philly, but he has been through the fire. No setback is so large that it can bring him down. He went back to Houston, where he runs a tennis club and works with a drug treatment center that is a model for others across the country.

The Alamodome

A key part of my second go-round with the Spurs in the late 1980s was helping to sell San Antonio on the idea of building a domed stadium that would serve as a new home for our NBA team and, hopefully, attract an NFL expansion team. The HemisFair Arena was hopelessly out of date and unsuitable for an NBA team. Most of the other NBA teams were building new arenas that included luxury boxes, club level seats, and other premium amenities that enhanced the market value of the teams and increased revenue. The revenue issue was critical because of the rapidly rising operational costs. Getting a new arena was at the top of my "to-do list" as soon as I bought the Spurs.

I was not the only person dreaming about a new multiuse complex for San Antonio. A number of civic and business leaders agreed with me that the city needed such a facility, but the leading advocate was San Antonio's dynamic mayor, Henry Cisneros. Henry had long hoped to attract an NFL team to San Antonio, and he knew it would not happen unless the city had a suitable stadium. In the late 1980s, we formed an advocacy group to sell the idea to the taxpayers of the city. We proposed to build a domed stadium that could serve as a venue not only for the Spurs and an NFL team, but also for everything from rodeos and college football bowl games. Financed by a half-cent sales tax, we were confident that the Alamodome would be an investment for the city that would be repaid many times over. I was equally confident that we could attract an NFL expansion team within five years of opening the new stadium. Nevertheless, that half-cent sales tax, like most taxes, was not easy to pass. But we did succeed.

Groundbreaking for the construction of the Alamodome was in November 1990, and it was open for business by May 1993. As it turned out, that half-penny sales tax paid off the entire $193 million cost in just five years, which made it possible to rescind the tax in 1994. We had a big reserve left that we used for operational expenses. With a seating capacity of 72,000, it gave the city of San Antonio a brand-new facility unlike any other it had had before.

It's strange to me, but we still have people who criticize the Alamodome. Although we did not realize our dream of getting an NFL team (for reasons I will explain in the next chapter), it served as a great home for the Spurs for almost a decade, and it has hosted the NCAA

Final Four basketball tournament, the Alamo Bowl games, and national conventions and events that attract forty to fifty thousand people for each event, among many other programs. Not only has the cost of building the Alamodome been paid off, it has brought hundreds of millions of dollars into San Antonio. For example, a study by the University of Memphis concluded that the economic benefit for hosting the NCAA Final Four tournament was more than $105 million. That doesn't even count the positive national exposure that the tournament brought to San Antonio, which is priceless.

Selling the Spurs

As the Alamodome neared completion, I realized that the time was right to sell the Spurs. We had excellent cash flow, and the team was playing well, but the franchise needed a broader base of ownership to make certain that the team would remain competitive and to provide the kind of long-term stability that would keep the team in San Antonio. In addition, I felt I had done all that I knew how to do with the team. We were in the playoffs every year, but we still hadn't won a championship. I decided that I had taken the franchise as far as I knew how to take it. I realized that I was in danger of losing my passion for it, and it was time for somebody else to try to get the team over the top, which is what happened.

In March 1993, before the end of the NBA season, I sold the Spurs for $75 million to a group of twenty-two San Antonio investors led by Peter Holt and Bob Coleman. The investor group, which assumed a 100 percent interest in the team, included Southwestern Bell (now AT&T) and the insurance giant USAA. With the sell of the Spurs to an investor group that included leading citizens of San Antonio and two corporations that are an integral part of our community, and with a new arena ready for the coming season, I could now rest assured that the Spurs would remain in our city. Not only have they remained in town, they have flourished, winning four NBA championships. When the Spurs finally won their first NBA championship in 1999, there couldn't have been anybody happier than me. That's what I had wanted to accomplish from the start, and I was satisfied that I had made my own contribution to their winning the championship.

The Civic Value of Professional Sports Teams

People in sports should never fear a philosophical discussion. Is this healthy? Is this right? Should we be talking about funding new stadiums, or finding a cure for cancer at M. D. Anderson Hospital? That's the real world. And this is the way things are: Owning a team is not a full-time job in terms of the hours worked, but it is full-time emotionally. Every place I go, from the car attendant to the chairman of the board, the first words I hear in San Antonio are about the Spurs. You have to understand that, acknowledge it, and respond.

I was making a speech on economic development to a group in San Antonio that was 80 percent female. During the question-and-answer segment, a woman identified herself and said, "This may not be germane to your speech, Mr. McCombs, but you're the only one who can answer this. I moved here months ago from another state. I find it appalling that so much civic and media attention is put on this silly basketball team. I find it unacceptable. Can you respond to this?"

I said, "Yes, I'm glad you gave me the opportunity. Last night the Spurs played a game before 17,000 people, a sellout. Another 250,000 watched or listened on television and radio. For those hours, they were able to put aside their cares and live or die with their team. In schoolrooms, hospitals, and business offices, in homes as neighbors were having coffee, the subject was positive because our team beat the Lakers last night. If that is silly, so be it." There was a standing ovation, which I did not expect. But the people attending that conference related to the point I was making. Sometimes you need a little candy for the soul.

The feelings I described were familiar to them; they understood. It was personal. All cities have great attributes that are important, and most of us support them: the arts, education, the medical center. Yet there is nothing quite like the impact of a sports team. The people who have trouble seeing that are the ones who have never embraced a team. All of this is part of what makes sports so important to a city. It is the most ecumenical thing we have. A winning team brings us together. Religion doesn't—it divides us. Music doesn't—some like jazz, others classical, still others country. Business doesn't—if steel prices go up, do Ford and Chrysler exchange high fives? And what the Spurs do for San Antonio cannot even be fully articulated—it was and still is the only major-league entry that San Antonio has into this huge world of sports.

Vikings owner Red McCombs with safety Robert Griffith, 1999. Photo by Jerry Holt. Star Tribune/*Minneapolis-St. Paul, 2010.*

Chapter Fourteen

PURPLE PRIDE

TO ME, THE TOP OF THE MOUNTAIN IN SPORTS OWNERSHIP IS A National Football League franchise. Beyond that, to have an NFL franchise in the division that originally started professional football in America attracted me in a way that is beyond what I can describe. It wasn't something that I coveted. It wasn't something I thought about all the time. But it was a thought that came up frequently over the years.

I was in the hunt for a professional football team in different ways for thirty years. In 1961, I gave serious thought to buying the American Football League's Denver Broncos. This was after the AFL's first season had ended and long before the AFL and the NFL merged. My goal at the time was to move the Broncos to San Antonio. The opportunity to relocate a team in the old AFL was not as difficult as it would have been in the NFL. That deal didn't happen because I couldn't find a partner.

Then one day in 1966, I heard on my car radio that Congress had passed a bill that protected the NFL and the AFL from the antitrust laws in the event of a merger between the two leagues. It was well known that representatives from the two leagues were involved in merger negotiations. I realized at that instant that a legal monopoly had been allowed that was going to create a great business opportunity. I decided to move as rapidly as possible to make a bid for an NFL franchise for San Antonio. I called my friend, Lamar Hunt, the founding father of the AFL and owner of the Kansas City Chiefs, to get his help to arrange a meeting for me with Pete Rozelle, the NFL commissioner. With Lamar's help, I was able to see Rozelle in his office in New York. Rozelle told me that the merger negotiations were not going well. A proposal to add a new franchise in San Antonio or anywhere else would complicate those difficult negotiations, so that wasn't going to happen.

I later realized that one reason for Rozelle's sensitivity about expansion teams was a political deal that he had already made with powerful U.S.

Senator Russell Long and Congressman Hale Boggs, both from Louisiana. In return for Senator Long's and Representative Boggs's support, which was critical to the successful passage of the antitrust exemption, the NFL promised to award an expansion franchise to New Orleans. Just one month after President Johnson signed the bill giving the NFL antitrust protection, the league announced the creation of the New Orleans Saints.

The Monterrey Golden Aztecs

During our meeting, however, Rozelle noted that he was very interested in determining the level of fan interest in Mexico for American football. He encouraged me to organize a team in Monterrey, Mexico, and put it in the Texas Professional Football League. San Antonio already had a team called the Toros in that league. Rozelle wanted to see how a team would do in Monterrey because of its close proximity to the United States. He offered the help of one of his top assistants, Jim Kinsel, to work with me to put the team together. Although I left Rozelle's office without a pro football franchise, my meeting with him did put me on the NFL's radar.

With the NFL's encouragement and Jim Kinsel's help, I established a professional American-style football team in Monterrey in 1969. Our team, which we named the Golden Aztecs, had forty players and four coaches. The other teams were located in Dallas, Fort Worth, Texarkana, Odessa, and Tulsa, Oklahoma. The season started at the first of August, but the Golden Aztecs were destined to last only until mid-September, when I had to close the club's operations.

It didn't take me long to learn that Mexico was not ready for American football. At first, however, I thought I had stumbled into an outstanding business opportunity. Our first game in Monterrey generated tremendous interest in the city. I promoted the game pretty strongly, of course, and we arranged to broadcast the game live to Mexico City, making this the first game of American football to be televised live in Mexico. I even persuaded Carta Blanca beer to sponsor the broadcast.

I only needed to average about 7,500 fans each game to make the enterprise work financially. When about 35,000 people showed up for that first game I felt like utopia was right under my feet. During the game I wandered through the stands to talk to fans. My confidence in our chances for success fell, however, as I tried to field dozens of the most basic questions about the game. "Why does everyone cheer when a player hits another player, but then another player does the same thing and those judges give him a penalty?" one man asked. Another wanted to know why the quarterback was allowed to pass the ball to another player. In other words, there was little understanding about what was happening on the field and why. I soon realized that most of our "fans" were there simply out of curiosity, the kind that attracts people to the two-headed-calf exhibit at the state fair.

That's when it really dawned on me that American football is a difficult game to explain. Those of us who grew up with football just understand it, but it is not an easy game to explain to people who have not been exposed to it. So I realized during the game that I had a serious problem. We attracted a large crowd because people wanted to see this new thing. They also were excited about the halftime show, which I had promoted heavily in the advertisements.

At our second game we had an attendance of 10,000. The third drew about 3,000. The only people who attended the last game were the players' families and girlfriends. We were playing a team from Chicago that last game, and the results made no difference in the league standings. At halftime, I talked to the coach and the owner of the team we were playing. I asked them what they would think if I could convince the officials to keep the clock running in the second half. Their response was, "Red, get us out of here as fast as you can." It turned out that the crew officiating the game was from San Antonio. The head referee was a guy named Bubba Wilson. I had played football with him at Del Mar College. I told Bubba that the other team had agreed to let the clock run during the second half. Would he please agree to do that? Bubba's response was, "Well, Big Red, how fast do you want me to run it?" I told him to run it as fast as he could and get us out of there. The record will reflect that we played the second half in seven and a half minutes.

I gave all of my uniforms and equipment to the University of Monterrey. I got my team on buses, turned out the lights, and headed north. That was the end of my American football experience in Mexico. But I was able to report to the NFL that although there were some pockets in Mexico, primarily Mexico City, where there were people who had attended school in the United States and were somewhat familiar with our version of football, it would be many years before the NFL could have a successful team south of the Rio Grande.

The NFL Hunt Continues

Although I continued to look for opportunities to get into the NFL, I was basically out of the hunt for more than twenty years. I finally saw my chance in 1992 when the NFL announced that it would add two expansion teams to begin play in 1993. I made formal application for one of the two slots to go to San Antonio. The Alamodome had been built, and we had everything in place to operate a successful NFL team. The new franchises, however, ultimately went to Jacksonville and North Carolina.

In 1993, after I sold the Spurs, I briefly toyed with the idea of buying the New England Patriots, but that deal had too many legal entanglements. I decided to back away. After that, I pretty much abandoned my hopes of joining the NFL. I believed that time had overtaken me. I no longer dwelled on the idea, because I didn't want to suffer that kind of torture after thirty years of being unsuccessful. My day-to-day activities were full, my life was contented, and I am not one to keep looking back.

An Unexpected Opportunity in Minnesota

In 1996, I learned almost by accident that the Minnesota Vikings franchise was having problems and might go on the market at some point in the very near future. The Fox television network affiliate in Minneapolis, owned by our company, Clear Channel, suffered a serious loss of revenue as a result of having to black out half a dozen of the Vikings' home games that had not sold out. Rip Riordan, who ran our television division, was based in the Twin Cities. During a phone call, I asked him why a team playing as well as the Vikings was having such difficulty selling game tickets. Rip said, "I just believe they are not taking advantage of all the opportunities that are here."

Rip's comments piqued my curiosity, so I began to investigate the possibility of acquiring the Vikings. I thought I had retired from chasing sports franchises. But I was like an old bloodhound that had picked up the scent. To begin with, I had no powerful hankering to spend my winters in Minnesota, where the well-traveled football coach Lou Holtz once referred to all the natives as having "blond hair and blue ears." How I acquired the Vikings really was not a case of perseverance or dogged determination on my part.

The Vikings franchise has an intriguing history. To the surprise of many, the NFL had decided suddenly to expand into Minnesota in 1960, persuading a group headed by Max Winter to renege on a commitment to the upstart American Football League. So the Vikings were born in a cradle of mischief and double-dealing.

In time, the Vikings thrived, up to a point. They reached the Super Bowl four times and lost them all. They became part of the lore of the game: the Purple People Eaters, the scrambling quarterback Fran Tarkenton, "Wrong Way" Jim Marshall, and coaches as opposite in temper as the explosive Norm Van Brocklin and the placid Bud Grant.

In 1997, before any public announcement had been made about the Vikings being on the market, I met privately in Minneapolis with the ownership group and their attorney. The franchise was owned by ten prominent and respected Minnesota business and civic leaders, led by Roger Headrick, who served as president. Having ten individuals who each had an equal share in the ownership was a real problem for the NFL. The league preferred that at least one owner have a minimum ownership stake of 30 percent. That prevents the league from having to deal with an ownership committee. So the Vikings were getting pressure from the NFL to change the ownership percentages. In addition, the group had owned the club for several years, and it was not doing well financially. They were ready to sell.

I told the owners that I wanted to buy the team. They responded that they planned to sell the Vikings at a silent auction. I was encouraged to make a bid when the time came. The owners warned me that they reserved the right to refuse any of the bids if they chose, but the bottom line was that the highest bid would win if the bidder met NFL approval. In addition, they stressed that the terms of the sale would require that the new owner keep the team in Minnesota. I told them that presented no problem for me, which surprised them. Frankly, moving the team to San Antonio was never on my agenda. This was Minnesota's team. I could not see it going anywhere else, and I told the owners that. This early meeting did not give me an advantage when they eventually announced the team was for sale, but it did help that we knew each other.

When the auction opened, I submitted a bid of $187 million. Eventually my bid and three others met all requirements, but two of the bids were higher than mine. The author Tom Clancy, whose spy novels had become automatic movie hits, was the winner with a bid of a little more than $200 million. He signed the preliminary agreement in February 1998. I was disappointed, but I had been given a clean shot and had no complaints. The sellers were very considerate and thanked me for being involved. At that instant I was quite sure the Vikings had been sold to the author of *The Hunt for Red October* and *Clear and Present Danger,* among others. I contacted Mr. Clancy, wished him well, and congratulated him.

Within days, reports were leaking out that Clancy was having personal problems that might keep him from closing the deal. Clancy asked the league for an extension in providing certain financial documents. He was involved in a very costly divorce, which had clouded his financial picture. I talked to my contacts within the ownership group and their attorney, and they verified that the deal was in deep trouble. It was likely that the Vikings would hold a second auction.

Victory at Last

In May 1998, the Minnesota Vikings announced that the deal with Clancy had fallen through. The attorneys notified us that they would mail out new applications to anyone who had already shown an interest. In short, the team was on the block again. I received this news with mixed feelings because I wasn't eager to benefit from another person's misfortune.

I had been very disappointed that I hadn't won the first auction, but suddenly I had another chance. I was determined not to let it pass me by. In calculating my bid, I was keenly aware of two very important developments. One was that the labor agreement between the league and the players' union was extended. A completed labor agreement is absolutely critical in estimating the monetary value of a franchise. With no labor agreement in place it is much more difficult to estimate potential salary costs. To have an agreement extension that would be in place for another six years made the Vikings and the other teams in the NFL more valuable.

The second development, which equaled the labor agreement in significance, was the NFL's new eight-year television package with four television networks worth $3 billion. That was a record for TV rights. I had to factor into the bidding an additional income stream for those eight years.

I soon realized that there was a third factor that I had to consider in determining the amount I would bid. In this second auction, my competition would include Glen Taylor, the owner of the NBA's Timberwolves, who had very deep pockets and was a Minnesota resident. The other bid would also come from Minnesota people. I knew there would be strong sentiment for local ownership, as there always should be. For that reason, I assumed that if I was to have any chance of winning, I would need to offer a substantially higher price than those made by the local bidders.

I confirmed that assumption when I called three of the ten owners that I knew best and I asked them: in this auction, if a homeboy is $10 million under the high bid, would you sell to homeboy or would you sell to the high bidder? Each one of those three men, not knowing I was asking the other two, immediately noted that $10 million would pay each owner an additional $1 million dollars. "We'd probably sell to homeboy," they answered, "and take a million dollars less." My next question was what if the high bidder was $20 million more than homeboy? "Oh, well," they said, "for two million dollars, forget homeboy; we're going to take the money." That was a great indicator to me that my bid had to be substantially higher than the others.

I hired Chase Bank's experts on sports businesses to help me prepare the bid. As we worked on a number, I read statements that my competitors had given in interviews to the news media about their plans for the Vikings if they won their bids. Those comments would have been meaningless to most people, but they gave me some important hints about what my competitors were thinking, which helped me estimate what their bids were going to be. Obviously they didn't think they had revealed anything, but they had. And that weighed a lot on my own bid.

I didn't tell anyone, including my longtime associate Gary Woods, if I was going to make a bid or how much it would be if I did make a bid. Gary has been an employee and partner of mine for thirty years, but Gary and I don't always see business deals the same way. Gary has never thought that investing in a sports team would generate the best return on your money. Gary didn't feel that I had been prudent when I bought the Spurs the second time or when I bought the Denver Nuggets. He certainly didn't feel like I was being prudent when I had made my first losing bid, and he told me that.

I appreciated Gary's opinion, but I did not agree with him. The deal was attractive to me. You can't evaluate a pro sports team the way you would any other business. It is unique, with great risks, many of which an owner has little or no control over. I can see why owning a team would not be your everyday choice of investment. It doesn't offer quite the same security as, say, U.S. Treasury bills. So as I developed my bid, I told no one what I was thinking.

Since the time I co-owned the Corpus Christi baseball team in 1953, I have said that I never invested in a sports team expecting a big return, but I always expected I could stay in the black operating a team. Up to this point, I had been successful in doing so, and I had every intention of maintaining that record. So my offer for the Vikings had to be high enough to win the bid, but not so high that it would be difficult to keep the financial operation in the black.

As we approached the bidding deadline, I had one of those Red McCombs moments where I was totally convinced that at last I was going to buy an NFL football team. I don't think anyone, including Charline, really shared my feeling that I would wind up with the Vikings. I just had a definite conviction that it was meant to happen long before it did. Can't tell you why. Don't know why.

On the day the bids were due, the deadline was five p.m. The sellers didn't know for certain if I was going to submit an offer or not. Gary Woods, my alter ego, was on a previously planned vacation to Europe. He left without knowing what I would do. The bankers I worked with at Chase, who had provided a lot of the information, were unsure. I played it as close to the vest as I could.

Several days prior to the auction deadline, I went over the terms of the contract and bounced back some issues I had to the Vikings lawyers, so there would be no surprises if I did submit a number. I had also gotten them to agree to accept my proposal by fax, meaning I could take it to the wire, if need be.

At one p.m. on the day of the bidding deadline, Gary's flight from London landed in Chicago, and he called me from the airport. I said, "Gary, I am going to send in a proposal around four this afternoon, and I expect it to be successful." Gary asked the obvious question: How much was I prepared to offer? I told him $250 million. "If you really want to close this deal," he responded, "and get this franchise, I think that number is too low." I said, "Well, I think it's going to be fifteen to twenty million dollars higher than the next bidder, and that's what I want it to be."

I ended the conversation by telling Gary, "I have never been so confident about anything in my life. This is going to happen, and it will be the right number."Then I called the Chase bankers in New York and gave them the news. Their response was the same as Gary's. "Red, if you want this," one of them said, "you're going to have to raise that price." Despite these pessimistic reactions, my comfort level was off the meter. I have bid on a lot of businesses. Sometimes you have a feel for it, sometimes you don't. In my mind, I knew this was going to work, even though I was the only one who seemed to think that way.

With the deadline set for five p.m. Wednesday, I assumed that the sellers would gather in their attorneys' offices the next day and exercise extreme care in looking at the offers because of the problems that had resulted from Tom Clancy's bid. I doubted that any decision would be made before Thursday and guessed they would delay the announcement until Monday. So I booked my calendar solidly for the rest of the week.

Gary returned home from his vacation and called me. He told me that he had just talked to John Moudy, the lead attorney for the sellers, all of whom were sitting in John's office. He had a couple of questions he wanted to ask me. "Are they questions of substance?" I asked. Gary said they were not. In fact, they were easily answered, lending further weight, he believed, that there would be no decision out of Minnesota that day. I had a totally different take. "You know what I think those two questions mean?" I said. "It means I own the Vikings."

Around noon the next day I was driving back to my office, and my mind was not too focused on my next appointment. The car phone rang, and Gary yelped, "Congratulations! John just called and they want to call you between three and three thirty to confirm the deal and wish you well."There I was, in my car on Loop 410, when I realized this quite remarkable event had happened. I immediately called Charline at the ranch in Colorado, and my first words were, "You're going to have to buy a lot of purple for your wardrobe because you're the new owner of the Minnesota Vikings."

She knew this was important to me, which was reason enough to be excited, although she wasn't quite sure what it all meant. Then reality jolted my reverie. I was going eighty miles an hour in a fifty-mile zone and I'm realizing that I've got to get control of myself because the Vikings owners are going to make the announcement to the world, and I haven't even made my plans to go to Minnesota. This was going to be a news item whether I wanted one now or not. I realized I had a lot of things to do.

I called Gary and said, "I'm going to invite the news media to a 4:30

p.m. press conference, and we're going to announce this in San Antonio before the word leaks out of Minnesota." I needed help. My next call was to Jim Dublin, who had done so much public relations work for us in the past. His office was closed, and every account executive was on vacation except one. I told her I was going to hold a press conference at 4:30. "I know it's not a good time," I told her, "but the TV news goes on at five, and it's the best I can do." Then I called my three daughters. I asked Marsha to find a place that was easily accessible to the press. I told her that I needed some props. I didn't even own a Vikings cap. I asked her to locate some Vikings memorabilia. She quickly discovered that the sports merchandise stores in San Antonio weren't exactly overstocked with Minnesota Vikings souvenirs. Her husband, John Shields, however, did manage to find a cap, which I perched on a little football helmet that I keep on my desk.

We somehow put the press conference together in time. Before it began, I was thinking that I needed a hook to get more publicity. A hook is something that differentiates you. It can be a phrase or a picture, or it can be any number of things. Your hook needs to be short for the media to make the most of it. Your hook needs to be easy to understand and it needs to be something that people will enjoy repeating. Suddenly the phrase "purple pride" popped into my mind. I had my hook. So I opened up my news conference by putting on a Vikings cap and declaring that "I'm happy to announce to the sports fans of the world that I am now the owner of the Minnesota Vikings: purple pride, purple pride, purple pride!"

The next day, I talked to the soon-to-be-former owners. I had gotten to know most of them over the years, and had originally indicated to that group, and the media, that I would buy 100 percent of the stock. Or, if anyone wanted to stay in, I would keep a minimum of 60 percent. As I began to get other calls, I started to revisit the NFL requirements and the scrutiny that would be involved. I decided on the spot that I would not take on any partners, and I notified all the owners. The NFL would have to scrutinize additional partners, which might lengthen the process. I did not want any delays. It was July, and the teams were ready to play football. They were all very gracious about it.

As it turned out, my offer was barely more than $20 million above the second bid. I had nailed it, and I had nailed it for, in my opinion, the very least amount that I could have bid and still won it. Once we started going through the lengthy process of approval, the first indication I had that we had crossed the goal line was when I received a phone call from Tom Benson, who owned the New Orleans Saints. Ironically, Tom was a close friend who had been a tough competitor in the car business when I started out in San Antonio in 1958. Tom had been on a conference call with the other members of the executive committee, and although they had not yet met, he felt secure in relaying their consensus. "Congratulations," he said, "you've been approved as the new owner of the Vikings."

NFL owners rarely have a unanimous agreement about anything, so when I attended my first meeting with them in New York, I assumed that at least a couple had voted against me. But when the NFL commissioner, Paul Tagliabue, introduced me to the group, he had a little lilt in his voice when he said, "Red, you are unanimously welcomed into the league." That was a wonderful surprise and honor.

Fan First, Owner Second

Owning the Minnesota Vikings was a unique opportunity that I never took lightly. At the outset, I told the people of Minnesota: "I'm a fan first and an owner second." I really believe that I represented the thousands of fans who would love to be owners. That's the way fans think about their football teams. I expected that the fans and the media would be apprehensive about the new custodian, an out-of-state guy who for five years had been actively pursuing a team for San Antonio. I embraced that head-on, knowing the issue would come up time and again.

My first order of business was to fly to Minnesota and let the media check me out. I stayed seven days and asked the Vikings staff to schedule me with media or fan groups from six a.m. to ten p.m. that entire week. I had lots of opportunities to tell the story of what my role would be. There was never any question about that. I had a passion for the Vikings. I operated as an owner, not an investor.

The head coach, Dennis Green, was on vacation in California when my offer was accepted, and he graciously volunteered to fly from California and join me for the announcement in Minnesota. I declined that. But from the time of that first phone visit, every conversation I had with Dennis, the more impressed I became. It had been suggested to me by more than one person that I was fortunate Dennis Green had only one more year left on his contract as coach. They assured me I would not like Dennis.

I had no preconceived notions, but I knew it would be brought up in my first press conference. It was about the third question: "Red, what are your comments about Green's book?" Dennis had authored a book, *No Room for Cry Babies*, which had been published several months prior to my purchase of the team. It had attracted a lot of notice from the media in Minnesota, largely because of Green's complaints about the local sportswriters in the Twin Cities area. I answered that I had not read Dennis's book nor did I intend to read it. "I don't want to read it because I want to like Dennis Green."

As I got to know Dennis Green, I recognized that he had excellent organizational skills. I was impressed that the Vikings had a number of players who were not big names when they came to the Vikings but who had developed into great players under Dennis and his staff. Soon after I bought the team, Dennis and I probably had about ten conversations by phone. In one of those, I asked him if he had any problem with my being in the locker room. I had been around sports and knew coaches had different feelings. I like to be in the thick of things. He kind of laughed and said, "I'm happy to have an owner who wants to be involved."

I had looked forward to addressing the team and all the football people when they were in training camp. My first day in camp at Mankato, they had just finished an afternoon practice and were already in the locker room. I had planned on meeting each player and coach individually. After I met the first several who were nearest the doors, I realized there were a hundred and fifty people in there—players, coaches, and staff. I could see this was going to be awkward. I'm sure my voice was carrying to every corner of the room, and I saw players coming out of the aisles and into the walkway. Fortunately, I spotted Cris Carter, who had taken off his jersey and shoulder pads and was undoing his pants. I solved my personal dilemma by walking all the way through the middle of the locker room, approaching, and saying: "Cris, I'm Red McCombs. Would you mind just turning around slowly so I can look at my money?" Laughter erupted on all sides, and that sort of broke the ice.

I addressed the staff and the players in the auditorium early in the evening, before they went into their breakouts. My remarks to them were very straightforward. I told them how proud I was to be associated with them because they and the men they play against are the best in the world at what they do. "Very seldom does anyone in life have an opportunity to compete at that level," I said. "So cherish the moment. Don't take it lightly. Recognize it, realize it, enjoy it." I think we had a special feeling between us from that moment on.

You've heard it said countless times, but this is what it's all about. You can talk about All-Americans. You can talk about Super Bowls. But their world is special, because so few ever get there. And I was about to make it my world.

Great Team, Bad Stadium

The fact is, I bought a much better football operation than I had ever dreamed would be there. We had some outstanding players. On the other hand, the business side, which I expected to be better, was disappointing. I've learned that when you buy a business, you're going to have surprises and they are not usually going to be pleasant. When I began my efforts to purchase the team, I had been aware that sooner or later the Vikings would need a new stadium to replace the Hubert Humphrey Metrodome, which is located in downtown Minneapolis. A few days before I closed the deal, however, as I learned more about the Vikings' business situation, I realized that a new stadium would be needed much sooner, not later. Called the "Metrodump" by some of the fans, our aging and poorly designed stadium was not up to the standards of most of the other teams in the NFL. The stadium's shortcomings meant that our revenue from concessions, parking, and luxury seating would be restricted significantly.

The Vikings lease the Metrodome from the Metropolitan Sports Facilities Commission. That lease runs through the year 2011. At the time I bought the Vikings, the Metrodome had many tenants, but the Vikings paid more than 80 percent of all the stadium's revenue. It is a very onerous lease as far as the Vikings are concerned. Although the lease is in effect through 2011, it does have a clause that clearly provides an exit, which states the penalty that will have to be paid if it is broken before 2011. That seemed to give us a legal way to get out, although we would have to pay a fairly large penalty.

I knew that there was one potential problem, however. Several years earlier, Commissioner Rozelle had given the sports commission a three-paragraph letter stating that as long as the Vikings were in good standing in the NFL, the league would not allow the team to be moved out of that stadium until the end of that lease. So we had a bit of an ambiguity between the letter and the actual lease contract. I asked my lawyers if Rozelle's letter prevented us from ending the lease. They analyzed the documents and reported to me that they did not think Rozelle's letter presented any legal barrier to our leaving the stadium. "The letter is not a contract," they said. "We don't even think the letter is relevant." It was clear to them that the letter was a pledge from the NFL not to leave the Metrodome before the revenue bonds had been paid off. Those bonds have been paid off for several years.

Before I closed my deal, I went to New York to get clarification from Commissioner Tagliabue about Rozelle's letter and the league's position on the matter. I asked him to examine the stadium lease and Rozelle's letter and give me his take on them. "I'm not saying I want to move the team out of Minnesota," I explained. "And I'm not saying that I want to move them out of the Metrodome. I just don't want to be obligated to not do it." Tagliabue said that he and his staff had concluded that the letter had intended only to satisfy investors that the bonds would be paid before the team would move out. The bonds had been paid off for years, so the letter had no effect. The lease would have to stand on its own as it was written.

Deeply concerned about the problems with the Metrodome, I met with Minnesota governor Arne Carlson, who was very near the end of his term in office. We discussed how we badly needed new facilities, but I stressed that we wanted them built in Minnesota. I told him that I had no intention of moving the team out of state. I also told Governor Carlson that a new stadium would require support from public funds. Whenever a new stadium is built, the NFL strongly prefers that the public provide two-thirds of the funding and the owner or other private investors the remaining one-third. The governor said that he understood the need, but he warned me that it would be a very difficult thing to get public funds from the legislature. It was possible, he stressed, but difficult.

So my goal from the time I bought the Vikings was always to get out of that facility before the 2011 lease ran out. I felt that I had the backing of the NFL and a cautious endorsement from the lame-duck governor.

The reason that these new types of facilities are critical is because the fans now want and expect something more than just to watch a ball game when they come to the stadium. They want an entertainment center.

From the owner's standpoint, that additional revenue stream can also make the difference between failure and success. To understand why, let me explain the basic financial arrangement in the NFL. Revenue generated nationally by television contracts is distributed equally among all the teams. The sale of sports caps and clothing is managed by NFL Properties, the New York–based licensing and marketing arm of the league, and that income is distributed in equal shares, no matter which team is the most popular. So when I saw a guy wearing a Green Bay Packers hat, I might have been unhappy that he was not a Vikings fan, but I was happy that he bought the hat because I got some of the revenue.

Seventy percent of our revenue came from the distribution of money from the sale of national products, most of that from the television package. The remaining 30 percent of our revenue came from a variety of local operations such as parking, ticket sales, stadium advertising signs, and food and beverage concessions. Every franchise, however, also needs revenue from sources other than traditional local operations. The reason is that some of the franchises have built new facilities that include luxury boxes and year-round entertainment centers, which generate significant amounts of cash. That extra cash gives them a competitive edge over those teams without such similar income sources.

I realize that many taxpayers strongly oppose using tax money to build sports facilities for privately-owned professional sports teams. The problem is that the public is generally unaware of the fact that in every instance where tax money has been used to build stadiums, those facilities have returned to the public far more than the public invested. I'm not talking about the fun and excitement; I'm talking about dollars and cents. Nearly all of them have been built after the public has voted to approve the use of public money. The fact is that these sports facilities do pay off. Public approval is not always granted. Sometimes the issue loses at the polls. Often the issue wins by a bare majority. In San Antonio, we passed the Alamodome project 53 percent in favor and 47 percent against. That's a victory, but not an overwhelming one.

The Magical Season: 1998

My consistent goal from the first day I bought the Vikings was to build a new stadium. But in the meantime, we had football games to play. While the Vikings were in their preseason training camp late in the summer of 1998, I really began to look at the team and our competition in a slightly different way. I came to the conclusion that there wasn't a game on the schedule the Vikings couldn't win. And the media had a field day with my saying so. Now, I didn't say we were going to go through the season undefeated. What I saw was a team coming out of training camp with a chance to win every week, including the so-called exhibition games.

To me, all games count. I have a problem with the term "exhibition game." When I asked my business staff what their plan was for selling out the preseason opener, they responded that the Vikings had never sold out an exhibition game. "Kids in the street play exhibition games," I replied. "The Vikings play preseason games, and I don't ever want to hear that other word again."

My prophecy, or maybe I should call it my fantasy, began to be fulfilled as the season progressed. We won all four of our preseason games, and I was convinced that we were headed for a special year. So, my juices were really flowing and I thought, what then can go wrong? Then it hit me. I was concerned about Dennis Green's contract, which would expire at the end of the season. I knew that, as the season progressed, the media would constantly ask if Green's contract would be extended and that it could distract the team.

When I bought the team, I told the media I wasn't going to redo any contracts until after the season. I changed my mind, however. I was impressed with Green's coaching skills and I liked him. He had the respect of his players, and I believed that extending his contract would be a boost to their morale. So before our first regular season game, I gave Green a three-year extension on his contract with a substantial raise in salary. It worked out beautifully. The team was excited, and we caught a few reporters by surprise with the news.

We began to see a team, week after week, not only winning, but having fun. We not only sold out every game, but also every product that we had licensed. I became aware that the Viking brand, as I called it, had a huge following beyond the borders of Minnesota. Wherever I traveled, I realized that the Vikings were big, and we were getting bigger.

We had a quarterback, Randall Cunningham, who was having a storybook season. We had two outstanding wide receivers, veteran Cris Carter and the explosive Randy Moss, who would set the season record for touchdown receptions by a rookie. We had a placekicker, Gary Anderson, who set a record with every extra point and field goal. And we had a punter, Mitch Berger, who put more balls inside the twenty-yard line than anyone had done in years. So there were great things happening around this team. And there was one other distinction worth noting: We had fifty guys on the squad, plus all the coaches, and not a jerk in the bunch, which is very rare.

We won our first seven regular season games, but then lost by three points to Tampa Bay on the road. It was the only game that I did not attend. I was too ill with a virus to get out of bed. There I was, stuck at home, rumpled and feverish, watching the team go down and feeling as if it was almost the end of the world. I never have really tried to claim that I keep sports in perspective, and I won't start now. I don't believe there is a perspective. It would be our only defeat during the regular season.

But we rebounded and started winning again, and then it was time to play the Dallas Cowboys on national television on Thanksgiving Day in my home state. I told the sports media before the game that I didn't know how it felt to have a team in a Super Bowl game because I haven't yet done one. For a guy from Spur, Texas, to go into Texas Stadium and win the ballgame, it doesn't get much better. If there is anything bigger, I'm ready to try it on.

The Vikings finished the season 15-and-l. We then won our playoff game against the Arizona Cardinals by twenty points, which put us into the NFC championship game against the Atlanta Falcons at home in the Metrodome. Although we were heavily favored, we lost the game in overtime by three points. That loss was not anything I could even imagine. I can't weigh or measure that kind of hurt. We had been through this joyous season, this magical sleigh ride, and there was never any thought that we might lose. I won't have another chance to be a rookie owner, with a once-beaten team, bound for the Super Bowl.

Jesse Ventura

During the 1998 football season there was a fierce political campaign for governor of Minnesota. To get acquainted with the political leadership in Minnesota, Charline and I arranged in the early part of the season to entertain gubernatorial candidates Hubert Humphrey Jr., the Democrat, and Norm Coleman, the Republican, as our guests. It never entered my mind to invite the Reform Party candidate, Jesse Ventura, a popular talk-radio host and flamboyant former professional wrestler.

On election day, Charline and I were at our home in San Antonio watching the local and state voting returns. At one point the crawl at the bottom of the screen said "possible upset in the race for governor in Minnesota." The Minnesota governor's campaign had been very unusual. The Democrats and Republicans are evenly split in the state, so the elections tend to go down to the wire, as we witnessed to an extreme example in the 2008 election for U.S. senator. But the presence of Jesse Ventura as an independent candidate in the gubernatorial campaign injected an unknown factor in the race. Most of the polls indicated that Ventura would not be a big factor, but Minnesota election law simply requires that whoever wins the most votes wins the election. The winner does not have to receive a majority of the votes.

I had met Jesse Ventura during the campaign, and I liked him personally, but Charline and I had not aligned with any candidate in the race. So as we watched the televised returns, I was shocked when it became clear that Ventura was going to win. I turned to Charline and said, "My God. I've got to start all over again." During the campaign, I had raised the stadium issue with Humphrey and Coleman, and they both assured me of their support for using public funds for a new facility. But I had no idea where Ventura was on this issue.

The day after the election, I called my general manager and asked him to get me on the telephone with Jesse Ventura as soon as possible. He didn't think that would be possible. National media reporters were swarming around Ventura because of his sensational upset victory, and it would be extremely difficult to get him on the telephone. I asked him to pull out all of the stops and see what he could do. About one hour later, he called back and said that he had made contact with someone on Ventura's staff. Later that morning, at eleven a.m., Ventura was going to do his daily radio show. He was going to take telephone calls from his listeners. My general manager had been able to get Ventura's staff to guarantee that my call would be accepted at exactly 11:15 a.m. and that our talk would be broadcast on the air. I agreed to make the call.

When I called, I was put on hold, but I could hear the program on the telephone while I waited. Ventura was talking about the campaign and how he had shocked the whole world with his victory. He talked about how he was more than a professional wrestler and that he would be a good governor. He said that no one wanted to talk to him yesterday, but today everyone in the world wanted his attention. "About three weeks ago," he said, "I was completely worn out after working day and night in the campaign. So I decided to take a Sunday off and go see the Vikings play. Can you believe that your governor-elect could not get a ticket?" He continued by asking "can you believe that the man who owns the Vikings is now on the telephone trying to talk to me?" Ventura said, "Okay, so let's talk to him. Good morning, Red, this is Jesse Ventura. Do you have any comments to make?"

Talk about eating crow. My reply was, "Yes, I do." I immediately congratulated him for his victory. Ventura asked me if I had heard what he said about not being able to get a ticket to the Vikings game? I told him that I did hear that, and that was history. "You not only have a ticket," I said, "but you can have as many as you want, whenever you want, and wherever you want, including my own personal suite." I invited him and his family to be my guests for the upcoming game that Sunday. He asked if the Vikings were playing in town or on the road next Sunday. I responded, "Governor, we will play wherever you want to play!" Of course, that was a great line for a radio talk show. It went over beautifully. People wrote about it for a week.

The fact was, however, that we were playing a home game. Ventura accepted my offer and said that he needed six seats. I told him to count on them. Then I asked if he would mind my presenting him at halftime to the 65,000 fans in the stadium. I also told him that he could address the crowd from the field. He accepted that invitation as well. That Sunday at the game we had a wonderful day, and he and his family enjoyed themselves. He received a standing ovation when he was introduced on the field.

A little later, Ventura's inaugural staff asked me to be the master of ceremonies at the party held the night after he took the oath of office as governor. I was pleased to accept. That party was one of the most enjoyable events I have ever attended. The governor showed up wearing his feather boa from his wrestling days, and he brought his motorcycle. It was a rip-roaring party that lasted virtually all night. I had a great time being master of ceremonies.

I like Jesse Ventura very much. He is a unique man and a straight shooter. Unlike the other candidates in the governor's race, Jesse told me flat out that the allocation of public funds for a new football stadium was "not going to happen." He maintained that position the entire four years he was governor. I was sorry he took that stance, but at least he wasn't wishy-washy. I must say that, although he did not support our new stadium plan, he did do a number of things for us while he was governor. I thought Ventura was an open, transparent, and fair governor. He had a very difficult situation with that state being so evenly divided politically and him in the middle as an independent. I think he served the people of Minnesota well. I consider him to this day to be a friend.

The Unhappy Season: 2001

When the good times are rolling in sports, you think they will never end. But, like puppy love, they always do. As warm and open as my relationship with Dennis Green had begun, it ended in a negative way. I sensed that something was happening to our friendship after the last game of the 2000 season, when we lost to the New York Giants for the conference championship and a berth in the Super Bowl. We were blown away, 41-0, at the Meadowlands. The loss was a bitter one for everyone associated with the Vikings. We had been heavy favorites to win the game. Not only did we lose, we really did not compete. Although no specific words crossed between Dennis and me, we never really got back on the same page from that point on.

There is a momentum to losing, just as there is with winning, and you start to expect bad things to happen. When training camp rolled around in July 2001, the team suffered a blow that made all else seem trivial. On the second day of camp during an unusual Minnesota heat wave, the popular Korey Stringer died of a heatstroke. He was twenty-seven, a two-time Pro Bowler, in his sixth season as an offensive tackle.

I feel guilty even thinking or talking about him in football terms. He was a dear person, devoted to his family, his wife, Kelci, and his son, Kodie, and steadfast to his friends. In my statement to the public after his death, I said, in part, that he was a true professional, a model of "dedication and preparation. He led by example. Words can hardly begin to express our sadness and grief."

Korey's death changed the look and feel of the 2001 season. A friend had died, yet his teammates couldn't afford to start thinking that what they do no longer mattered. Everyone had to work through that, and we tried to handle the tragedy as best we could, for the Stringer family and the players. There isn't a rulebook that covers such circumstances.

One way to show your respect is to carry on. As the season began, it looked as if we might be getting back into a football mode. We won all four of our preseason games. The 2001 season, I thought, was going to right itself and we would have a legitimate shot, again, to play for the Super Bowl. My early optimism took a pretty good jolt when we lost our home opener to Carolina, which turned out to be the only game the Panthers won that season, losing their next fifteen.

The season turned out to be a rollercoaster kind of experience. We would win a game and then lose the next. I had hoped that Dennis Green's leadership would put the program back together. But the team kept slipping and sliding, with the strain and pressure building with each loss. We didn't win a game on the road. In the last month, it was all downhill.

The other continuing story of the 2001 season was: What happened to Randy Moss? The question rolled through our ranks like a bowling ball wrapped in barbed wire. Randy was exceptional in every way, but his performance in 2001 was not on par with past seasons. A good deal of attention was focused on his new multimillion-dollar contract that featured an $18 million signing bonus. The bonus was spread over several years, but the first installment of $5 million was paid before the 2001 season, raising a question that is inevitable in anything as visible as professional sports. Did this big contract play a role in the drop-off in Randy's results?

I recognize that this idea of the Fat Cat Syndrome will always be open to argument, but I don't think so. The minimum contract in the NFL today is around $250,000. Kids come out of college, where they have been scrambling for gasoline money, and at twenty-one they feel rich overnight, whether the contract is for a few million or a bunch of millions. In my opinion, the magnitude of the money doesn't matter. Even at the minimum, each player is rich overnight on a relative basis.

I don't think his contract was an issue with Randy. There were other issues that troubled him and troubled me. It was obvious that Randy did not have the opportunities to catch the ball that he had before, and he was frustrated by this. Unfortunately, his frustration led him to make comments at midseason that would cause another distraction the team didn't need.

In November 2001, in an interview with Sid Hartman, one of the most respected sports columnists in the business, Randy was quoted as saying that he only played "when I want to." Randy never denied saying it, never offered any alibi. But he was branded with a label that critics were eager to pin on him: a gold brick, a guy who went hard only when it suited him. That isn't Randy Moss. I think he meant that the money didn't dictate how he played; his pride did. I know him as a competitor who wants to win as much as anyone on the team.

Despite our poor performance on the field in 2001, I was surprised by a message I received several days before our last game in Baltimore, which would be televised nationally on "Monday Night Football." I received a fax from Coach Green's attorney indicating that there were management issues that deeply concerned Dennis. I was surprised, but not entirely. Still, getting a memo from Dennis's lawyer, when I thought we had an open door between us, was just one level above getting a letter addressed to occupant. Dennis and I never got to discuss those management issues mentioned in the fax because from that point on we had no direct contact.

That message from Dennis's attorney made it obvious to me that I had to make a decision. Dennis still had two years left on his contract, but we now had an untenable situation. I had to make a quick decision or allow the speculation about our coaching uncertainty to turn into a media event and dominate the Monday night national telecast. I decided to buy out Dennis's contract and appoint an interim coach. We informed his lawyer that a change would be made.

I flew to Minnesota. Dennis handled the practice that Friday morning, then he met with the players and announced to them, and subsequently to the public, that he was no longer an employee of the Minnesota Vikings. An hour later, I announced that I had selected Mike Tice, who had been on the staff for the past six years, to take over the head coaching duties for the upcoming game on Monday night.

The situation was awkward for all concerned, but I was proud of Mike Tice for accepting a role that he had not sought nor expected. At the end of the season, I named him the head coach of the Vikings. He held that position until January 2006, when the new owners of the Vikings let his contract expire.

Heartbreaks and Frustration: 2002–2004

The 2002 football season, our first with Mike Tice as our head coach, began miserably. We dropped our first four games, blowing leads in the fourth quarter twice. Our struggles continued through most of the season. We entered the final three weeks with a dreadful 3-10 record. We finished the season on a strong note, however, winning our final three games to finish with a 6-10 record.

Thankfully, the 2003 season saw us back in the middle of the fight, winning our first six games. After that, however, we went on a skid and lost seven of our next ten games. Nevertheless, a win in our last regular season game against the Arizona Cardinals would have sent us to the playoffs. It was not to be. We lost that game by one point when the Cardinals scored a touchdown in the last second of the game. The Vikings became the second team in football history to miss the playoffs after getting off to a 6-0 start. It was yet another heartbreaker for the McCombs family, the players, and all of our fans.

The season following our heartbreaking loss to Arizona in 2003 was a copy of the previous season, with one significant exception. We made it to the playoffs in the wild card slot. Our quarterback, Daunte Culpepper, led the NFL in passing and broke the team's season record for touchdown passes. In the wild card game, we defeated our great rivals, the Green Bay Packers, by two touchdowns. In the divisional round of the playoffs, we lost to the eventual NFC champion Philadelphia Eagles by thirteen points.

Selling the Vikings

Near the end of his first term as governor in 2002, Jesse Ventura announced that he would not run for reelection; he was tired of fighting losing battles. Republican Tim Pawlenty was Ventura's successor as governor. I met with Governor Pawlenty and his staff soon after his inauguration. The governor agreed that there was a dire need for a new facility. He also agreed to help me achieve that goal. That was good news. Without the governor's visible support, I knew it would be impossible to get public funding.

Time passed, and Pawlenty kept promising his support, but he also continued to tell me to wait. At one point, I pledged to pay $100 million of the estimated $500 million cost of a new stadium to be located on the University of Minnesota campus in Minneapolis, and the NFL offered to contribute an additional $51.5 millon. That would leave approximately $350 million to be paid from public funds. Governor Pawlenty again urged me to wait. He argued that the Vikings were selling out every game and doing well financially, which was accurate. He explained that he needed to address immediate needs that were more important than a new sports facility.

After several frustrating years of my trying to get the Vikings a new sports facility, the citizens of Anoka County passed a bond issue to support the construction of a new stadium to serve as the Vikings' home. The proposed site in Anoka County is only fifteen minutes away from downtown Minneapolis. I appreciated the support we received from the officials in Anoka County. I wanted to build more than a stadium; I wanted to build an entertainment complex. We were going to copy what some of the other teams had done. I particularly like what the Green Bay Packers have done with their new facility. They keep it open twelve months a year with tours and other activities, which produces revenue in the off-season. And it is a great tourist attraction for the state of Wisconsin.

Early in 2005, the Minnesota state legislature approved a $330 million new stadium package for the Minnesota Twins baseball team. A similar package for a new complex in Anoka County for the Vikings was also at the legislature, but the state representatives adjourned and ended the session without addressing our project. I went immediately to Governor Pawlenty and said, "Governor, the citizens of Anoka County have passed a bond issue to support the construction of our new stadium. I'm ready to go. All I need is your blessing and support." The governor responded that I would have to wait. "I have waited," I answered. "I have waited now for four years. How much longer do I have to wait?" He replied that he could not give me a timetable. I realized that my patience had gone beyond its limits. "In that case," I responded, "I really have no other option than to sell the team."

I could tell that Pawlenty was alarmed by my announcement. He replied that he didn't want me to sell the team. "You put life back into the Vikings," he stated. "We want you in this state. You just have to wait your turn." I responded that my time had passed and that I would put the team up for sale. The bottom line is that I had to sell the Vikings because of what I felt was a failure of will on the part of the politicians in power in Minnesota.

In late February 2005, I accepted an offer of $600 million from a group of investors led by Zygmunt Wilf, who would be the general partner. Arizona businessman Reggie Fowler was another prominent member of the investor group. At first, Fowler was going to be the general partner, but he was unable to satisfy the financial requirements. The NFL approved the sale in May 2005.

The last thing that I did as the owner of the Vikings was trade our star receiver, Randy Moss, to the Oakland Raiders for linebacker Napoleon Harris and the Raiders' first-round draft pick. The trade was made nine days after we announced that the sale of the Vikings was pending. Moving Randy off the Vikings roster was directly tied to a couple of unfortunate incidents during the 2004 season. Randy left the field with two seconds left in our regular season loss to Washington, which displeased his teammates and his coaches and was widely noted by the media. The most publicized incident, however, came during our playoff game at Green Bay. During the game, Randy pretended to pull down his pants and moon the Green Bay fans. The NFL fined him $10,000 for that incident.

Randy had lost his place in the locker room, and he lost his place with our other leaders on the team. As an owner of a sports team, when you sense that you have a player who loses his place in the locker room, regardless of what kind of talent he's got, you have to make a move. I made a move. Oakland later traded Randy to the New England Patriots, where he has flourished, playing a key role in the Patriots' undefeated season in 2007.

I paid $250 million for the Vikings, but that is only partially true. My purchase of the Vikings included several additional assets. One asset was a very lucrative food concession company that served the entire Minneapolis-St. Paul urban complex, not just the Vikings games. It was a forty-million-dollar property by itself. When I sold the Vikings for $600 million, I didn't include that food concession company or three other companies that came with my original purchase. So my profit from selling the Vikings was considerably more than the $360 million difference from my purchase price.

The news media beat me up a little because I made so much profit on the sale of the Vikings. The accusation was that I had somehow taken that away from the people of Minnesota. The fact is I had increased the value of the Vikings during the seven years that I owned the team. I had taken a poorly performing asset and turned it into a major profit center. The revenue streams that I had built were far more than what I had purchased, so that if you looked at the purchase based on anticipated revenue, then Zygi Wilf actually paid less for the Vikings than I paid.

I realize that I have been severely criticized by some of the fans in Minnesota for making so much money from the sale of the Vikings. In my view, that is largely because of the news media in Minnesota, which loved to editorialize about this Texan who came in for seven years and then took all the money and left town. The truth is that I would love to have been able to stay for many decades, but I couldn't play with one arm tied behind me. I love the fans of Minnesota, and I appreciate the support they gave me. I can ask for nothing more. I just want to tell them that they need to get to work on their political leaders to get that stadium problem solved. It's not a McCombs or an owner issue. It is a state of Minnesota issue.

I've been asked if I wish I had managed the Vikings situation differently. My answer is yes, but that's also true for any number of things in which I have been involved. After the fact, there are always things that we look back at and wish we had done a little differently. Life is nothing but a learning curve. I hear people say, "Well, I'm seventy years old, and if I had it to do all over again I would do everything exactly the same." When I hear anyone say that, I know they are either stupid or lying or both.

But in the case of the Vikings, one thing I would do over is not keep Dennis Green as head coach as long as I did. I had an inflated opinion of Dennis, but I eventually recognized that I was the one who inflated it, not him.

As I have said before, there is no greater thrill than owning a professional sports franchise. So the question is: why did I ever get out? I owned the Spurs twice. I brought the Spurs to San Antonio. I created a market for professional basketball in San Antonio. There had been none. Why did I get out? I got out each time because I felt like I had done as much for that product as I could do. It needed someone else. My professional sports teams were always a business with me. It was a business that I understood very well. Each one has been successful, earning me great returns on my investment. But the reason for my success was that the fans always came first. I always told the players on my teams: "Keep in mind that you have a responsibility to our fans and to our sponsors. They are the ones who pay you. I do not pay you." My teams and staff knew how serious I was about that. As a result, I maintained excellent community relations with every sports team I ever owned.

Red McCombs and partner Bart Koontz at the groundbreaking for The Broadway, a luxury high-rise condominium in San Antonio, 2007. Photo by Mark Langford.

Chapter Fifteen

BLACK GOLD AND KOONTZ MCCOMBS

I HAVE ALWAYS BEEN FASCINATED BY THE OIL BUSINESS, AS FASCINATED as anything else in the business world that I ever knew. The fascination began when I was a boy, listening to stories of wildcatters who searched for what they called "black gold." My hometown, Spur, was not an oil town, but major oil fields were still being discovered in Texas when I was a kid. One of the most important oil regions in the world, the Permian Basin, is located to the south and southwest of Spur. It was being developed when I was growing up. We had many people pass through town on their way to work in the oil fields in the region, so there was much talk about the oil business even in a town where there was no oil.

My First Dry Hole

Many young men in Texas in those days found their first real jobs in the oil patch or in work related to the oil business. I worked as a roughneck on drilling rigs from the time I was in high school through college. But that wasn't the source of my fascination with the oil business. It came from knowing about the people who took risks, hit gushers, made and lost fortunes. That was always my fascination. As a matter of fact, an oil well was the very first thing I invested in when I left law school at the University of Texas. When I was in my second month selling cars, I had a fraternity brother who was working as a geologist for a small company in the town of Alice, located a few miles to the west of Corpus Christi. He asked me if I wanted to participate in a drilling venture they had up near Beeville, which is located between San Antonio and Corpus Christi. All I needed to invest was $800.

That was a very enticing proposition. Here was my chance to be a real oilman, or at least an oilman at the entry level. There was one problem, however. At that time I had absolutely no cash, not even $800. I somehow got my hands on $400, and then I borrowed another $400 against my next month's pay from the guys I worked with at the car lot. So, at a time when I had no capital to invest whatsoever, I put $800 into this well, which, as it turned out, was a natural gas well. We did hit the hydrocarbons, which today would be very successful. But in 1950 the price of natural gas was scraping the bottom, and we didn't have a pipeline in the area. We had to abandon the well, so it was the same as a dry hole.

Forging Ahead: My Partnership with Bill Forney

So my first shot at investing in the oil business was a loser, but I wasn't about to give up. As I advanced in my car-selling career and had a few extra bucks to invest, I took small interests in South Texas wells drilled by independent producers that I knew. When I moved to San Antonio in 1958, I met a guy named Bill Forney in a downtown San Antonio bar that was known as a hangout for oil people. The bar was in the Milam Building, which had mostly oil people as tenants.

Bill grew up in Kingfisher, Oklahoma, and graduated from the University of Oklahoma. After World War II, Bill moved to San Antonio, where he eventually became a successful independent oil and gas producer. We hit it off right away and launched a deep friendship that lasted until Bill's death about twenty years ago. Bill invited me to invest a few dollars in his enterprise, and I accepted the invitation. Our deal was sealed the old-fashioned way, with a handshake.

These were hit-and-miss ventures, primarily in South Texas. They didn't make much money, but they didn't lose much either. In 1960, Bill asked me to finance a lease that he had on a piece of property in South Texas, and *he* determined, not me, that we would become partners. So we formed a company that we named Forney & McCombs. Bill and I had a good run. We had solid discoveries in the McCaskill Field (1971) in Karnes County, Texas; the Charline Field (1978) and the Schreiner Ranch Field (1982), in Live Oak County, Texas; the extension of the S. E. Bonus Field (1983) in Wharton County, Texas; and many other oil and gas fields, primarily in Texas. In 1997, I bought out the Forney interest in the company, and it continues today as McCombs Energy. After Bill died, his two sons, Billy Jr. and Charles, assumed management. Billy Jr. is our company's president, and he operates the company out of Houston. Charles is vice president. We have been reasonably successful with it, having started all those years ago with no knowledge of the oil business, just my enduring fascination with it.

Over the years, we've had our share of opportunities; some have turned out okay, while others have been dry holes. One major opportunity, however, falls into neither category. It is a potentially fantastic opportunity in the Kurdistan region of Iraq that I have played with for a few years but have been unable to carry forward for a number of reasons.

In the spring of 2005, Bill Forney's son Phillip heard a lecture at a South Texas Geologic Society meeting by Bud Holzman, a retired army officer and geologist who was the president of a mapping company in Dallas. Holzman had extensive knowledge of the oil fields in Iraq because of his work as a consultant to the U.S. Army. Not long after the invasion of Iraq in 2003, the army had asked him to review a collection of maps documenting a French oil company's exploration in Iraq. Holzman's presentation convinced Phillip Forney that there were a number of exciting opportunities in Iraq for independent oil companies. Phillip called me, and then he and Rad Weaver and I had a meeting with Holzman to get more information. Holzman convinced us that we needed to figure out how to get into Iraq. I told Rad that I wanted him to find a way to smoke this deal out.

Soon after that meeting, in July 2005, Rad and Reeves Hollimon, the son of Chuck Hollimon of Hollimon Oil Company, went to London and attended a conference about the Iraqi oil fields. At the conference they met with officials from the National Oil Company of Iraq, who encouraged them about the opportunities for independents to get concessions for "small" producing fields.

After Rad returned, however, we soon realized that the Iraqi definition of small was much larger than our definition. It was obvious that we needed to partner with an independent company with more experience in working with large fields, so Hollimon Oil dropped out of the mix. In addition, the legal structure in Iraq was fuzzy to say the least. I had serious doubts about the viability of contracts in Iraq. It was unclear to us whom we would sign a contract with and what court would enforce it. The war in Iraq also got much worse as the insurgency escalated and most of the oil and gas exploration was suspended. It just made no sense to put our people at risk. We continued to monitor the situation, however.

Early in 2008, we realized that the Kurdistan region in Iraq would be the best area for our oil enterprise. Kurdistan is relatively stable, and it has a pro-American government that is operating on a semiautonomous basis within the Iraqi state. Its legal system is dependable enough to make contracts viable. The Kurds were granting large oil concessions, so I decided that it was time to jump in. We soon made a deal with Hupecol, an independent with a lot of experience working with a major oil field in Colombia, to be our operator on a fifty/fifty basis. An old Aggie friend of mine, Dan Allen Hughes, is the president.

Once we had an agreement with Hupecol, we began the complicated process of getting approval from the Kurdistan government for an oil concession. That began a back-and-forth series of meetings over a period of nearly eighteen months that involved negotiating with three different producing companies for an agreement to farm into their already existing concessions in Kurdistan. We were unable to complete a deal with any of them, however, because of their insistence on what we felt were unfavorable terms. We also had several meetings with different representatives of the Kurdish government, including Darbaz Kosrat Rasul, the son of the vice president of the Regional Government of Kurdistan (KRG), and Dr. Ashti Hawrami, the KRG oil minister.

Eventually, in the spring of 2009, Rad Weaver travelled to Kirkuk, the capital of Kurdistan, to meet with Dr. Hawrami at Prime Minister Barzani's palace to complete our negotiations for a concession, which was a block on the Bini Bawi structure, just north of the town of Irbil. The field adjacent to the block we were offered was producing 40,000 barrels a day. Rad and Dr. Hawrami reached an agreement on terms and sealed it with a handshake, contingent on my final approval and the approval of Hupecol. Ten days later, I met with Rad, Gary Woods, my daughter Marsha, and executives of Hupecol, including Dan Allen Hughes Sr., to evaluate the terms of the offer and to determine the prospects for a successful deal. By the end of the meeting, Hupecol decided to bow out. They were optimistic that they could find oil in the block, but they were seriously worried about the KRG reneging on the terms if they did find oil. In other words, if we found oil, could we keep it? Hupecol decided the risk was too great.

I appreciated Hupecol's concerns, but I still believed this Bini Bawi deal was a great opportunity. Hupecol's departure left us without an operator. I offered the deal to Tex and Charlie Moncrief in Fort Worth, but they declined. Unable to find an operator to partner with, I finally had to withdraw from the tentative agreement we had with Dr. Hawrami.

I haven't given up on the opportunities in Iraq. I'm still looking, but my involvement in the oil industry in that country will be determined by the degree of political stability and security the Iraqis are able to develop eventually. In the meantime, I've invested with Hupecol in Colombia, so McCombs Oil has become an international enterprise.

Despite our eagerness to take advantage of foreign opportunities, McCombs Oil continues to be very active in domestic exploration and production. We drilled eighty-two wells in 2008, which is a substantial and ongoing investment. Our success rate has been about 80 percent. As long as we hit pay dirt on 60 percent of our drilling sites, we can make it work. As of 2009 we had active onshore prospects in Texas, New Mexico, Oklahoma, Louisiana, Arkansas, and Alabama, as well as some offshore prospects in the Gulf of Mexico.

It's hard for me to believe, but I've been involved in the oil business now for more than fifty years. I have loved every minute. In all of these years, however, one thing has changed. Going to the well site was really a very exciting part of all this when I first started, but I haven't gone to one in years. I just want to get the report. Did we get the hydrocarbons? How much pressure do we have? It is something that plays a part in my life every day. I'm in contact with Billy Forney Jr. on a daily basis. The search for oil and gas, and the history of it, will always fascinate me. Although it has been a real up-and-down ride, I intend to continue in the business. It's the wheeler-dealer in me, I guess.

Koontz McCombs

It's difficult for any respectable wheeler-dealer to stay out of the world of commercial real estate development. In the late 1990s, I got very interested in the business opportunities resulting from rapid growth in San Antonio and other areas of Texas. Since the end of World War II, it seems as though everyone who has had the opportunity has moved to the Lone Star State. The vast increase in the state's population coupled with the economic boom set off a frenzy of development activity. I was eager to participate; I just needed the right partner. That partner turned out to be an energetic young whirlwind by the name of Bart Koontz. And I didn't find him, he found me.

Bart, who is a native of Victoria, Texas, and a graduate of Southwestern University, came to me in 1996 with a proposal to invest in some of his commercial real estate developments. Bart already had an outstanding track record backed with fifteen years of experience. He began his career in real estate in 1981 with Cushman & Wakefield in Dallas before moving to San Antonio to serve as a senior vice president of the Concord Property Corporation, a leading Central Texas commercial real estate development company. During his ten years at Concord, Bart not only developed large office parks and shopping centers, but also helped manage Concord's $200 million real estate portfolio. His personal projects included the Las Tiendas Plaza shopping center in McAllen, Texas, and the Concord Plaza office development in San Antonio.

Bart left Concord in 1993 to co-found HK Partners, Inc., an outfit specializing in large retail properties. HK developed more than 1.6 million square feet of commercial space for national retail chains like Target, Office Max, PetsMart, and Toys R Us. When he came to me, Bart not only sought my help as an investor, he also asked me to serve as a mentor and advisor for his business ventures. It didn't take me long to realize that Bart was the development partner I was looking for. I told him to forget the advising stuff. I wanted to be his full partner.

In May 1997, Bart and I formed Koontz McCombs as a multifaceted commercial real estate development, construction, and brokerage firm. The partnership has worked exceedingly well for more than ten years. As president and CEO, Bart is responsible for the company's strategic direction and long-term planning, as well as the development and implementation of the company's overall investment strategy. Bart Koontz is a high-energy guy. He was quoted in a business journal that "if you're not making dust, you're eating it." That makes sense to me.

From the beginning of our partnership, Bart and I have developed and acquired income-producing properties throughout the state. And in recent years we've expanded interests into other related areas. One unique quality about Koontz McCombs is that we own a construction company as well. In January 2000, we created Koontz McCombs Construction Ltd. to provide commercial construction services for the company as well as third-party entities. We built the Texas Center for Athletes in San Antonio, which is the home to the Spurs' doctors and the team's practice facility.

I'm proud that Koontz McCombs Construction has had an exciting run of successful construction projects, including several public schools, major medical clinics, churches, office buildings, apartment complexes, car dealerships, and retail properties. Our customers have ranged from school districts in San Antonio and Floresville, to retail stores such as Office Max. We even constructed the Early Childhood Development Center at the San Antonio Zoo.

Bart and I currently have active projects in San Antonio, Austin, and Houston. In the last ten years, we've been involved in the development, acquisition, or construction of over five million square feet of commercial property. In 2005, we completed the sale of our first multifamily development project, Las Ventanas Luxury Apartment Homes in west Houston. And we've built such projects as the San Miguel Apartments and the Montecristo Apartments in San Antonio.

The Broadway Condominium

One of most visible projects Bart and I have been involved in is our twenty-five-story high-rise condominium project on San Antonio's Broadway Street in the Alamo Heights district. In 2005, Bart and I could see that San Antonio was on the verge of a new urban housing trend incorporating resort-style, high-rise community living. We wanted to take advantage of this movement by building a suitable high-rise in the part of town that offered a convenient location and beautiful views. We could see that the most desirable location for a high-rise was just north of downtown at the busy corner of Broadway and Hildebrand.

That corner was occupied at the time by Earl Abel's restaurant, a very popular family diner that had operated there since the early 1930s. I would guess that nearly everyone who grew up in San Antonio during the last seventy years ate at Earl Abel's at least once. The place was a local landmark. It was at Earl Abel's that the late Congressman Henry B. Gonzalez famously punched out a fellow customer who called him a communist. It has been the site of untold numbers of first dates.

I felt that the corner of Broadway and Hildebrand was the best place in the entire city for a luxury high-rise, but I didn't know if we could swing a deal with Earl's son, Jerry, who had managed the place since his father's death more than twenty years ago. It turned out that Jerry, who is in his sixties, was open to the idea of selling out. As he told the news media, "the building is old and I'm old." He was tired of operating the restaurant. "Everything just came together perfectly," Jerry told the *San Antonio Express-News*. "The proposal from Koontz McCombs made so much sense." There was the usual fuss about San Antonio losing another "historical" icon, but that quieted down after the Abel family sold the name and the new owner reopened Earl Abel's on Austin Highway in 2006. The new place even has its much beloved old menu featuring its famous pies and chicken-fried steaks.

To take advantage of this prime, well-known location, we named the project "The Broadway." We decided to cater to a service-oriented type lifestyle. The Broadway is designed for empty nesters, corporate executives, Mexican nationals, and others who desire a "lock and leave" lifestyle in which they know their home is being well maintained while traveling. Before Interstate 35 was built, Broadway was the pathway into the city for traffic coming from the north. Bart and I feel strongly that The Broadway will create a new gateway from the north to downtown San Antonio, which will spur additional development along the Broadway corridor.

We initiated this major project just before the bottom fell out of the national economy. We had the good fortune of having locked in our funding from Amegy Bank, so the financing was committed right down to the last refrigerator. There is no question, however, that the national economic recession has impacted our development projects. Bart and I may have benefited, however, from some of the fallout. Our subcontractors have been able to do more on this job faster because other projects have been stopped or delayed. It is a tough economy for some folks, but San Antonio is still the economic high ground. I fully expect that the value of condos in The Broadway will spike, increasing as much as 50 percent over the next five years.

As Bart keeps reminding me, The Broadway is the first brand new residential high-rise tower to be built in San Antonio since the 1980s. So he and I believe there is a pent-up demand in this market. Despite the choppy economic waters, I see great opportunity in a project I never imagined would be part of my portfolio. We understand that there has been a change in the marketplace. But we're as happy about our project now as we've ever been. It's up to Bart Koontz to determine if another condo project makes sense for us. Bart is the creative member of this partnership.

Bart and I are working on some $170 million worth of projects in Texas, but it is The Broadway that has captured our attention. The Broadway is one of those developments that will stand the test of time. In the more immediate future, the development could help expedite efforts to create a true urban core in San Antonio, something the city is lacking. As this book is being written [2009] I'm focused on The Broadway, because I believe it will be a game changer for Broadway and for San Antonio. I'm totally convinced that one hundred years from today, The Broadway will remain a landmark in this city. I'm very honored to have my name attached to it.

SmartyPig

Finally, just so you don't think this old wheeler-dealer isn't hopelessly trapped in "dinosaur" businesses such as oil and construction, I have to tell you about my latest venture, which involves me in a cutting-edge, high-tech internet-based enterprise. In June 2009, I decided to purchase a substantial equity stake in the online social banking application SmartyPig, a company based in Des Moines, Iowa. This application, or "app" as they are known, is a high-tech piggy bank that allows users to open savings accounts online and to track their progress to meet specific savings financial goals. Those goals range from saving for a vacation, to planning for a new baby or wedding, to saving for a consumer purchase like a television. Users can even invite friends and family members to be a part of the process. I especially like the idea that SmartyPig can be an effective way of teaching children about being fiscally responsible from an early age. I believe this is a tremendous opportunity to change people's lives and help them break out of the vicious cycle of credit card debt. Making and saving money is an important life lesson, especially in these uncertain times.

SmartyPig offers one of the most competitive interest rates available and has partnered with major retailers to offer additional cash boosts on customers' savings goals. SmartyPig's innovative savings platform has proven extremely popular with consumers throughout the country. The company's customer deposits in the United States alone now total close to $100 million. Further, thanks in large part to customers who have been quick to share their positive banking experiences with their friends, SmartyPig's deposit base is expected to surpass $500 million by the end of 2009.

For its investors and business partners SmartyPig's online transaction engine generates detailed user information that serves as an effective tool for producing leads for the cross-selling of other products and services. The amazing thing about this to me is that this success has been accomplished with virtually no advertising costs. SmartyPig has already proven successful both inside and outside the United States, and I believe that within five years it will be a company with unusual growth internationally.

So this old wheeler-dealer has now gone into cyberspace. But I have to be honest. My investment in SmartyPig was the result of my relationship with Conrad "Rad" Weaver, an outstanding young man who is the head of New Business Development for McCombs Partners. In effect, Rad is our business opportunity scout, and he found SmartyPig for us.

Rad Weaver is an interesting story. His dad was a high school coach in San Antonio who died of a heart attack when Rad was still in high school. I'd known his dad casually around town as a high school football coach, but I didn't know Rad at the time. He was an outstanding high school athlete, but I hadn't heard of him because I have never followed high school sports that much. I met him through a scholarship program cosponsored by Ford Motor Company and San Antonio's Ford dealers. The year Rad was a senior it was my turn to present the scholarships to the fifty winners at a ceremony in McAlister Auditorium. Candidates for the scholarships had to write essays that were read and evaluated by a panel of local people who selected the winners. When I arrived at the auditorium, I was handed an envelope with Rad's essay in it. I was told to take it back to the office to read after the ceremony.

I gave out the scholarship awards and returned to my office. When I took my coat off that envelope fell on my office floor. If it hadn't fallen on the floor I might not have looked at it. I don't like to put things away to do later. I like to take care of business right away and get on with it. When I opened up that envelope and started reading, I was so impressed by everything Rad had done. He had lost his father a couple of years before, and his mother was a high school teacher. I was impressed with his writing and the goals he had set for himself. Rad was an all-state quarterback, and he was an all-state baseball player at San Antonio's Clark High School, but he wanted to play professional baseball. He also wanted to get a college degree and eventually open a sporting goods store. He'd been the president of everything in school from the time he was in the elementary grades, including the local Fellowship of Christian Athletes. The scholarship candidates had to have three testimonials written by their references. I read those, and my reaction was, "my God, this kid is something else."

I called Rad's house and left my number. When he got home from school he called me. After I congratulated him for winning the scholarship, I told him that I was impressed with his essay and wanted to offer him a summer job as my personal "gofer." He said that he already had a job as a roustabout for a local home-builder, but that he would rather work for me, even though my job paid much less than the construction job. He said that there were plenty of kids who could take his place at the home-building company. So we worked it out, and Rad came on board for the summer. He excelled at every task I gave him. Even at eighteen, Rad had a warm and outgoing personality with very strong people skills.

Rad and I bonded that summer. I continued to stay close to him throughout his college years. During his senior year in high school, Rad had been heavily recruited by Texas A&M as a quarterback, and he had been heavily recruited by several other universities as a baseball player. He even had an offer from the Houston Astros to play professional baseball as a right-handed pitcher. When the Astros made their offer, Rad and his mother asked me for advice. The Astros offered him something like $85,000, which was tempting for a family whose only financial support came from the mother's salary as a teacher. I didn't tell them to do one thing or the other, I just said, you know it's really not a big amount of money the Astros are offering. You will start at the bottom of their organization. I told his mom that Rad would have to be exceptional to make the big-league team. The odds were very much against him making it in the pros. His mother agreed. Rad decided to enter the University of Texas and play baseball for the Longhorns. He pitched, lettered all four years, and served as team captain his senior year.

While Rad was at the university he worked for me every summer and during school holidays. He would work day or night. He would do anything and go anywhere, whatever it took to do whatever I asked him to do. I have always been on the lookout for young, aggressive, and bright people to work with me. I could see that Rad was a young man to whom I could teach my business philosophy and tactics, so I gave him assignments in which he could learn the various things he should know about how to do business. Rad got acquainted with Charline and my three daughters, and my daughters could tell I was really taken with this kid. I mean I really liked him. I knew that after he graduated, I had to find a place for him in my business operation.

Two months after Rad graduated from the university, I purchased the Minnesota Vikings. This turned out to be a fortuitous coincidence for both of us. I was confident that Rad could handle a problem the Vikings had with calendars, media guides, and other branded merchandise products that the NFL allowed the individual teams to sell for themselves. This was a big revenue source for the teams that knew how to use it, but the Vikings hadn't paid attention to it. They essentially gave away most of the profit by farming the business out to vendors. I asked Rad to go to Minnesota and manage that part of the team's business. He jumped at the opportunity. The first year he took an operation that had never made more than $60,000 a year and turned it around and brought in $600,000.

Ever since then, I've thrown different things at Rad, and he has done an outstanding job with every one of them. He definitely is the CEO type, so I don't want to tie him to one part of the company. That's the reason I keep him here on the corporate staff. And with my daughter Marsha really taking my day-to-day leadership role, Rad is an ideal person to serve as a kind of freelancer to handle whatever needs attention. Rad's now thirty-two years old, and he has created a lot of wealth and opportunities for us and for himself, but he doesn't know yet how to turn loose of a deal that's not working. The reason for that is he's just so flat-out determined that he's going to make everything he does work.

That's one of the hardest things to teach people who are driven and refuse to accept failure. But that's what causes a lot of people to go broke. I'm trying to teach Rad that if he has given something his best shot and it's still not working, it is time to move on. I almost ignore defeats and things that don't work. I just don't want them around me. I don't mind selling stuff at a loss.

Fear of failure has never been a problem for me.

Red McCombs looks on as granddaughter Sita McNab throws the first pitch at the Red and Charline McCombs Field at the University of Texas at Austin. Courtesy of UT Athletics.

Chapter Sixteen

GIVING, SHARING, AND THE LONGHORNS

ONE OF THE TRAITS THAT I MOST ADMIRED ABOUT MY PARENTS was their strong belief in sharing whatever they could with others who were less fortunate. Mom and Dad didn't have material wealth, especially during the Depression. But they were rich with the spirit of helping and giving. The belief that you must always help others who need your help was something I grew up with. It was a lesson they taught me by word and action.

When I was growing up, my dad worked six days a week. I remember that when he came home on Saturday nights his pay envelope would have $24.75 cash in it. My mother would put the envelope on the kitchen table and take out $2.50, which she would put in another envelope for the First Baptist Church. One time, I heard her tell my dad that she wished that we could get ahead financially and make a gift to the church. I didn't understand it because I'd see her giving $2.50 every week to the church. So one day I made the mistake of asking Mother, "Why do you say you want to make a gift every week?" My mother's response was, "Are they teaching you anything in Sunday School? Are you playing hooky?" I said "no." She said, "Don't you know that that $2.50 is not a gift? We owe it. It is our tithe and a covenant that we have with God." That was something that I never forgot.

As I mentioned at the beginning of this book, during the Depression Mom and Dad often gave food to people who were out of work and were passing through town to find a job. In addition to that, Dad would go out when he had time off and fix for free the cars of people who didn't have the money to pay for the repairs.

The Joy of Giving

Because of my parents' influence, giving back and sharing have always been natural things for me. Charline has the same attitude. We have shared our resources with others all our lives, and we have taught our three girls to do the same. Marsha, for example, has been deeply involved with San Antonio's Cancer Center Council, the United Way, and the Partnership in Education, which supports the teachers and staff of local school districts. Our other girls do the same for causes in which they are interested.

Obviously, in the early years of our marriage Charline and I had much less to give than we have now. Frankly, when I started my business career and Charline and I were scraping for nickels and dimes, I made charitable gifts of $50 and $100 that were much more difficult for me to make than the million-dollar gifts I make now. We gave whatever we could afford at the time, but our donations never got any recognition until they began to have a lot of zeroes in the amounts. Now that we have a lot more resources, we have a lot more to share. And that is as fun as it is fulfilling. We both get a thrill out of our giving. The joy of giving is truly something that no one will ever understand unless they give. Our giving has made it possible for us to have that joy. We've never planned to leave a big estate for anyone to wrestle and fight over. We've been fortunate. We've made a lot of money, and we've given a lot of money away. If I'm fortunate enough to make some more money, we'll give even more away.

The McCombs Foundation

After my financial resources grew in the late 1970s and early 1980s, Charline and I established the McCombs Foundation to manage our philanthropy. We reached a point where the gifts were getting larger and larger, and it just made more sense from a business perspective to fund a foundation rather than give directly. It was as much a convenience issue as anything else, but it also puts in place something that will continue to do good after Charline and I are no longer here.

Guided by our three daughters, Marsha Shields, Connie McNab, and Lynda McCombs, our foundation makes an average of three hundred gifts every year. Over the past ten years, we have given about 3,500 grants for a total of approximately $200 million. We don't have a staff, so we have no expenses. Practically every penny we have is put into our grants, which go to various organizations that fund cancer research, youth activities, sports, religion, education, and leadership training. One of the things I'm especially proud of is the college scholarship program our foundation has established to benefit the children of the employees of our various businesses.

Charline and I have had a wide variety of philanthropic interests, not all of them in Texas. When I owned the Minnesota Vikings, for example, we raised $400,000 for the University of Minnesota Women's Athletics Department. Having raised three daughters, Charline and I have a strong interest in supporting women's sports. We were actively involved in numerous local charities and schools in the Twin Cities region, and we were successful in getting our players involved in that community. We also have provided support to make it possible for medical teams to travel to war-torn areas in Albania and Macedonia.

The gifts that I prefer to make are those that I feel are going to have an immediate and obvious result. I especially like to give to church programs that provide direct support to people who have immediate needs that can be met with a relatively small amount of money. You can help a lot of people with those types of gifts. You never know where a little bit is going to mean a lot to somebody.

We also like to make gifts to programs that may not have an immediate impact on any one person, but will make a huge difference eventually to a large number of people. Fundraising professionals often refer to those types of gifts as being "transformative." Those are always large gifts and they have the purpose of raising a program or an institution to a new level of excellence and service. My gifts to the University of Texas School of Business, M. D. Anderson, and Southwestern University were in that category.

M. D. Anderson

Charline's and my support for cancer research, treatment, and care is at the top of the list of things that have satisfied us the most in our philanthropic activities. Our support for the war on cancer has been directed largely to the M. D. Anderson Cancer Center in Houston. My interest in the program at M. D. Anderson dates back to 1986, when I visited a longtime friend of mine from Fort Worth who was being treated there. His prognosis was not good. I was aware of M. D. Anderson's reputation as the most respected facility of its kind in the world, but I had no association with its work. No one in our family had been stricken with cancer. We had been blessed.

There was nothing unusual or unexpected about my visit, but some vague feeling I could not identify tugged at me in the taxi to the airport and on the plane back to San Antonio. Eventually, I brushed it off, and my thoughts moved on to other things. The next week I went back to M. D. Anderson to revisit my friend. After I was greeted by a parking attendant, stopped at the information desk, and went up to the room, I realized what had eluded me the previous visit. I was witnessing one of the most unique approaches to caring and genuine concern I had ever known.

I remembered how, a week earlier, a guest who was visiting the other patient in the room had called out to a nurse as he was leaving. He held out a parking stub and asked, "Can you point me in the right direction? The last time I was here, I got hopelessly lost." The nurse called over a nurse's aide and said, "Would you take this gentleman to his car, please?" It was a small gesture, I suppose, and one that 90 percent of the visitors to a hospital, who are often distracted, would have missed. But the symbol was huge. These were people who really cared in a practical and attentive way.

After I left the room, I couldn't wait to call Dr. Charles "Mickey" LeMaistre, someone I had known since the 1960s. He is a former chancellor of the University of Texas System. I had lost touch with Mickey, although I knew he had been president of M. D. Anderson for several years. He invited me to stop by his office. When I did, Mickey directed me to a chair and said, "I'm glad you're here, Red. We have some catching up to do." I told him how impressed I was with his staff, and he handed me a mission statement that said, simply, "People who enter these doors, the patients and the people who visit them, are troubled. We need to be aware of this and go that extra mile in the care we give."

I told Mickey that I had witnessed an example of this service, and I thought it was remarkable, knowing that hospitals function seven days a week, twenty-four hours a day. He did not achieve all the high positions he has filled by being passive. "If you're that interested," he said, "why don't I get you on one of our boards?"

The next thing I knew, I was on the center's Board of Visitors, and I was asked to take on a couple of projects. Then, in 1994, Mickey asked me to chair the Institutional Initiatives Advisory Committee, a select committee to study all phases of M. D. Anderson as the hospital prepared itself for the next revolution in health care. I'm not much of a committee guy; in fact, I tend to run for the door when one is mentioned, but chairing this committee turned out to be one of the most satisfying assignments that I have ever accepted. At first, I resisted when he asked me to serve as chair, because I thought the head of the committee should be from Houston. But Mickey felt that it was critical that someone from outside of Houston lead the committee because M. D. Anderson serves the entire state of Texas, not just the citizens of Houston.

"Because He's the President of the United States"

One of the great pleasures of leading the committee was having former president George H. W. Bush as a member. After they left the White House in January 1993 and moved to Houston, President Bush and former first lady Barbara Bush decided that M. D. Anderson would be one of their retirement projects. So President Bush volunteered to serve on my committee. When Mickey LeMaistre called to tell me that the former president wanted to work on the committee, I was thrilled. I told Mickey that was great and that I would send the president a note and our meeting schedule. Mickey said, "Uh, I don't think that's the proper way to respond, Red." So I said, "Okay, well, I'll give him a phone call." I told Mickey that I had known Bush for years. "Red, trust me on this one," Mickey replied. "You need to come over here." I asked Mickey why I would want to take a day to go to Houston to respond to somebody who's already said that he wants to join our committee? "Because he's the president of the United States," Mickey answered succinctly. My answer was just as concise. "Oops, I get it. I'll come over there."

When Mickey and I met with President Bush at his office, the first thing Bush said was "Hey Red, what are you doing wearing a coat and a tie?" I told him it was because I had come to see a former president of the United States. "Well," Bush said, "I made it clear to Barbara that when we got out of Washington, the first thing I was going to do was get rid of my ties and the second thing I was going to do was get rid of my tuxedos. I've always loved the fact that you never had to fool with that stuff and here you are wearing a coat and a tie!" I said "Mr. President that's because of my respect for you." Bush smiled and said "Well don't do it anymore; you don't need to do that." He put in a lot of work, and he was a tremendous help to us on that committee.

We added some of the top CEOs in the Houston area to the committee. We submitted a series of recommendations to Mickey LeMaistre aimed at cutting expenses and making the business systems more efficient. Within two years after implementing our recommendations, M. D. Anderson went from an annual cash flow of minus approximately $15 million to a positive cash flow of about $50 million a year. And that was accomplished without any reduction in patient services or care. Our most important recommendation was to have the state legislature pass a bill giving M. D. Anderson more operational autonomy within the University of Texas System. We wanted the center to be free from unnecessary bureaucracy and to be more entrepreneurial.

And, of course, that didn't come easy because the system strongly opposed us. The system was pulling several million dollars a year out of M. D. Anderson's cash flow to fund other system projects. But we made the point to the legislature that the UT System was just the steward of M. D. Anderson, which had been created by the legislature back during World War II as a separate entity from the university. M. D. Anderson has a legal status that is completely different from the other entities in the UT System. After we pushed a lot of buttons and made some telephone calls, the legislature agreed with us. M. D. Anderson is still part of the UT System, but it has much more independence than the system's other units. Now M. D. Anderson's money stays at M. D. Anderson, which gives them more resources to battle cancer.

One thing led to another, as they often do. In October 1995, I was asked to chair the board for two years, succeeding Randy Meyer, who had been the CEO of Exxon. Later, I was appointed to a steering committee with Ben Love, the respected Houston banker, to raise $150 million in a five-year campaign. At nineteen, Ben had flown a B-17 Flying Fortress on bombing raids over Germany in World War II. It was no big stretch for him to provide the leadership, and we met our goal in two and a half years, half the time allotted. Sadly, Ben died in 2006 of cancer, the very scourge that he worked so hard to defeat.

I've continued to be active on M. D. Anderson's board of directors, including serving a term as board chairman that ended in 1997. Charline and I have made major gifts to the Basic Sciences Research Building, the Endowment for Innovative Cancer Research, and M. D. Anderson's "Fulfill the Promise" capital campaign. Charline has had a special interest in the Children's Art Project and other patient care programs.

The McCombs Early Detection and Treatment Center

In July 2005, Charline and I were so impressed with M. D. Anderson's plan to establish an Institute for the Early Detection and Treatment of Cancer that we decided to contribute $30 million to help make it possible. M. D. Anderson never even asked me for the gift. I'm a director emeritus at M. D. Anderson, and I get their mailings. In one of these flyers, I noticed that they were planning an institute that would bring together six already existing centers to work in a very integrated and focused way. The more I read, the more it seemed to me that within ten years the institute was going to change the way cancer is detected and treated.

The aspect of this institute that really excited me, however, was the plan to take the findings from this coordinated effort and bring them directly to the patients on a twenty-four-hour, seven-day-a-week basis. They will be able to go from the lab bench to the bedside and determine if the treatment is working or not. And they are concentrating on some of the most difficult cancers. I thought, now here is a simple and straightforward approach, what a genius of a plan.

I called M. D. Anderson's fundraising office to ask if they had a lead gift for the campaign to fund this new institute. The development officer said no, because they hadn't even started the campaign, but he said they had a good list of prospects for a lead gift. I asked if they had me on that list. He said no, because I had been so generous to M. D. Anderson with other gifts. I said, "Well, you won't need that list. I'm going to give you $30 million as a lead gift." John Mendelsohn, who succeeded Mickey LeMaistre as head of M. D. Anderson, called me back and said "Red, are you trying to make my whole career here just with one phone call?" I said, "John, this proposal is ingenious the way you're taking on the toughest cancers in the world. If we can get those, we know we are going to get these other buggers." I told him that I was completely turned on by the plan.

Mickey LeMaistre retired in 1996, with a superb legacy in place. I will always be grateful to him for inviting me to get involved with M. D. Anderson. It is one of a kind, and I don't feel I am slighting San Antonio by the time and effort I contribute there. The hospital isn't just for Houston. It is a treasure for all Texans.

The University of Texas Board of Regents gave Charline and me the great honor of naming M. D. Anderson's new program the Red and

Charline McCombs Institute for the Early Detection and Treatment of Cancer. The institute has a great slogan, "Making Cancer History." Charline and I have real expectations that this new institute will discover new cancer treatments, diagnostic tests, and screenings in the coming decades that will indeed make "cancer history." And we are well on the way down that path after only three years.

Mary Hull Elementary School

In 1994, I received a handwritten letter from a fifth-grade teacher at Mary Hull Elementary, near Lackland Air Force Base on the west side of San Antonio. She said that the authorities at the Northside Independent School District were threatening to close the school because not enough students were passing the state assessment tests. "We're on the list of nonperforming schools that can be closed," she wrote. "I gave up an accounting career as a partner with Ernst & Young because I wanted to help kids. My husband's a lawyer and he's getting transferred to Atlanta, so I'm not going to be here next year." She said that the school had never had a fifth-grade graduation ceremony. The last thing she wanted to do before she moved was to give the fifth graders that ceremony. She asked if I would be the speaker for their graduation to middle school. I'm not sure why I did it, because I get similar invitations all the time, but I called her and said that I would be happy to come out. But there was just something about her letter that touched me. I went out and gave a little speech and returned to my office and thought nothing else about it.

The Sunday after I had attended the fifth-grade graduation, I saw a brief story in the newspaper about a fire at Mary Hull Elementary. Vandals had torched a couple of classrooms. The next morning when I got out of bed I couldn't get this incident out of my head. So before I went to the office, I drove out to the school to see what had happened. And, of course, the kids were crying, there was a heavy odor of smoke, and two classrooms were badly damaged.

The principal was a real nice guy named Robert Zárate, but he seemed at a loss about what to do. I said, "Robert, what are we waiting for?" He replied that he was waiting for the school district to give him instructions. I said "Oh, nevermind the school district. Move these kids to the wing of the school that wasn't damaged and doesn't have the smoke odor. I'll get you a couple of front-end loaders over here and a dump truck and we'll clean this up." Robert's response was that he appreciated the offer of help, but he might get fired if he acted before he got his instructions. I said, "Well, if that happens you can go to work for me. You know that we can't have these kids standing around worrying about this." I asked the principal if he would send a note home with the kids asking their parents and other friends of the school to come back that night at six o'clock to help clean up. I would cook hamburgers for all. He agreed to do that. We had a good turnout, and we were able to get the place cleaned up by that evening. While this was going on, I just fell in love with those kids.

A couple of days later, I had a private meeting with the principal to learn more about the situation at his school. He explained that they were doing everything they could to keep the school from being closed for nonperformance, but it was looking bleak. Most of the students at the school are transitory. Very few of them ever enter at the first grade and go through to finish the fifth grade. Eighty-five percent are Hispanic. He asked for my help, so I agreed to make the school my personal project.

My goal was to get these kids invested in their school and to get them to take an interest in learning. I took them to the Spurs games, to the rodeo, and to the zoo. I had them come out to my ranch near Johnson City. But the most important thing that I did was to get most of the parents and many of their neighbors involved in the school and in our activities. I organized three different rallies for the neighbors to get them interested in the school. There are a large number of retirees living in the area. I told them that if an outsider like me was interested in those kids, the people who live in the neighborhood have to be interested. Many of them argued that they had no children in the school because their children were grown, so why should they be involved. I answered that they should be involved simply because these kids needed them. I'm not saying that I persuaded 100 percent of them, but I got most of them.

My role at the school was to be their guide and cheerleader. I made frequent trips to the school auditorium, where I gave pep talks to the assembled students. From the beginning, I stressed that they were going to be winners, that they were going to be the best. When I first went out there, I could just look in their eyes and see that they really didn't know what winning was about. And of course, my association with the Spurs gave me some credibility.

About a year after I started my program at Hull Elementary, my good friend former Texas governor Dolph Briscoe went with me to one of my school rallies. I hadn't planned to take him, but we were in a meeting in my office when I realized that I was scheduled to go out to the school. I explained to Dolph that I needed to speak to these kids in their school auditorium to pump them up about taking their state assessment tests. He readily agreed to go with me because he was interested in how we were carrying out our program. When we entered the auditorium, the place erupted. The kids went absolutely crazy. Their parents were also there. They had some of the student leaders lined up in front, so I went by and hugged each one and gave them high fives. Then I went up on stage and called out: "All right, who are we?" They yelled back in unison: "We are Mary Hull!" "What are we?" I asked. "We are number one, Mr. Red!"

I said "Okay, we've got a big day tomorrow. We're going to take the state test. Let's get prepared for it. Don't get nervous, because you're prepared. We're going to have a little cookout here this afternoon. I can't stay with you, but we've got some hamburgers and hot dogs and a lot of your neighbors are here. I want you to get totally relaxed, get a good night's sleep, and be here early in the morning because we're going to ace this, dude! Remember, we are Mary Hull, number one!"

That was typical of the type of rallies that we have had ever since I became involved. Within three years Mary Hull Elementary went from a being a non-performing school to being recognized as a National Blue Ribbon School. Instead of that being a place where teachers didn't want to go, it's now a place where they stand in line to be assigned.

I don't claim to be an educational expert or to have a special gift for working with kids or to have any deeply profound insights about how kids learn. My experience at Mary Hull Elementary, however, has convinced me that we can reach these kids when they are just starting out and are impressionable. But we can't just mail in our help. We all need to be involved personally at some level. It really does require more than good teachers. We need the parents to be involved, and we need the involvement of neighbors who may not have kids in school. It takes a lot of effort and hard work, but it is possible to get these kids fired up about learning and about staying in school. Mary Hull doesn't have to be an unusual or atypical example.

I do have to warn you, however. Once you get hooked, it's very hard to quit. Fifteen years later, I'm still helping them.

Southwestern University

Another one of our strong interests is in Southwestern University in Georgetown, Texas, just a few miles to the north of Austin, where Charline and I both spent some time in the late 1940s. Southwestern is a small private liberal arts school affiliated with the United Methodist Church. As the oldest institution of higher education in Texas, it has a rich historic past and a special place in our hearts. Charline and I donated six million dollars to the school in 1996. The university honored us by naming the student center, which houses dining facilities, a ballroom, and student life offices, the Red and Charline McCombs Campus Center.

When we made our gift, I challenged the administration and the faculty to develop a curriculum to help develop our future leaders. What changes the world is leadership. Southwestern has a great opportunity to make an important contribution in this area. Most of Southwestern's faculty members live in the small Georgetown community. The school has 1,250 students and a student-faculty ratio of something like eleven to one. Southwestern's faculty can spend much more time with the students than the faculty can at the larger state schools. We will always need scientists, mathematicians, engineers, and such, but what changes the world are not the Nobel Prize winners, it's what leaders do with what Nobel Prize winners come up with. Because it occupies a special niche in our state's educational system, Southwestern is well positioned to add significantly to our pool of future leaders.

UT Longhorns

Why does the University of Texas play such a big role in my life? Why do I devote so much time to that place? Well, for one thing, they couldn't run me off. I love the university. But there's a very selfish basic reason: because the place energizes me in a way nothing else does. As I've explained earlier, from the first day I walked on the campus I have felt that the UT campus is like a miniature of the world at large. It's all there in pretty compact packages, with all those different enterprises of learning.

Whenever I walk through the campus, I am exhilarated by what I see. Over there are the young engineers and architects; down there are young computer whizzes; up the road are student pharmacists, student nurses, student chemists, and student educators. Turn the corner and you see kids who are going to be our next generation of entrepreneurs strolling along with history and foreign language majors. And then you see the magnificent libraries, the museums, and the world-class intramural and intercollegiate sports facilities. The place literally is buzzing twenty-four hours a day with learning, discovery, and exploration.

I am so profoundly impressed with the realization that this is not only a repository of what has happened, although knowledge of the past is the basis of all learning, but it is also an incubator for what's going to happen. I wonder, as I walk around the campus, what exciting new things are being developed in all these buildings? Look at what's happening right here before my eyes. And as we say in the university's advertisements—"What starts here changes the world." Well, it truly does. Almost all of the good and wonderful advancements in our society originate at great institutions of higher learning. I've always been fascinated by that.

That's why I like to be on the campus in Austin and why I also like to make contributions to it. How do I do that? One way, of course, is with financial support when I can, but I also do it by being there and by encouraging the students and faculty. I advise them not to analyze things to death, because if they do they'll never find a reason for doing anything. If what you want to do makes sense, try to apply a little common sense to the knowledge you gain here and then *go for it.*

I realize that my involvement at the university has largely been associated with athletics, but that's just because I have had a deeply personal interest in athletics all my life. It's not because I think the athletic program is more significant than the academic mission of the university. As important as sports have been in my life, the truth is that I don't think I could have had the success I have had in my life without going to college.

One of the things that college did was stretch my imagination. And, of course, a general undergraduate education at a place such as the University of Texas arms you with basic knowledge of the world. It broadens your vision. Because of my college education I don't know a lot about any one subject, but I know something about a lot of important things. The other point about a college education is that it gives you access to so many things that are essential to success. It's much more difficult to get that access without college experience. Having gone to college also gives you more credibility when you go out into the world, no matter what it is that you want to do.

My involvement in the athletic program at the University of Texas is deep, not only because of my love for sports, but because in my mind the intercollegiate athletic program is an integral and essential part of the academic mission of the university. I don't see athletics and academics as being unconnected; I see them as integral parts of the whole picture.

The fact is that athletics, the football program in particular, makes the college experience so much richer for the students. Thousands of our students attend and enjoy the games and the events related to the games. Of course, not every student goes to athletic games, but not every student goes to the art museum, the LBJ Library, or to fine arts concerts, either. But very few people, at least anyone with any smarts at all, would advocate placing less emphasis on those programs. In my view, they should receive more support, not less, but the same goes for our athletic program. I know there are those who respectfully disagree, but I truly believe that the football, basketball, baseball, and other sports programs have been essential elements in the university's successful effort to attract gifts that are critical to the academic side of the institution.

My personal involvement in the university's athletic program began after I left the university and moved to Corpus, although that involvement was limited because I was working day and night building a business. One of the areas in which I did have time to participate was in the recruitment of high school football players. I helped the Longhorns' assistant football coach, Ox Emerson, recruit kids in the Corpus area. Emerson, who was an All-Southwest Conference lineman for the Longhorns in the late 1920s, was the freshman football coach for the university. I first met him when he coached at Del Mar College before he took his job with the Longhorns. That was great fun because I got to scout a lot of high school football games in the Corpus area during that time.

My involvement really intensified in 1957, when I was elected president of the statewide Longhorn Club. And naturally, I attended as many of the Longhorn football games as I could during those years, which is a habit I have continued. In December 1956, when the university was looking for a new football coach, I was president of the Longhorn Club. Darrell Royal was the head coach at the University of Washington at the time, and I was very aware of his growing reputation as an up-and-coming young coach. As a result, I played a very minor role in getting Royal hired. My dear friend, Bob Sorrell, who helped me acquire the Corpus Christi Clippers, was on the university's Board of Regents at the time. He served on the committee to recruit a new football coach. I was among those who lobbied Sorrell very hard to support Darrell Royal's hiring. Fortunately, Royal was hired, ushering in one of the most glorious eras in Longhorn football history.

Mack Brown

Although I am an active supporter of the athletic program, by and large I only do what the university asks me to do. I was not involved, for example, in the hiring of John Mackovic as head coach, and I wasn't involved when he was fired. The university did ask me to help with the search for Mackovic's replacement, however. Near the end of Mackovic's tenure as head football coach, Longhorn athletic director Deloss Dodds called me and said that he was going to reassign Mackovic after the game with Texas A&M. He asked if I would help with the search for a replacement. I told him I would do whatever I could, but I would not serve on a committee. As I've stated before, I'm not a big fan of committees. I did tell him, however, that the next coach should be the young guy who at that time was the head coach at the University of North Carolina, Mack Brown.

When Deloss replied that Brown was on his short list, I told him to tear up his short list and go straight after Mack Brown. "He has done a tremendous job at North Carolina," I said. "He has completely turned that program around." I also pointed out that he was the kind of guy the high school coaches in Texas would be crazy about. Mackovic had been widely disliked in Texas high school coaching circles and that had damaged our in-state recruiting. For the University of Texas to become a national title contender, it was absolutely essential that the next coach have a recruiting pipeline straight to the best high school players in Texas, and those high school coaches are crucial for that.

I told Deloss that I understood that Brown had a reputation as being an emotional guy who had a lot of pride. "I don't think he's going to put up with the typical kind of vetting process involving all of these committees, dinners, golf dates, and the other stuff that you guys like to put candidates through." I advised him that the bureaucratic process the university normally used for recruiting would kill any chance they had to get Brown. Deloss responded that the reality was that he was part of a bureaucracy and that he worked for other people. I told him that I understood that he had to get the university president and possibly the regents to sign off on whatever he wanted to do, but I urged him not to take the faculty committee route on this search. I knew that by the time the members of the faculty committee finished their navel-gazing, they would have lost Brown.

I strongly recommended to Deloss that he fly straight to North Carolina and offer the job to Mack Brown. I also warned him that Brown actually might have to be persuaded to come to Texas, so I suggested that he take a couple of former Longhorn football players who were successful businessmen, such as Bobby Moses and Corbin Robertson, with him to see Brown. "Oh, and the most important thing that you can do, Deloss, is take Darrell Royal with you," I stressed. "I can guarantee that when Coach Royal shakes Brown's hand, looks him in the eye, and says 'We want you at Texas, son,' there's no way Brown's going to say no."

Deloss listened politely and patiently to this presumptuous lecture, then he said, "Well, you know there is one other stop that I have to make even if I choose to go to North Carolina." I said, "You wouldn't happen to be thinking about going to Chicago?" Deloss said yes, he needed to talk to Gary Barnett, the head coach at Northwestern University. Barnett had turned one of the worst football programs in NCAA history into a winner. I asked, "Do you know Gary Barnett?" He answered, "No, only professionally." I told him that he didn't want Barnett. I knew people in the sports business that had worked with Barnett. "He is going to want to be more than the football coach," I argued. "He will want to run your entire athletic program." Deloss answered that he wasn't worried about his job. I said that it didn't matter, "You will have the title, but Barnett will be in charge if he comes to Austin."

Deloss did make that trip to Chicago, and he followed it up immediately with a trip to North Carolina. He took Coach Royal with him to see Brown, and within seventy-two hours after Mackovic was reassigned, Brown was in Austin to attend the press conference announcing that he had been hired. I'm not saying that my advice to Deloss made the difference or that he would not have hired Mack Brown if I had not recommended him. It was Deloss's decision to make, and he made it. I'm just proud of the relationship that I have with Deloss and the university, and I appreciate that he would ask my advice and that he was patient enough to listen to my strong opinion on the matter.

The Red and Charline McCombs Field

As a Longhorn fan, I am thankful for the job that Deloss Dodds has done as the university's athletic director. I think his record speaks for itself. I don't know of a better-managed collegiate athletic program in the United States than the program Deloss runs. It was his professionalism and leadership that helped convince Charline and me in 1997 to give $3 million to help fund a new $4.5-million stadium complex for the women's softball team.

One of the top facilities in all of collegiate softball, the stadium opened its doors on February 7, 1998, with a sellout crowd. The field sports the finest grass and clay infield available. When fans and opponents arrive at McCombs Field they are treated to unobstructed grandstand seating, a great concessions area, and easily accessible parking. Under talented softball coach Connie Clark, the women's team has produced an impressive record. We are proud that the gift was the largest ever made in support of women's athletics at the university, because we believe that it will bring even more attention to women's sports. And we were profoundly honored when the UT Board of Regents named the stadium the Red and Charline McCombs Field.

The Red Zone

Mack Brown, of course, has more than fulfilled the hopes we had for him when he became head coach in December 1997. He has restored the Longhorn football program to the glory days it enjoyed under Coach Royal. The night we beat Southern Cal to win the 2005 national championship in the Rose Bowl ranks near the top of my list of all-time thrills. I firmly believe that there are other national championships yet to come under Coach Brown, and I will do everything that I can to help him and Deloss Dodds make that happen. One of the ways that I decided to help was to provide $6 million in support of the multimillion-dollar renovation of the university's Darrell K. Royal–Texas Memorial Stadium.

When Deloss asked for my help with the stadium renovation, he said that the university also wanted to name something at the stadium for me. I told him I would be pleased to do that, but I had a stipulation. It couldn't just be lettering on a wall. If my name was going to be on it, I wanted it to be a place that would inspire a feeling like the one that started giving me goose bumps so long ago when I first got hooked on Texas football. Deloss and I agreed that the expansive new north end zone should be that place, so it was named the Red McCombs Red Zone.

The atmosphere that is going to be created in the Red Zone during football games is going to be one of the greatest in sports. That's where the Longhorns are going to feel good. That's where they're going to soar. I want the stadium to have an aura like The Swamp at Florida, or Ohio State's Horseshoe. The Red Zone will be an eardrum-splitting, high-decibel den that inspires Longhorn legends. You will see superhuman efforts in the Red Zone. It will be where the action is. It's going to be hard for guys to score on us down there. And it's going to be easier for us to score. Your home ground is your castle. Nobody should ever want to come into your place.

The McCombs School of Business

As I said earlier, I'm not a one-note guy when it comes to my appreciation for the University of Texas. It's not all about athletics. That's why I decided in the year 2000 that my largest gift to the university to date, which totals $50 million, would be directed to support the academic program at the School of Business.

I believe that business is the core of society. Whether you practice business or any other profession, or you're involved in a church or a non-profit, if it's going to reach its ultimate level, there has to be a core business involved in the entity, helping it to grow and stretch its vision. From planning, to fundraising, to financing and operating, there is a business at the heart of every organization. And that is precisely why I made that gift to the business school at the University of Texas.

Charline and I make philanthropic decisions based on the same two questions that we ask of every proposal: "How great is the need?" and "What will be the impact of the gift?" We all know the School of Business is a great school, but I don't know how many people think about the kind of impact this school has. It is the blood supply for the growth and hopes of Texas and the nation. Throughout this state, the nation, and the world, there is someone from the UT Business School operating the central core of a multinational company, a three-man business, or a start-up—it's amazing!

It would never have even entered my mind that there would be any possibility that the UT School of Business could become the Red McCombs School of Business, even with all of my ego and love for the school. It was something that just dawned on me as I assisted UT President Larry Faulkner and Dean Bob May with the university's capital campaign. Our discussions centered on how to make people more aware of the business school's quality and impact and how to take it to the next level of achievement. We eventually came to the conclusion that we needed a heavy hitter—a donor the caliber of which the school had never seen.

Since the gift I had in mind was so large, I called my family together for their guidance. I didn't make any big presentation about it. But almost before I could get it out of my mouth, they were saying, "Dad, go for it, that will be great!" With that rousing endorsement, I set in motion my proposal to give $50 million in cash, completely unrestricted, over the next seven years.

At the May 11 press conference, my emotions ran high. I told the students at the press conference that, aside from my family, everything else I have ever been involved with in my life paled beside this. It was truly the defining moment of my life. I decided to make the gift unrestricted because I wanted to leave decision making to the academic officials. They know better than I do about what needs to be done. But ever since I made the gift, I've been delighted to continue to be involved in efforts to promote and shine a light on the great things the school has to offer, as well as its primary product: the students.

I should also point out that one of the reasons I chose the School of Business for this gift was because of the influence its greatest dean had on me. That dean was the late George Kozmetsky. I didn't meet Dean Kozmetsky when I was a student at the university because he wasn't there at the time. It was much later, long after I had entered the business world, that I got to know him. The university brought George Kozmetsky to campus in 1966 to take the School of Business to a new level, which he more than accomplished during his sixteen years as dean. A co-founder of the Teledyne Technologies back in 1960, Kozmetsky built that firm into one of the most successful enterprises of its type in the country. Within six years of Teledyne's founding, it made the Fortune 500.

I was fascinated when the university stepped out and took a man of his stature from a successful background in business and academia to lead the UT business school. I thought it was giant leap. I was fortunate to have benefited many times from his advice and guidance over the years. He was a great man who truly made a difference. He brought significant improvements to almost every facet of the school, transforming it from a regional institution that just taught basic courses to a nationally recognized powerhouse for research and business education. During this time, he also founded the IC^2 Institute, a think-tank charged with researching the intersection of business, government, and education. He was absolutely and hopelessly in love with the University of Texas. My name may be on the School of Business, but it has Kozmetsky's stamp on every department and program.

I have been very happy with the progress that the McCombs School has made these last few years. It pleases me to think that the additional resources that I have provided may have made a significant contribution to that progress. We have a new and talented dean, Tom Gilligan, a visionary who I believe will continue to push the school up the ranks of the best business schools in the country. The results of various surveys published in 2009 indicated that the McCombs School's national rankings included first place for its accounting program; second place for its business ethics program; sixth place for its BBA program; and eleventh place for its MBA program. The ranking that most pleases me is first place for the school's MBA program for Hispanics. That ranking was determined by *Hispanic Business Magazine*.

The University of Texas has given me many honors, including a Distinguished Alumnus Award in 1998, and it has seen fit to place my name and Charline's name on buildings and programs on campus. But the greatest honor for both of us has been our close and continuing association with the leaders, faculty, and students of one of the greatest institutions of higher learning in the United States. That association has enriched our lives immeasurably. As I said earlier, I'm just glad they let old Red hang around campus. They can't run me off!

The Question

There is a truth that I've known since I was ten years old. There is one area in life in which we are all totally equal and that is the fact that God gives all of us twenty-four hours a day. Nobody gets any more or any less. So the question is what are you going to do with those twenty-four hours? Every night when I go to bed I think, now what did I do today? That question is not all about making money. I also question if I was a better husband, a better father, a better friend. Is there anyone out there who really needed me and I didn't help? Is there some worthy cause with which my philanthropy might make a real difference? And some days I find myself deficient. Did I create anything worthwhile today? Anything? So I grade myself, and I want to make every day count, because I realize, at the end of the day, we're all a speck of sand. But, while I'm here, I want to make a difference.

Red McCombs speaks to graduates of the McCombs School of Business at the University of Texas at Austin, May 2010. Courtesy of the McCombs School of Business.

Conclusion

GO FOR IT!

I AM FREQUENTLY ASKED IN INTERVIEWS BY THE MEDIA AND IN sessions after my lectures if I think it's more difficult now for a young entrepreneur to succeed than when I began my career.

That's the greatest question. The questioners don't like my answers necessarily, although they should. But I nearly always see frowns when I answer that question in front of a bunch of students. I tell them what I believe—this is the easiest time in the history of the world for young talent to make a mark. Just think about it for a minute. We've been through eras where young people did not have a value except as being readily available to carry a rifle. Otherwise, you had to "pay your dues," and you had to be at least forty years old and have twenty years experience in business before anyone would think you knew anything.

That was the way things went, and that was what I bucked when I started out. I didn't like that attitude when I was young, and I don't like it now that I have few decades behind me. When I was in my early twenties, I resented the sarcastic reactions from my "elders" whenever I had a good idea. "That guy has an idea? What has he done? Nothing." But today the premium is actually on youth because what the high-tech, dot-com, and "green" businesses have done is shown us that brilliance and innovation is coming from very young minds. How old were Michael Dell, Steve Jobs, and Bill Gates when they changed the computer world? They were nineteen, twenty-one, and twenty, respectively.

What those three and many others did at an early age changed the business environment for all young people. Now youth is at a premium, and if you're forty years old and haven't done it, you've got an uphill climb. Although you might have done pretty well in those fifteen years since you've been out of school, that's often not good enough for those of us who are looking at people as potential partners in business. So number one: is this a more difficult time for youth? No—it is absolutely the best of times. It is the best of times because if you're young and have any kind of credentials in the form of education or experience, and you've got an idea, it is easier for you to access capital than at any time in the history of the world. Never before has it been this way. So thank God you're young because you've got a lot of advantages other than just having energy and strength. You've got a market that is saying it wants you. Frankly, I couldn't be happier about that. Why? Because it gives me great hope for the future.

I've already mentioned that I'm not much of a forward planner, but I have some thoughts I have as to where I think McCombs Enterprises will be five years from now. We are well positioned to make some serious leaps in several different businesses. Our structure is exactly where I want it. We have Gary Woods, who has been here for more than thirty years. His number one man is Steve Cummings, who has been here twenty-five years. My daughter Marsha is my successor, and she has the legal authority to make all the decisions that she wants to make. Marsha has been hugely successful with our automotive sales division, and I expect that we will expand in that area. Five years from now we will have at least double or triple the number of locations that we currently have selling vehicles. Hopefully those will be in San Antonio but if not, at least nearby in South Texas. Assisting her on the sales end we have Tim Cliver, a twenty-five-year employee.

Our big star for the next five years is going to be Rad Weaver. Rad got the responsibility about seven or eight years ago to put together our outside investments in already established businesses. I'll repeat again that what we really look for are businesses that are beyond the startup phase and well under way with products that we like. We want someone who is well-schooled, well-timed, and well-placed with a product that we think has at least a national (hopefully even an international) opportunity to expand. Rad is a very fast learner, and he has a great catalog of contacts plus the drive and passion necessary to make something happen.

We always have a lot of people contacting us with proposals, because in my entire business career I've been known as a person who will at least look at most deals. If the business looks halfway decent on paper, then I will probably give you an audience. I can make a pretty quick decision. So we see a lot of deals. But this also gives us a lot of new opportunities. We feel like our strength will be in recognizing opportunities and then being able to help an entrepreneur who already has his or her company started. We will be able to add management to that business from our side, which will allow the entrepreneur to do more and to do it a lot faster. I anticipate that the new business we will bring in through McCombs Partners in the coming five years will double the market value of McCombs Enterprises. That's a big step involving a lot of action. I'm really bullish about the future. I think we have all the people in place to do it. McCombs Partners, under Rad Weaver's leadership of a team that includes Tony Rimas, Shawn Rosenzweig, Dave Schlagel, Bruce Knox, Carson Rubey, Jack Nelson, and Steven Moya has already added more than thirty companies. The value of these transactions exceeded $800 million. The biggest compliment Rad Weaver and McCombs Partners can get is an introduction from one of our current partners to a new deal opportunity. With the addition of the Formula One racetrack in Austin, the international attention to McCombs Partners is at an all-time high.

The oil exploration business has been a very productive area for us. That business will continue to grow under the leadership of Bill Forney and his two brothers, Charles and Phillip, along with Bill's two sons. Bart Koontz leads our major real estate development firm. We are well positioned there to continue to add great properties and grow that company just as we have for the past ten years.

Marsha will be overseeing all of this, but I hope to add whatever I can to this effort. I don't ever plan to retire. I will continue to offer the best that I can right up until the last breath that I draw. That's not because of any greed, it's because of my need to satisfy what I believe is God's intention for all of us, which is to be productive and to do things pleasing to Him. Business has always been something I look forward to doing. It's not something I look at as work.

Our foundation will continue to grow, which will enable us to help a lot of people in the communities where we work and live. I feel good about the legacy of sharing and giving that Charline and I have established.

From a family standpoint, Marsha is now a seasoned executive. We have eight grandchildren; the only one active in the company right now is the oldest, Carson Rubey. I feel like that over the next five or six years, we'll probably have at least three or four more of the grandkids become involved with the business. Charline and I certainly hope that we do. We would like for all of our grandkids to be involved with McCombs Enterprises, but that will be their decision.

One of my dreams is that McCombs Enterprises will be a productive entity on its one-hundredth anniversary. Since we started in 1953 we are more than halfway there. I know that Marsha can add many years on to this record. I hope the grandkids will pick up from her, and our future will continue. We are structured to allow anyone in the family to exit the business by selling their shares back to the group. We hope that doesn't happen, but realistically it probably will. I feel like God has been very generous with Charline and me. We love what we do, and we know that our daughters love what they are doing. I have a strong belief that the grandchildren will feel the same way.

I've never believed that there is any such thing as status quo. I think status quo is really a phrase that should be abolished from our vocabulary because it doesn't ever exist. If you're not going up, you're coming down. I've always felt that people who think they are at status quo, with everything rocking along the same, more than likely have already started down and don't know it. I know our family shares my vision and enthusiasm, and I feel very good about where that may take us. Hopefully, in fifteen or twenty years Marsha and her sisters will have something exciting to write a book about.

I'm excited about the future. Again, I'm not a long-range planner, but now that I've had my eighty-third birthday I'm thinking that planning five or six years out is not really long range. And it maintains my optimism, which is a true gift, because, at my age, I could easily slide into grumpy-old-man status. Seeing those classrooms at the McCombs School of Business full of brilliant eager entrepreneurial wannabes of both genders soaking up knowledge and ready to conquer the business world just thrills the heck out of this redheaded good old boy from Spur.

I admit that some of my feelings stem from selfishness. I want my grandkids to grow up and enjoy the lifestyle made possible by the entrepreneurs, scientists, technicians, and other brilliant people who have flourished in our great system of free enterprise and individual liberty. So those young people at the McCombs School give me hope and a strong faith that the world my grandkids will live in will be just fine.

My message to them is this: The world is now yours to conquer, so go for it.

INDEX

Page numbers in *italic* refer to illustrations.

T